# GOD'S UNIVERSAL COVENANT

## A Biblical Study

# GOD'S UNIVERSAL COVENANT

## A Biblical Study

**WALTER VOGELS**

University of Ottawa Press

BS
680
.C67
V64
1986

**ISBN 0-7766-0164-4**

© University of Ottawa Press 1979, 1986
Published 1979. Second Edition 1986
Printed and bound in Canada

*To my Father and Mother,
Lieve, Magda
and their families.*

## PREFACE

For a number of years I have been interested in the topic of universalism in the Bible. Through my courses, seminars and workshops in Canada, the United States and Africa, I have shared my ideas with numerous students. The results of some of my research have been published in a variety of periodicals, in French, English and Dutch.

Though many biblical texts have yet to be analysed in full detail, I believe that some type of synthesis is already possible and it is my hope that this book will be a less technical presentation of such a synthesis. Therefore, I will avoid justifying various positions and discussing different interpretations of the texts. If desired, the reader can find such information in some of my previous writings, which I have listed in the footnotes together with some further bibliographical references to studies on specific topics or texts. I generally have not included references to the commentaries. These may be known to the reader or are easy to find. This should make the text easier to read while introducing what in my mind is fundamental to the Bible: God's universal covenant with mankind.

I wish to thank in a very special way Fr. Stanley Haskell, w.f., and Sr. Margaret Ferguson, g.s.i.c., for correcting the English in my manuscript, the Research Centre of Saint Paul University, Ottawa, which has made this publication possible, and Dr. Kenneth Russell, researcher at Saint Paul University, for preparing the second edition of this book.

W.V.

# ABBREVIATIONS

| | |
|---|---|
| Ant. | *Antonianum* |
| A.T.A.N.T. | *Abhandlungen zur Theologie des Alten und Neuen Testaments* |
| B.A. | *Biblical Archaeologist* |
| B.A.S.O.R. | *Bulletin of the American Schools of Oriental Research* |
| B.B.B. | *Bonner Biblische Beiträge* |
| Bib. | *Biblica* |
| Bib.Or. | *Bibbia e Oriente* |
| Bijdr. | *Bijdragen* |
| Bi.Leb. | *Bibel und Leben* |
| B.K. | *Biblischer Kommentar, Altes Testament* |
| B.T.B. | *Biblical Theology Bulletin* |
| B.V.C. | *Bible et Vie chrétienne* |
| B.W.A.N.T. | *Beiträge zur Wissenschaft vom Alten und Neuen Testament* |
| B.Z. | *Biblische Zeitschrift* |
| B.Z.A.W. | *Beihefte zur Zeitschrift für die Alttestamentliche Wissenschaft* |
| C.B.Q. | *Catholic Biblical Quarterly* |
| Coll.Mechl. | *Collectanea Mechliniensia* |
| Conc. | *Concilium* |
| C.R.B. | *Cahiers de la Revue Biblique* |
| Cu.Bib. | *Cultura Biblica* |
| Égl.Th. | *Église et Théologie* |
| Est.Bib. | *Estudios Biblicos* |
| E.T.L. | *Ephemerides Theologicae Lovanienses* |
| Ev.Th. | *Evangelische Theologie* |
| Ind.J.T. | *Indian Journal of Theology* |
| Interpr. | *Interpretation* |
| Isr.E.J. | *Israel Exploration Journal* |
| J.A.O.S. | *Journal of the American Oriental Society* |
| J.B.L. | *Journal of Biblical Literature* |
| J.N.E.S. | *Journal of Near Eastern Studies* |
| J.R.H. | *Journal of Religious History* |
| J.S.O.T. | *Journal for the Study of the Old Testament* |
| J.S.S. | *Journal of Semitic Studies* |
| Ned.T.T. | *Nederlands Theologisch Tijdschrift* |
| N.R.T. | *Nouvelle Revue théologique* |
| N.T.S. | *New Testament Studies* |
| O.T.S. | *Oudtestamentische Studiën* |
| Par.Miss. | *Parole et Mission* |
| R.B. | *Revue Biblique* |
| R.Cl.Afr. | *Revue du Clergé africain* |
| Riv.Bib.It. | *Rivista Biblica Italiana* |
| R.S.R. | *Recherches de Science religieuse* |

| | |
|---|---|
| **R.T.L.** | *Revue théologique de Louvain* |
| **S.A.N.T.** | *Studien zum Alten und Neuen Testament* |
| **S.B.T.** | *Studies in Biblical Theology* |
| **Sc.Eccl.** | *Sciences ecclésiastiques* |
| **Sc.Espr.** | *Science et Esprit* |
| **Scot.J.T.** | *Scottish Journal of Theology* |
| **Script.Vict.** | *Scriptorium Victoriense* |
| **S.T.** | *Studia Theologica* |
| **Sw.J.T.** | *Southwestern Journal of Theology* |
| **Th.Dig.** | *Theology Digest* |
| **Th.Phil.** | *Theologie und Philosophie* |
| **Th.Tod.** | *Theology Today* |
| **Th.Z.** | *Theologische Zeitschrift* |
| **T.T.St.** | *Trierer Theologische Studien* |
| **T.T.Z.** | *Trierer Theologische Zeitschrift* |
| **V.T.** | *Vetus Testamentum* |
| **V.T.S.** | *Supplements to Vetus Testamentum* |
| **W.M.A.N.T.** | *Wissenschaftliche Monographien zum Alten und Neuen Testament* |
| **Z.A.W.** | *Zeitschrift für die Alttestamentliche Wissenschaft* |
| **Z.K.T.** | *Zeitschrift für Katholische Theologie* |
| **Z.M.R.** | *Zeitschrift für Missionswissenschaft und Religionswissenschaft* |
| **Z.T.K.** | *Zeitschrift für Theologie und Kirche* |

## CONTENTS

| | PAGE |
|---|---|
| **Preface** | ix |
| **Abbreviations** | x |
| **Introduction** | 1 |
|     I. *Covenant* | 1 |
|     II. *Universalism* | 7 |
|     III. *The One God's Revelation* | 9 |
| **Chapter 1: The Primitive Universal Covenant** | 15 |
|     I. *In Yahwistic Prehistory* | 17 |
|     II. *In Other Biblical Traditions* | 28 |
|         The Noah Covenant (Gen. 9:1-17) | 28 |
|         The Covenant of Brotherhood (Am. 1:9) | 30 |
|         A Covenant with the Beasts (Hos. 2:20) | 31 |
|         The Covenant with Adam (Hos. 6:7) | 31 |
|         The Eternal Covenant (Is. 24:5) | 32 |
|         The Covenant of Peace (Is. 54:9-10) | 32 |
|         A Covenant with the Day and the Night (Jer. 33:20-25) | 33 |
|         A Covenant of Peace (Ezek. 34:25) | 33 |
|         The Covenant with All the Peoples (Zech. 11:10) | 34 |
|         The Eternal Covenant (Sir. 17:12; 44:18) | 35 |
| **Chapter 2: The Place of the Nations in the Historical Covenant with Israel** | 39 |
|     I. *The Promises to Abraham—Blessing for the Nations* | 39 |
|     II. *The Covenant—Service to the Nations* | 46 |
|     III. *The Relations between Israel and the Nations* | 49 |
|         Covenant with the Midianites (Kenites) (Ex. 18:1-12) | 51 |

|  |  | Covenant with the "Inhabitants of the Land" (Ex. 23:32; 34:12,15; Dt. 7:2; Jgs. 2:2) | 54 |
|---|---|---|---|
|  |  | Covenant with the Gibeonites (Jos. 9) | 56 |
|  |  | Covenant with the Tyrians (1 Kgs. 5:15-26) | 58 |
|  |  | Covenant with the Aramaeans (1 Kgs. 15:19 = 2 Chr. 16:3; 1 Kgs. 20:34) | 59 |
|  |  | Covenant with Assyria (Hos. 12:2) | 61 |
|  |  | Covenant with Egypt (Hos. 12:2) | 62 |
|  |  | Covenant with Babylon (Ezek. 17:13,14,15,16,18) | 62 |
|  | IV. | *The Nations, Witnesses of the Covenant* | 64 |
|  | V. | *The Nations, Yahweh's Instrument of the Curses and Blessings of the Covenant* | 68 |

**Chapter 3: Parallel Covenants with the Nations?** — 71

  I. *The "Exodus Experience" of the Nations and their Belonging to Yahweh* — 72
  II. *The Judgment of the Nations* — 80
   Oracles against Neighbouring Nations (Am. 1:3-2:16) — 80
   The Condemnation of Egypt (Ezek. 29:1-12) — 84
  III. *The Restoration of the Nations* — 87
   The Restoration of Egypt (Ezek. 29:13-16) — 88
   Egypt my People (Is. 19:16-25) — 95

**Chapter 4: The New Universal Covenant** — 111

  I. *Centripetal Universalism* — 111
   The Pilgrimage of the Nations to Jerusalem (Is. 2:2-4) — 112
   The Liturgical Tradition — 116
   • Jerusalem, Mother of all Nations (Ps. 87) — 117
   The Prophetic Tradition — 117
   • The Feast at Zion (Is. 25:6-8) — 118
   • Jerusalem, City of Light (Is. 60) — 118
   • Jerusalem, the Throne of Yahweh (Jer. 3:17) — 119
   • Jerusalem, Place of Peace (Hag. 2:6-9) — 120
   • The Favour of Yahweh in Jerusalem (Zech. 8:20-23) — 120
   • The Eschatological Battle, the Splendour of Jerusalem (Zech. 14) — 120

- The King of Heaven in Jerusalem
  (Tob. 13:11; 14:6-7) 121
II. *Centrifugal Universalism* 122
   The Mission of the Suffering Servant 123
   The Mission of Jonah 127
   "Tell among the peoples his deeds" (Psalms) 128
   The Mission of the Disciples (Mt. 28:18-20) 130

**Conclusion** 143

# Introduction

Many books and articles on universalism in the Bible have already been written.[1] So, one may wonder about the possibility or the usefulness of still another text. Since my approach towards universalism tends to differ from that of previous works, I feel that there is definite room for such a study. If in the past the concept of election-covenant has too often been seen as an obstacle to universalism, it is my intent to show the very strong link between these two concepts.[2]

This essay is based on the results of recent biblical research, which I shall present before I develop my thesis. For this reason my introduction may seem to be rather long.

The three main points which I should like to handle in the introduction are: (I) the modern understanding of *Covenant*, (II) some notions on *Universalism*, and (III) some problems of methodology linked with the concept of *God's revelation*.

## I. COVENANT

If we wish to speak about God, it is necessary to use images of human experience. When biblical writers wanted to explain the relationship between Yahweh and Israel, they chose familiar images: the husband-wife relationship; the father-son relationship; and the more frequent image of covenant: $b^e r\hat{\imath}t$.

Research in the field of covenant in the last twenty years has been extremely rich. Some extra-biblical texts, known as treaties, have been of great help in understanding the biblical concept of covenant. It seems very likely that biblical writers were inspired by these extra-biblical contracts. One particular kind of treaty, known as the vassal treaty, regulated the relations between a Great King or Suzerain and his vassal. This relation-

---

1. One of the most recent studies is by P.-E. DION, *Dieu universel et peuple élu. L'universalisme religieux en Israël depuis les origines jusqu'à la veille des luttes maccabéennes*, Lectio Divina 83, Paris, 1975.
2. For a summary of my position: W. VOGELS, "Alliance et Universalisme", in *Par.Miss.*, 14 (1971), n. 56, pp. 219-227; or "Covenant and Universalism. Guide for a Missionary Reading of the Old Testament", in *Z.M.R.*, 57 (1973), pp. 25-32.

ship was considered by biblical tradition as a very appropriate image to express the relation between Yahweh and his people.³

Since this discovery more progress has been made through further research. A treaty was never abruptly concluded between two unknown partners. Certainly some events must have preceded the formal conclusion of the covenant, which in turn was only the beginning of several other possible events in this new relationship, like faithfulness, unfaithfulness, punishments, promises, renewal. Different studies have shown how the same attitudes and events are present in the Bible. These different situations of the covenant can even give a synthesis of the whole biblical history.

It is not my intent to restate already established facts, but only those aspects relevant to my thesis. Therefore what follows is a brief summary of the different moments of covenant relationship between Yahweh and Israel.

The first step in each vassal treaty was the *PROMISE of the future covenant*, which is composed of three elements.⁴

(I) *Cry for help*. A minor king, who was in trouble and in need of assistance, would request the aid of a major king.

(II) *Promise of salvific action*. The Great King would then promise to come to the rescue of this minor king.

(III) *Request for submission*. Normally the Great King would ask that the minor king submit to certain, as yet unrevealed, conditions. After his rescue by the Great King, the minor king would then yield to his new protector.

This procedure is found in the beginning of Exodus: Israel, enslaved in Egypt, cries out for help; Yahweh accepts and promises to bring Israel out of Egypt into the promised land; once this has happened, Israel will be asked to serve Yahweh. Note that the "out-into" aspect of salvific action will become very important in covenant theology.

Two texts in which these three elements are clearly present are Ex. 2:23b-26; 6:2-8 belonging to the P-tradition and Ex. 3:7-8,12,16-18 of the JE-tradition.

---

3. For a survey on this question: W. VOGELS, *La promesse royale de Yahweh préparatoire à l'Alliance. Étude d'une forme littéraire de l'Ancien Testament*, Ottawa, 1970 (with bibliography pp. 171-181); D. J. MCCARTHY, *Old Testament Covenant. A Survey of Current Opinions*, Growing Points in Theology, Richmond, 1972; P. BUIS, *La notion d'alliance dans l'ancien testament*, Lectio Divina 88, Paris, 1976; R. KOCH, L'Alliance et les 'Formulaires d'Alliance' dans le Pentateuque", in *Studia Moralia* XIV, Rome, 1976, pp. 77-104. Some exegetes question the validity of this approach: L. PERLITT, *Bundestheologie im Alten Testament*, W.M.A.N.T. 36, Neukirchen, 1969; E. KUTSCH, *Verheissung und Gesetz: Untersuchungen zum sogenannten "Bund" im Alten Testament*, B. Z.A.W. 131, Berlin, 1973; M. WEINFELD, "Berît-Covenant vs. Obligation", in *Bib.*, 56 (1975), pp. 120-128. The whole issue was discussed at the XXIIIrd Biblical Conference at Louvain (August 23-25, 1972), and published in *Questions disputées d'Ancien Testament*, ed. C. Brekelmans, Leuven 1974. Of special interest: E. KUTSCH, "Gottes Zuspruch und Anspruch. Berît in der alttestamentlichen Theologie", pp. 71-90; and D. J. MCCARTHY, "Covenant-relationships", pp. 91-104.

4. W. VOGELS, *La promesse royale de Yahweh...*, pp. 45-75, 133-152.

This promise of the future covenant is only the prelude to the real covenant. It is only the day on which the vassal is freed from his enemies that he stands before his Suzerain and finds out what his requested submission entails. Now we can speak about the *CONCLUSION of the Covenant*.[5] This moment of the treaty practice is perhaps best known to us, and again we see how biblical tradition has used this to express the Yahweh-Israel relationship. This is the well-known "Bundesformular", the Covenant Formulary, which consists of the following structural elements:

(1) *Preamble*. The Great King presents himself with his name and his titles.

(2) *Historical Prologue*. The Great King recalls all that he has done to help the minor king and cites the historical benefits. He affirms that his promise of assistance has been successfully realized, and that he now expects an answer from his new vassal.

(3) *Stipulations*. The Great King now stipulates his conditions:
—in general, from now on the Suzerain requests total loyalty from his vassal.
—in particular, the Suzerain makes clear what this total submission means, namely, the paying of taxes, protection in case of war, or some other form of dependency.

(4) *Witnesses*. To satisfy the requirements of a legally valid contract, one needs witnesses. In extra-biblical treaties the gods of the two partners are called upon as witnesses of the agreement. Such gods may include (deified) nature such as heaven, earth, mountains.

(5) *Blessings and Curses*. Each party to the contract believes that the witnesses will bless the vassal if he is faithful, but curse him if he is unfaithful.

This way of treaty-making was adopted by biblical tradition and applied to the relation between Yahweh and Israel. Examples are to be found in Ex. 19:3-8; Ex. 20; Jos. 24; 1 Sam. 12:

(1) the characteristic name of the covenant-God is "Yahweh". This name is revealed during the exodus, and his title is "your God";

(2) "the" historical event which is the basis of Israel's submission is precisely this exodus event and the gift of the promised land ("out-into");

(3) many juridical texts stipulate how Israel is asked to submit to Yahweh;

(4) further, the Bible often calls nature to witness to the relationship between Yahweh and Israel;

---

5. G. E. MENDENHALL, *Law and Covenant in Israel and the Ancient Near East*, Pittsburgh, 1955; K. BALTZER, *The Covenant Formulary in Old Testament, Jewish and Early Christian Writings*, Philadelphia, 1971; D. J. MCCARTHY, *Treaty and Covenant. A Study in the Ancient Oriental Documents and in the Old Testament*, Analecta Biblica 21A, Rome, 1978.

(5) in long lists of blessings and curses one may read what will happen to Israel if she remains faithful and what will happen if she becomes unfaithful (Lev. 26; Dt. 28).

Biblical tradition has also a *PREACHING and a TEACHING of the covenant* to remind Israel of her duties and responsibilities.[6] Here again the same elements are used:

—*past history*, what Yahweh has done for Israel is the basis of

—*Israel's submission*, which she has to accept if she wants

—*blessings*.

The book of Deuteronomy and the whole of Deuteronomistic tradition incorporate precisely such a teaching.

Though severe curses were a part of the treaty formula, vassals did rebel against their Suzerain. When this occurred the vassal might be called to trial. We find this in the *COVENANT-LAWSUIT* or Rîb-pattern, of which we now cite the most important elements.[7]

(1) *Witnesses* are called to be present at the trial and are necessarily the same as those who were present at the conclusion of the covenant.

(2) *Historical Inquiry*.

—Yahweh's kindness to Israel is retold, and the historical benefits are cited.

—There is a statement of Israel's response to this treatment, her refusal to submit and failure to observe the covenant stipulations.

(3) *Declaration* that Israel is guilty.

(4) *Condemnation*. Israel is deserving of the punishment announced in the curses. In some lawsuits this last element is not yet a punishment, but an admonition. In this case, Israel gets another chance to change her conduct.

This structure is frequently found in the prophets when Israel is accused of unfaithfulness: Is. 1; Jer. 2; Mic. 6; Ezek. 20:1-38; Dt. 32.

Having received a judgment of his guilt the unfaithful vassal may ask pardon of his Suzerain. In the case of Israel, she addresses God in a special *PRAYER for Restoration*, which is called *Tôdāh,* and which consists of the following elements:[8]

---

6. N. LOHFINK, *Das Hauptgebot. Eine Untersuchung literarischer Einleitungs-fragen zu Dtn. 5-11*, Analecta Biblica 20, Rome, 1963; J. L'HOUR, "Formes littéraires, structure et unité de Deutéronome 5-11", in *Bib.*, 45 (1964), pp. 551-555; D. E. SKWERES, "Das Motiv der Strafgrunderfragung in biblischen und neuassyrischen Texten", in *B.Z.*, 14 (1970), pp. 181-197; B. O. LONG, "Two Question and Answer Schemata in the Prophets", in *J.B.L.*, 90 (1971), pp. 129-139.
7. H. B. HUFFMON, "The Covenant Lawsuit in the Prophets", in *J.B.L.*, 78 (1959), pp. 285-295; J. HARVEY, *Le plaidoyer prophétique contre Israël après la rupture de l'Alliance. Étude d'une formule littéraire de l'Ancien Testament,* Studia 22, Montréal, 1967; G. W. RAMSEY, "Speech-Forms in Hebrew Law and Prophetic Oracles", in *J.B.L.*, 96 (1977), pp. 45-58.
8. W. BEYERLIN, "Die Tôdāh der Heilsergegenwärtigung in den Klageliedern des Einzelnen", in *Z.A.W.*, 79 (1967), pp. 208-224; M. GILBERT, "La prière de Daniel. Dn. 9:4-19", in *R.T.L.*, 3 (1972), pp. 284-310.

(1) Israel's acceptance that Yahweh is just in his punishment because she is guilty.

(2) Recollection of the historical benefits that Yahweh has bestowed upon Israel.

(3) Israel's confession of unfaithfulness and of her refusal to submit.

(4) Her prayer for pardon, her request that the punishment cease and that the covenant be renewed.

It is easy to see how the same essential elements of other covenant situations are present in these prayers, of which we find examples in Jer. 32:16-25; Ezra 9:6-15; Neh. 1:5-11; 9:6-37; Dan. 9:4-19; Bar. 1:15-3:8.

So it is evident that a broken treaty was not necessarily the end of a relationship between a Suzerain and his vassal. Under some conditions a renewal or a new treaty could be established. Such an arrangement is present also in the relationship between Yahweh and his people. When the final punishment has befallen unfaithful Israel, there is still hope. Israel, living now in exile, receives the *PROMISE of a new covenant*, which interestingly enough is composed of essentially the same elements as the promise of the first covenant, with some changes.[9]

(I) *Cry for help—conversion*. A person in trouble may cry for help, but if his cry arises out of punishment for his own unfaithfulness, then such a cry must be a cry of conversion. Israel while in Egypt cried out for help, but when she was in exile, which is the final judgment of God, her cry had to be one of conversion.

(II) *Promise of salvific action*. Yahweh accepts Israel's conversion. And we find in his acceptance the same terminology of the first covenant: Yahweh will "bring out" Israel "into" the promised land. The return from exile is like a new exodus and a new conquest, a repetition of what happened centuries before. But a new element is added: God promises to renew the heart of Israel. An interior change is announced.

(III) *Request for submission*. For such clemency, Yahweh expects deep and long-lasting fidelity from Israel.

The prophets frequently spoke of this new covenant which would come in spite of Israel's unfaithfulness, and also of the punishment she would undergo prior to its establishment: Hos. 2:9b,16-25; Jer. 32:36-41; Ezek. 11:17-20; Zech. 8:7-8; Lev. 26:40-45; Dt. 30:1-10.

Treaty relationships were not merely documents, but living realities. Since all this expressed so well the relation between Yahweh and Israel, the biblical tradition had no scruples about using this juridical extra-biblical material to describe the different mutual attitudes which existed between Yahweh and his people. The same three basic elements are used in these different structures: historical benefits, submission and blessings-curses. Because Yahweh had done something for Israel, he had the right to request her submission, the only condition for her happiness.

---

9. W. VOGELS, *La promesse royale de Yahweh...*, pp. 76-132.

This concept of the covenant gives a perfect unity to the whole of salvation history, which moves from promise to promise.

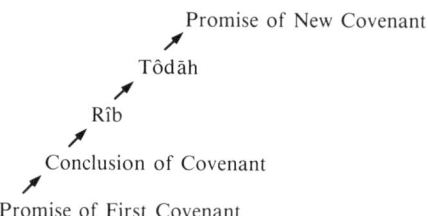

This pattern may also be considered as a perfect circle. After the failure of the first covenant, the cycle starts all over again. But there is more; this new covenant is not simply a restoration of the first, but goes deeper, and requires an interior renewal.[10]

Not only does the whole of the Bible become more meaningful through this insight, but also many details of the biblical texts receive a new light. Words and sentences which belong to this technical language of the covenant receive special richness when read with the covenant relationship in mind. To express Israel's total submission to Yahweh, the biblical tradition uses a distinctive vocabulary: serve, know, fear, love, obey, listen to his voice, forget not. If one comes across the formula: "I brought you out of Egypt into the promised land", it is usually a clear indication that the text belongs to one of the preceding covenant situations. It may be still in the future as a promise, or in the past as a request for submission, or an accusation of unfaithfulness.

Several theological conclusions could be developed from this particular way of presenting the relationship of Yahweh and his people. It is a very personal, mutual relationship; Yahweh is "our", "your", "their" God, and Israel is "my", "your", "his" people. It is God who acts first in history. He has done something, he has revealed himself through the events. This is why he can expect an answer from his people, an answer of gratitude, but also of obedience. This answer is a total gift of oneself, which must be lived in the details of daily life. Some specific stipulations determine this total submission, giving a new understanding of what the biblical law means.[11] Even if there are curses and punishment, God's final word seems to be blessing and hope.

A well-known biblical expression summarizes all this in a few words:

I am your God,
you are my people.

---

10. W. VOGELS, "Je vous donnerai un cœur de chair..." (Ezek. 36:26). Conversion—Renouveau—Réconciliation", in *Kerygma*, 7 (1973), n. 21, pp. 103-116.
11. J. L'HOUR, *La Morale de l'Alliance*, C.R.B. 5, Paris, 1966; W. VOGELS, "Le Sens de la loi dans l'Ancienne Alliance", in *R.Cl.Afr.*, 25 (1970), pp. 421-432.

We never read "my nation", which is more a political designation associated with state and government, but always "my people", which implies a blood relation or family-tie, and insists on the human dimension.[12]

## II. UNIVERSALISM

If the covenant between Yahweh and his people seems to make a synthesis of the whole biblical tradition, then the question arises: what about the other nations? Is there any room for them? Do they have any role to play?

It would be ridiculous to deny that the election of Israel and her covenant with Yahweh are central. The Bible describes the history of a people, and even if it is salvation history, the events concern concrete historical situations of Israel: her battles, her victories, her defeats.

But on the other hand, we very often read about the nations. Israel evidently is not living alone. Her history is connected with the history of others, and as we will see, salvation history does have something to offer to these nations. A superficial reading of the Bible quickly shows how frequently the "nations" are mentioned, often in opposition to "my people". We are all aware of the rather negative texts of the curses, the destruction and the killing of the nations. But there are many other texts which refer to these other nations in a positive light.

Consequently, universalism has often been studied as a theme of biblical theology, but generally distinct from the covenant theme.[13] A typical example of this approach is the work of the eminent English biblical scholar H. H. Rowley. His first book dealt with the question of election: *The Biblical Doctrine of Election* (London, 1950); he then devoted another book to universalism: *The Missionary Message of the Old Testament* (London 1955). This is a classical and typical way of presenting salvation history.

Contrary to the approach just mentioned, the purpose of our study is an attempt to show the close link that exists between the covenant with Israel and the salvation of the nations. In a certain sense, we might even say that *covenant is universalism*. This is the meaning behind the title of our book: *"God's Universal Covenant"*. The importance of this approach

---

12. E. A. SPEISER, "'People' and 'Nation' of Israel", in *J.B.L.*, 79 (1960), pp. 157-163; A. CODY, "When is the chosen people called a *Gôy*?" in *V.T.*, 14 (1964), pp. 1-6; N. LOHFINK, "Beobachtungen zur Geschichte des Ausdrucks *'ām YHWH*'", in *Probleme biblischer Theologie, Festschrift G. von Rad*, ed. H. W. Wolff, München, 1971, pp. 275-305; R. MURPHY, "'Nation' dans l'Ancien Testament", in *Conc.*, n. 121 (1977), pp. 99-105.
13. A. GELIN, "L'idée missionnaire dans la Bible", in *L'Ami du Clergé*, 66 (1956), pp. 411-418; R. MARTIN-ACHARD, *Israël et les Nations. La perspective missionnaire de l'Ancien Testament*, Cahiers théologiques 42, Neuchâtel, 1959; J. BLAUW, *The Missionary Nature of the Church. Foundations of the Christian Mission*, London, 1963; P. TERNANT, "Bible et Mission (Bibliographie)", in *Par.Miss.*, n. 28 (1965), pp. 144-152; A. DE GROOT, *The Bible on the Salvation of Nations*, De Pere, 1966.

is rather evident. We have spoken for a long time about the Church, in reference to its being institution, diocese, parish, while simultaneously referring to the missions as a separate entity. We are becoming more and more conscious that the Church *is* mission. If the Church merely looks at herself, she will die; it is only when she looks around her that she can be a dynamic Church.

The Bible speaks in different ways about the election of Israel,[14] the first step towards covenant. Yahweh had first to elect Israel, before he could make a covenant with her. In many of these texts, we find reference to the other nations. "For you are a people holy to Yahweh, your God; Yahweh your God has chosen you to be a people for his own possession, out of all the peoples that are on the face of the earth..." (Dt. 7:6). This is one of the clearest texts affirming the election of Israel, while at the same time indicating that she was chosen from among the others. To choose necessarily implies that there are alternatives. As many other texts say, Yahweh is master over all the nations, but he took one particular nation for one special purpose. Why?

Some special titles given to Israel to express her election can be very instructive with regard to universalism: "Israel is my firstborn son" (Ex. 4:22) normally implies that other sons exist; "Israel ... the first fruits of the harvest" (Jer. 2:3) says very clearly that the harvest is only beginning. Thus, the election of Israel implies that other nations, other peoples, are called. This is the meaning of universalism.

These few texts may already have shown that election, far from being opposed to universalism, is very much related to it. As a matter of fact, election is not a privilege to profit from, but a privilege which implies service to be rendered. The major sin of the chosen people was precisely their refusal to serve, to assume responsibility, and their belief that because of their election, they were protected against all dangers: "...do not presume to say to yourselves 'We have Abraham as our father'!: for I tell you, God is able from these stones to raise up children to Abraham" (Mt. 3:9).

We would like to show that what has just been said about election can also be said about covenant. We shall see how the covenant itself implies universalism, and how several biblical writers use the vocabulary, the images and the different structures of the covenant (which we have just studied) to speak about the nations. These are the limits of our investigation. We do not want to analyse all universalistic texts or to repeat everything that has been said about universalism.

---

14. T. C. VRIEZEN, *Die Erwählung Israels nach dem Alten Testament*, A.T.A.N.T. 24, Zürich, 1953; H. WILDBERGER, *Jahwes Eigentumsvolk. Eine Studie zur Traditions geschichte und Theologie des Erwählungsgedankens*, A.T.A.N.T. 37, Zürich 1960; P. ALTMANN, *Erwählungstheologie und Universalismus im Alten Testament*, B.Z.A.W. 92, Berlin, 1964; B. E. SHAFER, "The Root *bḥr* and Pre-exilic Concepts of Chosenness in the Hebrew Bible", in *Z.A.W.*, 89 (1977), pp. 20-42.

The word *universalism* can be used in many different ways. Some texts speak about Yahweh, the God of Israel, as creator of all nations. All mankind has the same origin and, therefore, Yahweh is master over all the nations. This is called universalism of *creation*. But the nations may also share in the privileges of Israel and so enter into the universalism of *salvation*.

How will the nations come to know this salvation plan of God? Some texts say that the nations have to come to the centre, to Jerusalem, to Israel, and there they will receive the light; this is called *centripetal* universalism. How and why they come to the centre can vary. Sometimes it looks as if they are compelled to come; sometimes they seem to have been impressed by Israel's witness and come spontaneously. But instead of waiting for others to come, the centre may decide to go out to the nations. In such cases we speak of *centrifugal* universalism.

There is clearly a difference between universalism and *mission*. Even if the notion of mission is presently much discussed, and even if not everybody agrees on the definition, the word mission is normally only used for centrifugal universalism. It is only when the chosen people go out to others that we speak of missionary texts in the strict sense.

### III. THE ONE GOD'S REVELATION[15]

Most books on universalism limit themselves to one period: some speak about universalism in the Old Testament, others about universalism in the New Testament. Those which analyse the whole Bible make clear divisions between the two parts. In studies of the New Testament one may sometimes read about the missionary method of Paul. These approaches are based on the commonly accepted distinction between Old and New Testament. But this is quite disputable. If we believe that *all* these books are God's revelation, why do we use the term "old", often with a kind of disdain suggesting *dépassé*, and boast of having the "new", in a manner that suggests that we have something better?[16]

The question: "Where does the New Testament start?" gives rise to some strange answers. Some people say it begins with John the Baptist. But why would he be considered "newer" than Jeremiah or any other of the prophets? Normally the answer is that the New Testament starts with Jesus. But this is precisely the difficulty we face when it comes to universalism in the Bible. We all know how Jesus limited his mission to Israel. "I was sent only to the lost sheep of the house of Israel"

---

15. W. VOGELS, "Het éne, oude en nieuwe Testament" in *Objektief*, 10 (1976), n. 1, pp. 4-9.
16. On the question of the relation between Old and New Testament: L. DEQUEKER, "Pourquoi les chrétiens lisent-ils encore l'Ancien Testament?", in *Coll.Mechl.*, 54 (1969), pp. 329-341; "Signifiance de l'Ancien Testament pour la foi chrétienne", in *R.S.R.*, 63 (1975) (the whole issue n. 3, pp. 297-406, is on this topic); L. SABOURIN, "The Bible and Christ: The Unity of the Two Testaments", in *B.T.B.*, 8 (1978), pp. 77-85.

(Mt. 15:24), and when he sends his disciples on their first mission, we encounter the same limitation: "Go nowhere among the Gentiles, and enter no town of the Samaritans, but go rather to the lost sheep of the house of Israel" (Mt. 10:5-6). We have to wait until Jesus' resurrection to see the apostles with a mission to the whole world. Then we have something new.

The time-honoured distinction between the Old Testament, as the time of the justice of God, and the New, as the period of his love, is no longer valid, if we properly understand all of covenant theology. Everything was not perfect in the "Old" Testament, and the so-called "scandals" of killing, lies and sexual disorders are well-known; so too we know that everything was not perfect in the "New" Testament. The apostles themselves were not perfect, neither was the primitive Church. Texts such as "you shall love Yahweh your God with all your heart, and with all your soul, and with all your might" and "you shall love your neighbour as yourself" are not originally from the "New", but from the "Old" Testament (Dt. 6:5 and Lev. 19:18). The most recent books of the "Old" Testament were composed in the last century before Christ, a time which was very close to the first writings of the "New" Testament. Why call everything before Christ "Old" and everything after him "New"? What is one century in the history of mankind?

Would it not be better for us to speak of God's revelation as a unity with several periods, with evolution, with growth, with some periods more important than others, and some periods newer? In this way we should refrain from referring to one part of the Bible as "Old" and therefore of no use to us. Similarly we should refrain from referring to the other part as "New" or, in other words, the fullness of revelation. The fullness lies not in one section, but in the totality.

The presentation of God's revelation of his plan of salvation, as a single unit which can be divided into three main periods, might be more clearly understood than our present division of the Bible into Old and New Testament.

The first period is summarized in the first eleven chapters of Genesis. We find there God's universal plan for mankind. In order to distinguish it from later periods we will call this the *Primitive Universal Covenant*. In this era mankind lives in peace with God, but later, sin breaks the relationship. This situation becomes worse and worse until we reach a totally disrupted relationship. People no longer understand each other and are scattered over the earth in a kind of exile of mankind, for indeed this is what the story of the tower of Babel tells us. This exile could have been the end. But there was still hope.

And so we enter the second period of the plan of salvation in the person of Abraham. God promises him that he will be the father of a nation, and through him (through Abraham and his people) others will share in his blessing (Gen. 12:1-3). This promise is the key to our understanding of God's plan of restoration to dispersed mankind. God wants to start with one people and from this one group proceed to others. He had limitless options but this is what he chose. This is the period of the *Historical Covenant with Israel*. God continues to reveal himself and to build up his people. As different periods of history come and go, with their different leaders and prophets, God's plan of salvation unfolds itself with a deeper revelation. Each period brings something new, until we reach the important revelation of Jesus, God's own son: "In many and various ways God spoke of old to our fathers by the prophets; but in these last days he has spoken to us by a Son..." (Hebr. 1:1-2). And now it becomes suddenly very clear why Jesus limited his preaching to Israel. This was God's plan, "for salvation is from the Jews" (Joh. 4:22). Israel must first receive the total revelation. Nobody can give to others what he does not have himself. After Jesus' death and resurrection, when Israel has received the final word of God, she can then share with others: "And (Jesus) said to them, 'Go into all the world and preach the gospel to the whole creation...' So then the Lord Jesus, after he had spoken to them, was taken up into heaven, and sat down at the right hand of God. And they went forth and preached everywhere..." (Mk. 16:15-20). This is the end of the second period.

Now begins the third period, in which the revelation given to Israel can be offered to all mankind. This is the *New Universal Covenant* promised through the prophets and instituted by Christ with his last words. Christ affirmed that it will last until his return at the eschaton. This covenant will restore to mankind what was lost in the Primitive Universal Covenant.

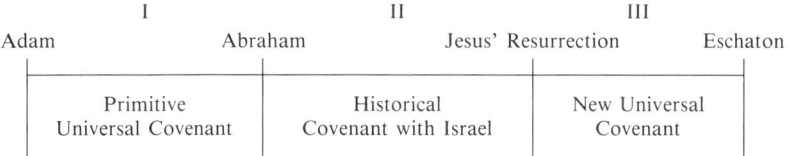

This scheme, of course, does not respect historical proportions. This second period is insignificant when seen against the whole history of mankind. We can indeed put dates on it. According to a number of historians, Abraham may have lived in the nineteenth century before Christ, so the whole period between him and Christ's resurrection is only twenty centuries.

We have been speaking of different periods and even about dates, a procedure which calls for some caution, because God's plan is not only *history*, but *salvation history*. Chronologically speaking, mankind is living in the twentieth century after Christ, so on the level of history we are in the third period. However, since we are speaking about salvation history, such may not be the case. We know that some nations are still in the first period, because they have never heard of God's revelation. Another group is already in the second period, but has not reached the end, for part of Israel remains closed before the person of Jesus, since she has not been able to accept this last part of God's revelation. When we move from groups to speak about individuals, things become even more complicated.

Because of this view of God's one single revelation, no distinction will be made in this book between universalism in the Old and in the New Testament. The whole Bible will be used; even more texts are quoted from the "Old" Testament than from the "New", since this last covers only a few years—however important they may be—and God's revelation lasted not a few years but centuries.

With this we reach the difficult option one has to choose when it comes to the study of a biblical theme, in view of the much discussed question of the *methodology* of biblical theology.

One may choose an historical approach, a diachronic study of the Bible, going from the oldest to the more recent texts. Such an approach would show how Israel gradually became conscious of universalism. Some authors have wrongly simplified this as an evolution from polytheism to monotheism, and only then to universalism. More objective research has shown a much more complex growth. Some of the oldest texts, such as the yahwistic tradition, already have a very strong universal spirit, whereas other more recent texts can be very narrow-minded. The historical situation in which Israel lived was a determining factor in her attitude. In a time when Israel was strong, she did not fear the nations, but when she was oppressed and nearly disappeared, she needed to fight first of all for her own survival and identity. This last tendency existed, for instance, after the exile. A study of the texts according to their origin would show how universalism appeared, developed, and sometimes lost its importance.

This diachronic method has serious difficulties, since we are far from certain about the dates of several texts. Sometimes the discussion is based on doctrinal *a priori*'s. Simply stated, a summary of this kind of argument would be: "this text is a very universal text, so it cannot be very old". Further, such an approach does not give a clear synthesis, since the consciousness of universalism has known its ups and downs during the many centuries of Israel's history.

The method we have chosen is more synchronic. We take the Bible as it is offered to us—God's plan of salvation going from Adam and Eve in Genesis to the expectation of the return of Christ in the Apocalypse. God's plan started, of course, in the beginning, but the texts of the beginning in Genesis are not the oldest. In an historical approach we should be obliged to study these texts later. This, however, does not mean that we completely neglect history and historical data. God's plan of salvation is intimately linked with history. In spite of all the difficulties of our chosen method, we hope to come to a better general view of God's plan of salvation through it.

\* \* \*

This introduction, it is hoped, has made the aim and the method of this book clearer. We want to follow *God's total plan of salvation* for mankind included in the Old and in the New Testament—what God had in mind for man and how it would be accomplished. So this book is not intended to be a manual for missionary methods, although such methods might become clearer once we have understood God's plan. This book will, it is hoped, give an answer to the *why* of mission. Once this is understood, the *how* will become easier to find.

God's plan of salvation is based on the *covenant*. The covenant experience that Israel lived herself, and the way she understood it and formulated it, has also taught her to understand how God acts with the nations. The biblical tradition, reacting perhaps against some narrow-minded popular attitudes which insisted upon Israel's privileges, was not afraid to use the words, formularies and structures of Israel's own covenant of which she was so proud, and to apply all equally to God's relation with the nations. These texts are the most important for us, and consequently many other universalistic texts will not be considered.

Based upon our view of God's one single revelation, our book will be divided into four chapters.

*Chapter one* will treat this first period of the *Primitive Universal Covenant*. This period of unknown length has been summarized in only a few chapters: the first eleven chapters of Genesis. But we also find some references to it in the rest of the Bible.

*Chapter two* will consider the second period of the *Historical Covenant with Israel*. We will not develop what this meant for Israel (we have already given a small synthesis of this in the first paragraph of our introduction), but will rather show the *place of the nations in this Historical Covenant with Israel*. We shall examine the question: Has this covenant with Israel anything to do with the nations?

*Chapter three* again reflects upon this second historical period in the history of mankind. Since Yahweh made a special covenant with Israel, it could well be that he did the same with other individual nations. In other words, we raise the question as to whether we can speak about *parallel covenants with the nations*?

*Chapter four* will cover the third period and reflect upon what the Bible has to say about this *New Universal Covenant*.

Chapter One

# The Primitive Universal Covenant

If one wants to write the history of a nation, one starts with the period in which this nation was born and traces how it developed further, how it became independent, and so on. One may even try to go a bit further back in history to discover the ancestors of this nation and where they came from. This is also how Israel wrote her history. Her real beginning lies in the exodus event and with Sinai, where Israel became Yahweh's covenant people. This was but the beginning; Israel had still to conquer the promised land and to become a kingdom. But biblical tradition also went back as far as it could to find Israel's ancestors, and these are presented in the stories of the patriarchs.

However, not too many national histories go as far back as Adam and Eve. The Bible seems to be an exception in doing so. This is understandable because the Bible is not only history, but also salvation history. What is God's plan in history? We do not only read pure facts but also ask some questions. Why is it, for instance, that Yahweh will bring Israel out of Egypt? The answer is that "God remembered his covenant with Abraham, with Isaac and with Jacob" (Ex. 2:24). But where then do these patriarchs come from?

Israel experienced Yahweh first as her saviour, but from there she also became conscious of Yahweh as creator. The day Israel believed Yahweh to be creator, she inevitably admitted that he was creator of all mankind, and master of universal history. But then necessarily an important question must have arisen: Why is it that this universal God is only recognized and known by Israel? Why do the other nations not adore their own creator? The first eleven chapters of Genesis supply the answers to these questions.

Not only the fact that biblical tradition has reflected upon these questions is important, but also significant is the place these chapters received in the final redaction of the Bible. It has already been noted that, contrary to all other national histories, the Bible does not start with Israel's own history, but with a very broad view of the world and mankind. All these problems could well have been treated but put somewhere else in the Bible. By placing them right at the beginning, the whole perspective is changed. Those chapters are going to enlighten the rest of salvation history, and will even give the key to the understanding of the election of Israel.[1]

But what could biblical tradition really know about this enormous period extending from the beginning of the world to the period of Israel's own patriarchs? There were, of course, no sources available to give objective information and besides, this was not the purpose of the biblical writers. These writers did not want to write a book of science, or a scientific history; their purpose was salvation history. In other words, they were more interested in God's relationship with mankind than in events. To discover this relationship, these writers had the experience of their own history. Yahweh revealed himself to Israel in history. Through the understanding the writers got from this, they could reflect upon the past. Like the prophets who were able to understand the events of their own days and from that point project into the future and predict what the next step of Yahweh would be, so these writers looked not into the future, but into the past. It has been said, therefore, that these eleven chapters of Genesis could be called a prophecy of the past.

The reading of these chapters is not very easy. It is apparent that the text does not constitute a harmonious unity. Sometimes the story is repeated. After we have read that God created everything, we read that he starts creating a second time. To repeat oneself is not a problem, but if one text seems to contradict the parallel text, then we are in trouble. Further, one group of texts has its own vocabulary, style and theology, distinct from another group of texts with its own characteristics. For all these reasons modern biblical research agrees, generally speaking, in the division of these eleven chapters into two different traditions: the oldest called the yahwistic tradition (J) and the more recent, the priestly tradition (P).

In the first section of this chapter we will study the yahwistic view of prehistory. The tradition, reflecting upon Israel's covenant experience, has projected this experience into the past in an attempt to apply it to God's attitude towards mankind. For this reason we speak about the primitive universal covenant. We have chosen the yahwistic tradition since the purpose of this book is to show the relation between covenant and universalism. The priestly prehistory also has a universalistic perspective but it is presented differently.

In the second section, we will go through the rest of the Bible to see how this concept of a primitive universal covenant is not restricted to the Yahwist, but is present in several other texts belonging to different traditions.

---

1. H. GROSS, "Der Universalismus des Heils. A. Nach der biblischen Urgeschichte Gen. 1-11", in *T.T.Z.*, 73 (1964), pp. 145-153; W. VOGELS, "L'universalisme de la préhistoire. Gen. 1-11", in *Egl. Th.*, 2 (1971), pp. 5-34.

## I. THE PRIMITIVE UNIVERSAL COVENANT IN YAHWISTIC PREHISTORY[2]

The yahwistic writer used several stories to cover the period from Adam and Eve to Abraham. Most exegetes now attribute the following narratives of the book of Genesis to this particular tradition: paradise (2:4b-25) and fall (3:1-24); Cain and Abel (4:1-16); the descent of Cain (4:17-24) and of Seth (4:25-26 + 5:29); the sons of God and the daughters of men (6:1-4); the flood (6:5-8; 7:1-5,7-10,12,16b,17b,22,23; 8:2b, 3a,6-12,13b,20-22); Noah and his sons (9:18-27); fragments of the table of the nations (10:1b,8-19,21,24-30); the tower of Babel (11:1-9); and a few verses on the family of Terah (11:28-30).

The origin of the stories contained in these texts is far from clear. Some have a more mythological origin, others are etiologies, or wisdom reflections, or stories about tribes. For instance, the narrative of Cain and Abel could well have been a story to explain the origin of the mysterious tribe of the Kenites.[3] But whatever the origin of all this disparate material may have been, the yahwistic tradition no longer considers the local situations of Palestine or of the neighbouring tribes, but rather it projects all of it into the dark period of prehistory. Cain and Abel are no longer tribes, but are the sons of the first human couple. The Yahwist is certainly not concerned about Israel, whose name is even, surprisingly enough, absent from the table of the nations. He speaks about mankind before Abraham. Some of his verses make this very clear: "the man called his wife's name Eve, because she was the mother of all living" (3:20), or "these three were the sons of Noah; and from these the whole earth was peopled" (9:19).

There is no doubt that we are at the level of the world of mankind, and as such, in universalism. Though the writer may have changed the original meaning of all this material, he used Israel's experience to give a perfect image of mankind in its relationship with God.

In these narratives, a certain number of themes appear regularly: God gives some benefits to mankind but mankind rebels and sin increases more and more; as a consequence, God punishes, but at the same time God shows his pity and forgives. This pattern is developed not only once, but several times. It is not very difficult to recognize, in these different steps, the narrative scheme of biblical salvation history. Consequently, for the Yahwist salvation history starts with the first men. But there is much more than this very general parallel between the major themes of prehistory and

---

2. W. VOGELS, "L'Universalisme de la préhistoire. Gen. 1-11", in *Egl. Th.*, 2 (1971), pp. 5-34, II. L'Universalisme dans la préhistoire Yahviste, pp. 19-33; H. W. WOLFF, "The Kerygma of the Yahwist", in *Interpr.*, 20 (1966), pp. 131-158; P. F. ELLIS, *The Yahwist. The Bible's First Theologian*, Notre Dame, 1968.
3. A. IBAÑEZ ARANA, "La Narración de Cain y Abel en Gen. 4:2-16", in *Script. Vict.*, 11 (1964), pp. 281-319.

the history of Israel. Some much richer comparisons can be made.⁴ When the Yahwist composed his prehistory he was living salvation history. But in a very special way, he was imbued by what was central to it—the whole covenant idea and practices. To explain the different questions he had about mankind, he applied salvation history to prehistory, and he dared even to project Israel's covenant experience upon mankind.

We shall see now how the different elements of the covenant formulary are used in the narratives of yahwistic prehistory—indeed, not only the elements, but even the characteristic vocabulary of covenant theology.⁵

(1) *Preamble*: the Great King presents himself with his name. One of the norms by which to distinguish texts belonging to the yahwistic tradition from those of the priestly tradition in prehistory is the divine name, "Yahweh" as used in J., and "Elohim" (God) as used in P. In other words, according to the yahwistic writer the name Yahweh was already known in that period of mankind. He even says it very clearly of Enosh, the son of Seth: "At that time men began to call upon the name of Yahweh" (4:26).

All of this is rather strange, since biblical tradition is very positive about the fact that the name of Yahweh was revealed to Moses (Ex. 3:14 according to the E-tradition, and Ex. 6:3 according to the P-tradition). It is the special name of the God of the exodus. When Moses is sent to bring Israel out of Egypt, he asks this question: "If I come to the people of Israel and say to them, 'The God of your fathers has sent me to you', and they ask me, 'What is his name?' what shall I say to them?" (Ex. 3:13). This is the moment when the name Yahweh is revealed. And this event becomes basic to the covenant, as can be seen in such stereotyped expressions as: "I am Yahweh your God, who brought you out of the land of Egypt" (Ex. 20:2).

According to the yahwistic tradition, this name has already been revealed to Enosh. The choice of this person is also very significant. The name Enosh is a more poetic term referring to "man" in general. In other words "man" already knew Yahweh.

What the Yahwist says symbolically is very simple. He knew as well as anybody else that, historically speaking, the name Yahweh was related to the time of Moses, but he projected this, theologically speaking, into the past. The first men adored the true God, whom we now call Yahweh,

---

4. Scholars have compared the theology of the yahwistic prehistory with the theology of the royal court: W. RICHTER, "Urgeschichte und Hoftheologie", in *B.Z.*, 10 (1966), pp. 96-105; or have pointed to similarities with the Succession Story (2 Sam. 9-20; 1 Kgs. 1-2): W. BRUEGGEMANN, "David and his Theologian", in *C.B.Q.*, 30 (1968), pp. 156-181.

5. The similarities between Gen. 2-3 and the Covenant have been suggested by L. ALONSO-SCHÖKEL, "Motivos sapienciales y de alianza en Gn. 2-3", in *Bib.*, 43 (1962), pp. 295-316. There is an English summary, "Sapiential and Covenant Themes in Genesis 2-3", in *Th.Dig.* 13 (1965), pp. 3-10. His views were followed by R. KOCH, *Grâce et Liberté humaine. Réflexion théologique sur Gen. 1-11*, Paris, 1967, pp. 83 ff., 96 ff.; P. F. ELLIS, *The Yahwist*, pp. 181 ff.; and others. I have expanded this approach to the whole yahwistic prehistory.

whatever names they may have given him.

The true God revealed to Moses is the same God mankind knew in the beginning.

(2) *Historical Prologue*: the Great King recalls the historical benefits he has bestowed on his vassal. We have seen before how this element in the salvation history of Israel comprises the "out-into" concept. We read over and over again that Yahweh brought Israel out of Egypt into the promised land. This double movement is the great salvation of Israel. The prophets who spoke about the new covenant projected this experience into the future: Yahweh will bring Israel out of exile back into the promised land.

What these prophets did for the future, the Yahwist did for the past. He projected this "out-into" experience into prehistory.

Yahweh created man in the desert. This is, in fact, what the land described in 2:5 means. Already the idea of a desert could remind us of the desert at the time of the exodus. After Yahweh planted the garden in Eden, he brought man into this paradise. "Yahweh God took the man and put him in the garden of Eden" (2:15, cf. 2:8). So we find here this double movement: "out" of that desert, "into" the paradise.

It is not only the theme which is important, but also the choice of the vocabulary that is typical. The same verb, translated here by "took", is used in many biblical texts to express the idea of a bringing out for the purpose of an entry (Dt. 30:4; Ezek. 36:24; 37:21; Is. 14:2). The verb contains at the same time the idea of election. All this, of course, is no longer evident in our different translations. To express the entry into paradise the writer uses the verb "put", which also can belong to the technical vocabulary for the entry of Israel into the promised land. The verb includes the idea of peace and rest after migration (Dt. 3:20; 12:10; 25:19; Jos. 1:13, 15; 21:44; Ezek. 37:14).

As mentioned earlier, the prophets, in speaking about the restoration of Israel, used to do the same thing as the Yahwist did for the past. Note, for example, Is. 14:1: "Yahweh will have compassion on Jacob and will again choose Israel, and will put them back in their own land", where the ideas of election and settlement are present.

After her sojourn in the desert, Israel could then enter the promised land, which was also presented as a paradise, "a land flowing with milk and honey" (Ex. 3:8), a land which Yahweh has given her, and therefore the land of God. The first man was taken out of his desert to enter a paradise, full of water and richness: "you were in Eden, the garden of God" (Ezek. 28:13).

The profound meaning of exodus is not a pure local movement from one place to another, but rather from being the servants of the Egyptians to becoming servants of Yahweh. It was a movement from slavery to service.[6] The first man, according to the Yahwist, was chosen by God and

---

6. Cf. the title of the book by G. AUZOU, *De la servitude au service. Étude du livre de l'Exode*, Paris, 1961.

introduced into intimacy with him. Right from the beginning man was placed in this freeing movement of salvation history.

(3) *Request for submission*: What the Great King had done for his new vassal gave him a right to gratitude and submission. This included, as we have seen, a request for total loyalty as well as other specific stipulations. Israel's covenant is not only related to Yahweh's saving actions, but is also a demand for her *total submission*.

This aspect is used by the Yahwist and projected into the relationship between God and mankind in prehistory. Adam's exodus experience entailed for him also a fundamental obligation. Yahweh took Adam out of the desert and brought him into paradise, it is said, "to till *('ābad)* it and keep *(šāmar)* it" (2:15).

This sentence has always caused some difficulties. Did this marvellous paradise and garden of God, with all the trees good for food (2:9), need to be cultivated? And what could be the meaning of "keep this garden"? Against whom? The understanding can well become much easier when seen in the context of the covenant.

The two verbs indeed belong to the technical vocabulary of the covenant, if they are used in a covenant context. The verb *'ābad* is often used in the first section of the Book of Exodus with a very interesting wordplay attached to it. It is often said that Yahweh will bring Israel out of Egypt, out of the house of "servitude", where they were "slaves", and had to "serve" the Egyptians with a hard "service". All these words are derived from the same root *'ābad* (Ex. 1:13-14; 2:23; 20:2 etc.). The deliverance of Israel out of Egypt has a very precise aim, in view of their "service" to God, which is expressed by the same root *'ābad*. "And you shall say to Pharaoh, 'Thus says Yahweh, Israel is my first-born son, and I say to you, "Let my son go that he may serve me" '" (Ex. 4:23; cf. also 3:12; 7:16,26; 8:16 etc.). This service to God is nothing other than the service that Yahweh will ask of his people at Sinai, in other words the total submission of the covenant partner. At the great covenant celebration at Shechem, the verb is again used in the same context: "...for it is Yahweh our God who brought us and our fathers up from the land of Egypt, out of the house of bondage...therefore we also will serve Yahweh, for he is our God" (Jos. 24:17-18); "And the people said to Joshua, 'Yahweh our God we will serve and his voice we will obey'" (Jos. 24:24). The same verb is often used in the book of Deuteronomy, which is so deeply imbued by the covenant idea (Dt. 5:9; 6:13; 7:4 etc.). We may conclude that the verb *'ābad* is one of the characteristic verbs used to express total loyalty and submission expected from the covenant partner. This now may enlighten the meaning of the text taken from Genesis, where the Yahwist uses the same verb to express the request for total submission from Adam, playing also on the double meaning of this verb: work in the garden and service to God.

What has been said about the first verb may be equally applied to the verb "to keep". This is another verb expressing total submission to the demands of the covenant, and acceptance of its laws (Ex. 15:26; 19:5; Lev. 18:4,5,26,30 and very often again in Deuteronomy 4:2,6,9,40; 5:1 etc.).

God has introduced mankind into his garden, into his intimacy, but he expects in return gratitude and total submission on the part of man.

But in every treaty, after the request for total loyalty, some *specific stipulations* are given to clarify what this service means. Yahweh has given Israel long lists of laws, and above all he has given the decalogue (Ex. 20:1 ff.; Dt. 5:6 ff.).

In the relation between God and man in paradise, following the request for total submission, God adds a more precise order: "You may freely eat of every tree of the garden; but of the tree of the knowledge of good and evil you shall not eat" (2:16-17). This sentence is stylistically formulated as a negative apodictic law. The biblical tradition has two kinds of laws: apodictic laws, "you shall" or "you shall not"; and casuistic laws, "if...then". Most of the extra-biblical laws are presented in the casuistic form. This raises the question about the origin of the apodictic form. One possible explanation refers to the extra-biblical treaties in which some stipulations have such a formulation, and may explain the apodictic form of some of the biblical laws, since they are covenant stipulations.[7] The Yahwist again applies this to this particular stipulation from God to man, confirming again the covenant idea which seems to be present in the whole passage.

But what exactly is behind the symbolic language of this command? The other images used in the text, like the serpent, suggest idolatry and the cult of fertility rites.[8] Adam and Eve certainly refused to recognize the true God; they even wanted to become like him (3:5). The Yahwist says in very symbolic language that God expects mankind to observe the *first commandment*: "You shall have no other gods before me" (Ex. 20:3), which is also formulated as an apodictic negative law.

The Mosaic law had many other stipulations telling the Israelite how he was supposed to serve his God, such as the many laws pertaining to different feasts and sacrifices. The Yahwist, of course, knew these laws, since he himself lived according to them, and he now projects some of them into his prehistory. Mankind was already living the Mosaic law in anticipation, we might say, as we notice when God prefers Abel's sacrifice to that of Cain. We can find several reasons to justify this preference for

---

7. In this line, for instance, J. L'HOUR, "L'Alliance de Sichem", in *R.B.*, 69 (1962), pp. 15-16. This explanation is not accepted by others, who see the origin of these apodictic laws in the wisdom tradition: E. GERSTENBERGER, *Wesen und Herkunft des 'apodiktischen Rechts'*, Neukirchen, 1965 and by the same writer "Covenant and Commandment", in *J.B.L.*, 84 (1965), pp. 38-51, but see a critical reply by M. J. BUSS, "The Covenant Theme in Historical Perspective", in *V.T.*, 16 (1966), pp. 502-504 and J. J. STAMM and M. E. ANDREW, *The Ten Commandments in Recent Research*, S.B.T. II 2, London, 1967, especially pp. 45 ff.
8. G. LAMBERT, "Le drame du jardin d'Eden", in *N.R.T.*, 76 (1954), pp. 917-948, 1044-1072; P. F. ELLIS, The Yahwist, pp. 61-65, 165-172.

Abel on the part of God. First, Abel's sacrifice was in perfect accordance with the much later law. Abel did not sacrifice just anything, but "of the firstlings of his flock" (4:4) because according to the law, the firstlings belonged to Yahweh: "All that opens the womb is mine, all your male cattle, the firstlings of cow and sheep" (Ex. 34:19). Abel offered even "of their fat portions" (4:4). These portions, being the best, were reserved to God according to the law: "Then from the sacrifice of the peace offering as an offering by fire to Yahweh, he shall offer its fat..." (Lev. 3:9-11, 14-16).

In the story about the flood the yahwistic tradition distinguishes between clean and unclean animals (7:2), a distinction which is not made by the more recent priestly tradition (6:19). So again, to express how faithful mankind was living with the true God, the Yahwist projects into his prehistory this Mosaic distinction between clean and unclean animals (Lev. 11; Dt. 14:3-21). Noah is obliged to take seven pairs of clean, but only one pair of unclean animals, because he can eat only the clean and he also requires some of them for his sacrifice. "Then Noah built an altar to Yahweh and took of every clean animal and of every clean bird, and offered burnt offerings on the altar" (8:20), according to the law of the burnt offerings (Lev. 1). It is, therefore, not surprising to see that Yahweh is pleased with Noah's offering: "Yahweh smelled the pleasing odour" (8:21), according to a technical expression of the Israelite ritual (Ex. 29:18,25,41; Lev. 1:9,13; Num. 28:13 etc.).

For the Yahwist there was no doubt. Mankind from the beginning was supposed to submit totally to God by observing the first commandment with everything that it entailed. The Mosaic law not only regulated the vertical relation between mankind and God, but was also concerned about the horizontal dimension between mankind and his fellowmen. These relationships are indeed a very important aspect of biblical revelation, and, therefore, one cannot exist without the other.[9] For instance, the prophets often reject all sacrifices to God, when a poor relationship of justice exists between men. If one has no respect for God what will govern one's relationship with others? Likewise if one despises one's fellowmen, how can one really love God?

This concept is also present in the yahwistic prehistory. Once man has rejected the true God, what then is going to control him? Sin has entered into the world, and it now continues. The second step is the story of Cain and Abel. Cain, jealous about his brother's success, got angry and finally "killed him" (4:8). This is, of course, directly opposed to the *fifth commandment*, "You shall not kill" (Ex. 20:13). And so evil grows. After rejecting this respect for his fellowman, man becomes his own centre and pleasure becomes the norm of his life. This is what the Yahwist says

---

9. W. VOGELS, "The Social Dimension of the Bible's Teaching", in *Attentive to the Cry of the Needy*, Donum Dei 19, Ottawa, 1973, pp. 11-26.

in his next story. Lamech took two wives (4:19) against the original plan (2:24), and by doing so, he is acting against the *sixth commandment*, "You shall not commit adultery" (Ex. 20:14). Into this world of increasing violence and evil, God sends his flood, but even this lesson is not enough. The first story after the flood is again a story of sin. One of the sons of Noah dishonours his father: "Ham... saw the nakedness of his father..." (9:22). The important aspect of the narrative is the insistence upon the relation between father and son (cf. the repetition of the word "father", 9:22,23, and "sons", 9:18,19,24), suggesting that we have a violation of the *fourth commandment*, "Honour your father and your mother" (Ex. 20:12), and also of the laws of respect for one's relatives in the field of sexuality. "None of you shall approach anyone near of kin to him to uncover nakedness... You shall not uncover the nakedness of your father..." (Lev. 18:6 ff.).

So the major commandments of the decalogue, charter of the Sinai covenant and even some very precise Mosaic laws were the concrete stipulations which mankind was supposed to observe to manifest its gratitude and submission to God, who had taken it into his intimacy.

(4) *Witnesses*: In international treaties the gods of the two partners were called to be the official witnesses of the contract; at other times deified nature was called. The latter could only be used in biblical texts to bear witness to the covenant between Yahweh and Israel. "I call heaven and earth to witness against you this day..." (Dt. 4:26; cf. Dt. 30:19; 31:28; 32:1; Is. 1:2; Mic. 6:1-2; etc.).[10] However there are occasions when the calling of witnesses is not mentioned.

One particular verse belonging to the yahwistic tradition might be used to explain this element of the covenant formulary. God promises after the flood never to destroy the earth again as he had done before. As a guarantee he points to the regularity we observe in nature. In a certain sense nature is a witness of God's gracious promise to mankind: "While the earth remains, seedtime and harvest, cold and heat, summer and winter, day and night shall not cease" (8:22). While this is certainly not a very clear point in our thesis and remains rather weak, it is a normal situation since the problem of witnesses in the covenant always remained obscure. No gods who were the witnesses in the extra-biblical texts could be called upon to testify between Yahweh and his people.

(5) *Blessings and Curses*: These are determined by the faithfulness or unfaithfulness of the vassal. This element of the covenant formulary is present. In this respect let us return to the text of Gen. 2:15-17, in which we have already distinguished God's benefits, a request for total submission and a very precise stipulation; we also find there a curse linked with

---

10. M. DELCOR, "Les attaches littéraires, l'origine et la signification de l'expression biblique 'prendre à témoin le ciel et la terre'", in *V.T.*, 16 (1966), pp. 8-25.

the commandment: "for in the day that you eat of it you shall die" (v. 17).

Here then we have a perfect example of a curse, and indeed not just any curse, but a very classical curse, well-known and formulated exactly in the same manner as is to be found in several of the juridical texts (Ex. 31:14,15; Lev. 20:2,9,10,11,12,13,15,16 etc.).

This is not the only text in which the Yahwist speaks of a curse for we find other curses in his prehistory (3:14,17; 4:11; 5:29; 9:25) and likewise there is a blessing (9:26). In the later history of Israel, the people were faced with a choice of either being faithful to Yahweh and thereby receiving his blessings, or being unfaithful and struck down with curses: "see, I have set before you this day life and good, death and evil..." (Dt. 30:15-20). In other words, the people are divided into two groups. In the priestly tradition's prehistory no such division is made. When presenting the descendants of mankind from Adam to Abraham it gives only a single line of the generations from the beginning to the end. But the Yahwist follows a different approach; with him we find that from the beginning mankind faced a choice, as is the case at the later stage with Israel. Because of this choice mankind is divided into two groups right from the start. Even before the flood two groups arose from the first couple. We have the sons of Cain, the one who killed his brother. In his family and his descendants evil grows and people turn away from God (4:17-24). Parallel to this group, we have the other section of mankind, the sons of his brother Seth (4:25 ff.). In his descendants men start to call upon the name of Yahweh (4:26) and also to receive a promise of better times to come (5:29). The same division between good and evil reappears immediately after the flood with the sons of Noah: "cursed be Canaan" (9:25) but "blessed be Yahweh, the God of Shem" (9:26).

We have, therefore, discovered nearly all the elements belonging to the covenant formulary. The Yahwist knew this structure because it was part of the theology of the covenant between Yahweh and Israel. The Yahwist used these elements very freely and projected them into the past to present the relation between God and mankind as a covenant relationship. But he did even more.

Israel was often unfaithful to her covenant obligations, and so the prophets accused Israel of rebellion. They put Israel on *trial*, with a very special formulary: the rîb-pattern or lawsuit, as we have seen in the introduction. The Yahwist uses also some of this thinking in his prehistory.

After their sin, Adam and Eve are put on trial by God (3:8 ff.) with all the juridical procedures of questions and answers, inquiry and excuses. Even the vocabulary of the text refers once more to the covenant vocabulary. Adam's answer, "I heard your voice ... and I was afraid" (3:10), contains two verbs which are sometimes used as technical terms in covenant theology.

"To hear the voice of Yahweh", which can also be rendered by "to listen to his voice", "to obey his voice", is very common in Deuteronomy (Dt. 4:30; 8:20; 9:23; 13:5,19 etc.). It is one of those verbs expressing total submission to the stipulations of the covenant,[11] very often in the context of curses and blessings (Dt. 28:1,2,15,45,62). A comparison with one particular text of Deuteronomy might be enlightening: exile for Israel will be the supreme curse (30:1), but then Israel will be converted to Yahweh, and return to him. This is expressed with the same verb, "listen to his voice" (v. 2); then Yahweh will bring his fallen people back (v. 3 ff.). In this particular context the word is used to express Israel's conversion. So the answer of Adam that he heard God's voice might contain some regret and indicate perhaps the beginning of his conversion. The Yahwist seems to suggest this by comparing Adam's present attitude— he listens to the voice of Yahweh—with his sin, for which he is blamed by God: "you have listened to the voice of your wife" (3:17).

The second verb, "to be afraid", "to fear" is also a very technical term to express the right attitude of man towards God (Gen. 22:12; 42:18; Ex. 1:17; etc.), and as such is very appropriate for the faithfulness of the partner of the covenant in observing the different stipulations (Dt. 6:2,13,24; 10:12,20; Jos. 24:14; Jer. 32:39; etc.).[12]

Besides this first trial, we also have the trial of Cain (4:9 ff.) and, of course, above all the great trial of the flood.

Until now we have seen in the yahwistic prehistory several aspects of salvation history: God's benefits, human unfaithfulness and divine punishment.

But the history of salvation does not end with punishment; there is hope because of God's *mercy* and *promises* of salvation. This most important element is not absent from prehistory. God showed his patience to Adam and Eve, who did not die the day of their sin as the curse had said (2:17); God even blessed them with new life (3:20), and he clothed them (3:21). Although the punishment of Cain was more severe he still received divine protection (4:15). In a world of growing violence and evil, Noah found favour in God's eyes (6:8), since he was the only just person (7:1), and because of him and through him, his family shared in Noah's salvation (7:1). We see in God's treatment here the typical biblical idea of the remnant.[13]

And above all, two promises are of supreme importance. The text, often called the Protevangelium (3:15), promises the victory of mankind over the powers of evil. Some understand this as a victory obtained by collective mankind, while others think of it as obtained by the messiah

---

11. A. F. FENZ, *"Auf Jahwes Stimme hören". Eine biblische Begriffsuntersuchung*, Wien, 1964.
12. H. A. BRONGERS, "La Crainte du Seigneur, *yir'at JHWH, yir'at Elohim*", in *O.T.S.*, 5 (1948), pp. 151-173; J. BECKER, *Gottesfurcht im Alten Testament*, Analecta Biblica 25, Rome, 1965; L. DEROUSSEAUX, *La crainte de Dieu dans l'Ancien Testament*, Lectio Divina 63, Paris, 1970.
13. G. F. HASEL, *The Remnant. The History and Theology of the Remnant Idea from Genesis to Isaiah*, Andrews University Monographs, 5, Berrien Springs, 1972.

representing mankind.[14] After the flood God strongly promises "never again" (8:21).

The four main elements of salvation history are present: God's benefits, man's sin, punishment and hope, and all this is imbued by covenant thinking.

In this study of the yahwistic prehistory we have not mentioned the last narrative: the story of the Tower of Babel (11:1-9),[15] which plays a very particular role. When men rebel against God out of pride, trouble starts all over again. It is a kind of re-edition of the sin of the first couple, but now it is a collective sin of mankind. The builders have a very specific purpose: "lest we be scattered abroad upon the face of the whole earth" (11:4). The divine punishment will be precisely their dispersion: "Yahweh scattered them" (repeated twice v. 8,9). Undoubtedly the verb "to scatter" is most stressed in this text. This same verb has a very important meaning when applied to Israel. It is the technical term for the supreme punishment of unfaithful Israel: "I will scatter you among all the nations" and in the promise of the restoration: "I will gather you again from all the peoples where I have scattered you" (Dt. 28:64; 30:3; Jer. 9:15; 13:24; 18:17; 23:1; 30:11; Ezek. 11:16,17; 12:15; 20:23,34,41; 22:15; 28:25; etc.). Yahweh has shown his patience with Israel for a long time, but then he inflicts the supreme punishment upon the unfaithful partner of the covenant: Israel is sent into exile. All prehistory has also shown God's patience with mankind. There have been many trials, but "nothing that they propose to do will now be impossible for them" (11:6), and therefore follows the supreme punishment for mankind; we could call this the *exile of mankind*. Men will no longer live in mutual understanding, but in dispersion. As Israel's exile was to be to Babylon, this story happened in Babel. Contrary to all other trials in prehistory, where some hope always persists, this story finishes with a punishment. As exile seemed to be the end of Israel's history and her covenant, the history of mankind and the primitive universal covenant seem to end with this exile.

As in the moment of despair some prophets announced the new covenant to Israel, so also we shall see that new hope will arise for mankind. We shall show this in chapter two.

---

14. Some exegetes claim that this verse has no message of hope: G. VON RAD, *Genesis*, The Old Testament Library, London, 1961, p. 90; C. WESTERMANN, *The Genesis Accounts of Creation*, Philadelphia, 1964, pp. 33-34; B. VAWTER, *On Genesis: A New Reading*, Garden City, 1977, pp. 82-84. For the message of hope and the discussion on the messianic meaning: J. COPPENS, "Le Protévangile. Un nouvel essai d'exégèse", in *E.T.L.*, 26 (1950), pp. 5-36; B. RIGAUX, "La femme et son lignage dans Gen. 3:14-15", in *R.B.*, 61 (1954), pp. 321-348; W. WIFALL, "Gen. 3:15. A Protevangelium?", in *C.B.Q.*, 36 (1974), pp. 361-365; A. FEUILLET, "Le triomphe de la femme d'après le Protévangile", in *Communio*, 3 (1978), pp. 8-19.
15. K. SEYBOLD, "Der Turmbau zu Babel. Zur Erstehung von Gen. 11:1-9", in *V.T.*, 26 (1976), pp. 453-479; C. HOUTMAN, "'...opdat wij niet over geheel de aarde verspreid worden'. Notities over Genesis 11:1-9", in *Ned.T.T.*, 31 (1977), pp. 102-120; B. W. ANDERSON, "Unity and Diversity in God's Creation. A Study of the Babel Story", in *Currents in Theology and Mission*, 5 (1978), pp. 69-81.

The Yahwist has presented his prehistory in a very broad universal perspective. He applies to mankind what Israel considered as her privilege: the covenant. He composes his prehistory with the scheme of the great salvation history and even more precisely with the elements of the covenant. In this we find in miniature what we will read in the rest of the Bible. Mankind experienced an exodus-entry event; it was taken into the intimacy of God. Men already knew the true God, his revelation and his demands. They were expected to answer in gratitude by total submission, faithful observance of God's commandments, and especially by observance of the decalogue, the charter of the covenant. But mankind became unfaithful and experienced punishment, though God showed his patience and mercy, and hope was always there. In final punishment, men have been scattered and instead of living in harmony with God and among themselves, mankind now lives in a world of misunderstanding.

If this is the right interpretation of the yahwistic view on prehistory, one might be surprised not to find the word $b^e r\hat{\imath}t$, "covenant". The Yahwist used the vocabulary, the structures and the theology of the covenant, but not the term itself. Why does the text never say that Yahweh made a covenant with mankind?

This omission in itself is not a very big problem, since similar examples exist in the Bible. One very typical example is the absence or the rare use of the word "covenant" by many of the pre-exilic prophets. The texts of some of these prophets contain the vocabulary, the structures and the theology of the covenant, but not the term itself. There have been several explanations offered. Many exegetes believe that these prophets avoided the word on purpose.[16] Popular beliefs in Israel too often considered the "covenant" as a privilege, and the term alone was enough to produce misdirected confidence in her election. The prophets, on the contrary, insisted upon the duties involved, something which Israel was inclined to forget. So the absence of the term does not mean that these prophets did not believe in the covenant, but rather that they avoided the term for a very precise purpose.

The Yahwist too may perhaps have had some particular reasons to avoid the term. The yahwistic tradition was put into writing during the reign of Solomon, which was a period of expansion. Israel had conquered many neighbouring nations and also had initiated rich international trade relations. So it was a time of luxury and of national pride. But all this brought on the tendency to oppress others, a tendency arising from having suffered from others for so long. But surely Israel must have asked herself some theological questions: why is it that all nations do not par-

---

16. R. E. CLEMENTS, *Prophecy and Covenant*, S.B.T. 43, London, 1965, p. 55; B. VAWTER, "Recent Literature on the Prophets", in *Conc.*, n. 10 (1965), pp. 61-67, II. The Prophets and the Covenant, pp. 63-64; D. J. MCCARTHY, "Covenant in the Old Testament. The Present State of Inquiry", in *C.B.Q.*, 27 (1965), pp. 217-240 especially pp. 231-232; L. PERLITT, *Bundestheologie im Alten Testament*, Das 'Bundesschweigen' bei den Propheten des 8 Jahrhunderts, p. 129 ff.

ticipate in the covenant with Yahweh? Why do they not share the blessings of Israel? How could they be conquered? The most simplistic and probably popular answer must have been: "we are the elected people. Yahweh is with us". The yahwistic tradition has gone deeper, reflecting upon Israel's own experience. When Israel was conquered in the past and had lost her independence, how did she interpret this? No doubt she saw it as a punishment for her unfaithfulness to her covenant with Yahweh. The situation of other nations must then be explained in a similar way: mankind has been unfaithful to "its covenant" and the humiliation of the nations is punishment for their sins.

But as Israel had always experienced salvation after oppression, some salvation will also be offered to mankind. The Yahwist goes on to describe how this will happen. We will treat this in our second chapter. The yahwistic writer, who has an intense universal theology, is perhaps reacting against some narrow-minded popular beliefs. He might have been afraid, though, that his view of this period of national pride would be rejected if it were too clear. This is why he avoids saying explicitly that God concluded a "covenant" with mankind. But what he did was clear enough for those who were ready to accept his theory. He reminds Israel not to be too proud, because her privilege in having a covenant was once the privilege of all mankind.

## II. THE PRIMITIVE UNIVERSAL COVENANT IN OTHER BIBLICAL TRADITIONS[17]

We will now investigate whether or not the concept of a primitive universal covenant as proposed by the Yahwist, one of the oldest biblical traditions, is limited to him or if other biblical writers and traditions have adopted this same view. Do we find in those texts what was absent in the Yahwist, the term "covenant" itself? While going through the whole Bible we will study those texts where the word "covenant" is used in this sense.

THE NOAH COVENANT (Gen. 9:1-17)

The Yahwist avoided the term "covenant" for a very special reason. The priestly writer, who composed his prehistory many centuries later and lived, therefore, in a different historical context, used the term without hesitation (Gen. 6:18; 9:9,11,12,13,15,16,17).[18] To the priestly writer there is no doubt that God concluded a "covenant" with mankind, long before his covenant with Israel. We can enumerate the characteristics of this primitive covenant.

It is first of all a *natural* covenant. Like every contract, it contains divine promises and demands from men. God promises to maintain the

---

17. W. VOGELS, "L'Alliance primitive universelle", in *Egl.Th.*, 3 (1972), pp. 291-322.
18. P.A.H. DE BOER, "Quelques remarques sur l'Arc dans la Nuée (Gen. 9:8-17)", in *Questions disputées d'Ancien Testament*, ed. C. Brekelmans, Leuven, 1974, pp. 105-114; L. DEQUEKER, "Noah and Israel. The Everlasting Divine Covenant with Mankind", *ibid.*, pp. 115-129.

established order in creation, the cosmos will never become a chaos again (v. 11,15) and God expects men to respect this order. There is no "supernatural" revelation; the laws imposed upon Noah could be called "natural law principles" for mankind: "be fruitful and multiply, and fill the earth" (v. 1,7), which is a directive and at the same time a blessing. Respect for life relates to relations between mankind and animals, where mankind is master (v. 2-5), but also relates to relations between men mutually (v. 5-6). The sign of this covenant is found in nature in the form of the rainbow (v. 12-17).

This covenant is not concluded with one individual person or with one particular nation, but with all mankind, and as such is *universal*. God speaks to Noah after the flood as if to the father of the new mankind and his sons (v. 1,8): "Behold, I establish my covenant with you and your descendants after you" (v. 9). The covenant covers not only men, but also the world of all living creatures (v. 10,12,15,16): "every living creature of all flesh that is upon the earth" (v. 15,16). This very universal aspect is underlined by the frequent use of "all", "every" (v. 10(3x),11,12, 15(3x),16(2x),17).

The notion of universality also includes the idea of the brotherhood of man. Man should respect his fellowman because they are brothers: "For your lifeblood I will surely require a reckoning ... of every man's brother I will require the life of man" (v. 5). All men belong to the same family, since they are all made by God "in his own image" (v. 6). This is confirmed by the priestly tradition in its table of the nations (Gen. 10), where all the nations of the earth are related to the three sons of Noah. The Noah covenant is a universal *fraternal* covenant, or a covenant of brotherhood.

The Noah covenant is also a covenant of *peace* for mankind. The divine promises ensure the stability of the cosmos. God commits himself to keep the powers of nature under control; they will never destroy the earth again, "and never again shall there be a flood to destroy the earth" (v. 11,15). The animals ought not to be a danger for mankind (v. 5) nor men be in danger from men but between themselves they must respect the peace intended by God (v. 5-6). As a consequence we shall have a world in which men can live peacefully and free from constant fear of the violence which caused the flood (Gen. 6:11,13). There will be security and rest, as the root of the name Noah itself suggests.

And finally, this covenant with Noah is an *eternal* covenant. God commits himself: "with your descendants after you" (v. 9), "for all future generations" (v. 12). In his promises we also see the expression "never again" (v. 11,15). We find the term explicitly in "the everlasting covenant" (v. 16). The lasting aspect of this covenant is also expressed by the verbs "establish", "maintain" (6:18; 9:9,11,17). This covenant is going to stay, because God has committed himself as protector of mankind. All men will always be bound by it; no subsequent covenant will ever abrogate this one. The Noah covenant precedes every other covenant, because it is the expression of the natural order and the basis for the salvific order to come.

We first spoke about the priestly tradition, because it very clearly makes use of the term covenant in its prehistory and gives some distinct characteristics of this primitive universal covenant. It is interesting to see how these aspects reappear in several other biblical texts belonging to different periods. We will now consider these texts without going into all the details or discussing them fully, for we have done this elsewhere. We will rather give a kind of general survey of the most important texts which possibly refer to this primitive universal covenant. We do not say that these texts have copied the P-tradition, since many of these texts are older. We are not entering into the problems of what depends on what, or if there was a common source. This is irrelevant to our study here, as we said in our introduction.

### THE COVENANT OF BROTHERHOOD (Am. 1:9)

In his oracles against the nations, the prophet Amos accuses Tyre of her crimes, because she "did not remember the covenant of brotherhood" (1:9). This expression is unique in the Bible, so one must wonder if this text contains the same ideas as we have seen in the Noah covenant, which is characterized by the universal brotherhood of men.

The text is far from being clear, as is evident from the many different interpretations given to it.[19] We will have the opportunity of discussing this text again on several occasions. For our purpose here, it might be enough to say that one particular interpretation given is in reference to the ideas expressed in the Noah covenant by the priestly writer.

What was asked of mankind in the Noah covenant was that man respect his fellowman, because he is his brother (Gen. 9:5). This is the accusation of Amos. Tyre did not respect other people "because they delivered up a whole people to Edom" (1:9). Interestingly enough, in his next oracle against Edom, Amos says something very similar: "because he pursued his brother with the sword" (1:11).[20]

This may well be a possible interpretation for this expression; that is the least we can say. Amos accuses some nations of not respecting their

---

19. There are three major explanations given for this expression "covenant of brotherhood". (1) *A political international treaty between Tyre and another nation, possibly Israel*: J. PRIEST, "The Covenant of Brothers", in *J.B.L.*, 84 (1965), pp. 400-406; F. C. FENSHAM, "The Treaty between the Israelites and Tyrians", in *V.T.S.*, XVII (1969), pp. 71-87; (2) *The Covenant of consanguinity between Israel and Edom*: H. W. WOLFF, in *B.K.* XIV / 2, Neukirchen, 1969, p. 194 where he quotes other authors who opt for this interpretation; (3) *The Noah-Covenant*: A. NEHER, *Amos. Contribution à l'étude du prophétisme*, Paris, 1950, pp. 59-67, and partially A. FEUILLET, "L'universalisme et l'alliance dans la religion d'Amos", in *B.V.C.*, n. 17 (1957), pp. 17-29.
20. M. FISHBANE, "The Treaty Background of Amos 1:11 and Related Matters", in *J.B.L.*, 89 (1970), pp. 313-318; R. B. COOTE, "Amos 1:11: *RḤMYW*" in *J.B.L.*, 90 (1971), pp. 206-208; M. FISHBANE, "Additional Remarks on *RḤMYW* (Amos 1:11)", in *J.B.L.*, 91 (1972), pp. 391-393; J. R. BARTLETT, "The Brotherhood of Edom", in *J.S.O.T.*, 4 (1977), pp. 2-27.

neighbours, an attitude which demonstrates unfaithfulness to the basic universal covenant.

A COVENANT WITH THE BEASTS (Hos. 2:20)

The prophet Hosea accuses Israel of her unfaithfulness to the covenant in a long lawsuit (2:4-15), but he also adds some promises of restoration (2:16-25). Israel will be re-established in her now broken covenant: "You are my people ... Thou art my God" (2:25), and in v. 20 the prophet also speaks about another covenant to come.[21]

It is a very strange text about something more than a covenant between Yahweh and Israel: "I will make for you a covenant with the beasts of the field, the birds of the air, and the creeping things of the ground" (v. 20a). This can easily be compared with the Noah covenant: "I establish my covenant ...with every living creature that is with you, the birds, the cattle, and every beast of the earth with you" (Gen. 9:9-10). The restoration will be a return to the harmony in nature, in order that man will again be master over the animals (Gen. 9:2).

This future covenant will also bring the end of wars: "I will abolish the bow, the sword, and war from the land" (Hos. 2:20b). Man has nothing to fear anymore from his fellowmen. This is another aspect of the Noah covenant—man has to respect his fellowmen (Gen. 9:5-6).

The prophet Hosea too seems to know about a kind of natural, universal peace covenant, which he believed to have existed in the past, since he projects it as a restoration for the future: "in that day".

THE COVENANT WITH ADAM (Hos. 6:7)

One very interesting text is an oracle by the same prophet Hosea. The prophet blames the people of his days for their unfaithfulness by comparing it to the rebellion of Adam.

> But like Adam they violated the covenant,
> behold they dealt faithlessly with me (6:7).

The prophet makes a clear comparison. The people have violated the covenant as Adam did. This implies that Adam lived in a special covenant relationship with God, which he broke.

This could be a very important text to prove that other people also accept what the Yahwist has said. Hosea here does not speak about a covenant with Noah, but with Adam himself.

But since the person of Adam does not appear often in biblical tradition, and also for some other reasons, many exegetes attempt to correct

---

21. H. W. WOLFF, "Jahwe als Bundesvermittler", in *V.T.*, 6 (1956), pp. 316-320; U. DEVESCOVI, "La Nuova alleanza in Osea (2:16-25)", in *Bib.Or.*, 1 (1959), pp. 172-178; W. BRUEGGEMANN, *Tradition for Crisis. A Study in Hosea*, Richmond, 1968, pp. 115-116.

the text.[22] This is why in several translations all reference to the primitive covenant with Adam is eliminated.

## THE ETERNAL COVENANT (Is. 24:5)

One explicit statement on the primitive universal covenant appears in the so-called "Apocalypse of Isaiah" (Is. 24-27), which is post-exilic.

The context of Is. 24:5 speaks about a universal judgment. This is evident from the repetition of the word "earth" (v. 1,3,4(2x),5,6(2x)). This term can have the meaning of the promised land, but certainly indicates here the whole world. The parallel with "world" in v. 4b proves this very clearly. The text speaks about the whole of mankind, the "inhabitants" of the earth (v. 1,5,6(2x)).

Mankind is accused of having broken "the everlasting covenant" (v. 5). This certainly cannot be the covenant concluded with Israel, but must refer to a universal covenant between God and mankind such as, for instance, the universal covenant with Noah (Gen. 9:1-17), which also was called "everlasting" (Gen. 9:16).

Men have broken this covenant because "they have transgressed the laws, violated the statutes" (v. 5). Mankind has broken the law to which it was bound. The text specifies further the nature of this transgression: "the earth lies polluted under its inhabitants" (v. 5a). This expression in the Bible often refers to bloodshed: "you shall not thus pollute the land in which you live; for blood pollutes the land, and so expiation can be made for the land, for the blood that is shed in it..." (Num. 35:33 ff.; Ps. 106:38; compare also with Gen. 4:10 ff.; 6:5ff.; Dt. 21:1-9). This is precisely what happened in this case according to the context (Is. 26:21). This situation then corresponds to the natural law of mankind under the Noah covenant: "to respect life and not to shed blood" (Gen. 9:5).

## THE COVENANT OF PEACE (Is. 54:9-10)

Deutero-Isaiah compares the new covenant, which Yahweh will establish with Israel, with the Noah covenant, this primitive covenant with mankind (Gen. 9:1-17). We find the same characteristics in the two texts. It is a covenant of *peace* (v. 10), it is *eternal*, which is suggested by "no more", "shall not be removed" (v. 9,10), and is said explicitly to be "everlasting" (v. 8). This covenant is also *natural*. Just as in the time of Noah the rainbow was the sign of the stability of the Noah covenant, so here the mountains and the hills are a kind of sign of stability (v. 10). Deutero-Isaiah, who is very universal in his teaching, foresees that the covenant of peace will one day unite all mankind in harmony; this is another reason for comparing it with the *universal* covenant with Noah.

---

22. The Hebrew text reads $k^e$'ādām ("like Adam", or "like a man"). The correction often suggested is $b^e$'ādām ("at Adam"): "they have violated the covenant at Adam". Cf. e.g. The Jerusalem Bible, The Revised Standard Version, The New English Bible.

This text clearly shows a belief in a primitive universal covenant, which serves as the example for the new covenant.

### A Covenant with the Day and the Night (Jer. 33:20-25)

The text of Jer. 33:17-26 has a purpose similar to the preceding text of Deutero-Isaiah. To reassure Israel of the stability of the new covenant, Deutero-Isaiah compared it with the Noah covenant of the priestly tradition. The present writer also refers to prehistory to encourage the people (v. 24). He speaks about the creation of day and night (v. 25a, cf. Gen. 1:5, P-tradition), with their regular succession (v. 20b, cf. Gen. 8:22, J-tradition). The stability in the cosmic order, which cannot be interrupted by men, is the image of the stability of the new order. And this order in nature is called by the writer "a covenant of Yahweh with the day and the night" (v. 20a). Just as each covenant includes obligations, this one also has its laws. God has established "the ordinances of heaven and earth" (v. 25b), the natural laws that will direct this order (cf. Jer. 31:35-37).

The writer of this paragraph unites creation with salvation history under the common concept of covenant. There is the covenant of creation (v. 20a); the covenant with Abraham (v. 22a, with clearly the language of the promises to Abraham, Gen. 13:16; 15:5; 22:17; etc., cf. also in v. 26 "Abraham"); the Sinai covenant (v. 24b, "my people"); the Davidic covenant (v. 21a); and the covenant with Levi (v. 21b).

However, besides all the different covenants which are concluded in favour of the elected people, there is yet another one, which could be called natural, with natural laws for creation. The natural covenant precedes all the others and is their guarantee. We can now surely speak of a primitive covenant.

### A Covenant of Peace (Ezek. 34:25)

The prophet Ezekiel has a text (34:25) very similar to Hos. 2:20, which we have just studied. The same ideas are repeated. The prophet mentions "a covenant of peace": there will be no danger any more from the animals (v. 25,28), neither from one's fellowmen (v. 28,29), and thus there will be "security" (v. 25,27,28).

There is a difference, however, from the text of Hosea, which says that Yahweh will make a covenant with the animals in favour of Israel: "I will make for you a covenant with the beasts of the field..." (Hos. 2:20). Ezekiel on the contrary says: "I will make with them a covenant of peace" (Ezek. 34:25). According to Hosea, Yahweh will make a covenant with the animals in favour of Israel; but contrariwise Yahweh chases the animals: "I will banish wild beasts from the land" (v. 25b). Israel, and therefore man, becomes the partner of the covenant: "I will make with them a covenant of peace". Both concepts, the one of Hosea and the one of Ezekiel, are present in the Noah covenant: "I establish my covenant with you (Ezekiel), ...and with every beast of the earth (Hosea)" (Gen. 9:9-10).

Ezekiel, speaking about the restoration of Israel, predicts the return of a natural order which existed in the primitive covenant. In doing so he shows that he too believes in the existence of such a covenant.

THE COVENANT WITH ALL THE PEOPLES (Zech. 11:10)

The section of Zech. 11:4-17, often entitled the "allegory of the shepherds", is one of the most obscure and frequently discussed texts of the Bible.[23] Many aspects of it remain mysterious. One of the difficulties is the formula: "the covenant which I had made with all the peoples". It is unique in the whole biblical tradition, but could be very interesting for our topic.

One possible and well-accepted interpretation would be to understand it as a covenant between Yahweh and all the peoples of the earth. Shepherds in Palestine have two rods, one to chase the wild beasts and the other, the real staff, to guide the flock. By breaking the first rod, "Grace", the flock is no longer protected against wild beasts. In other words, Israel is again vulnerable to the attacks of the nations, since Yahweh has broken his covenant with the peoples. One could compare this text with the texts of Hosea 2:20 and Ezekiel 34:25, where the same ideas are expressed. In the study of these two texts we have shown the relation with the Noah covenant and how those two prophets indirectly reveal their belief in a primitive covenant. In accepting these similarities, we must be aware that there is an important difference. For Hosea, Yahweh made a covenant with the beasts in favour of Israel; for Ezekiel, Yahweh concluded a covenant of peace with Israel, but here the partner of the covenant is directly the nations: Yahweh has made a covenant with all the peoples. It is perhaps interesting to note that the prophet does not refer to a covenant with all the "nations", but with all "peoples". This term is always used, as we have seen before, when Israel is referred to as covenant partner, but never the term "nation". The peoples now are really in a covenant relationship with God. This text (Zech. 11:10), then, speaks even more clearly and more directly than either the Hosea or the Ezekiel text about this universal covenant as expressed in the Noah covenant (Gen. 9:1-17). One of its characteristics is the fraternity between all men, which, according to one possible interpretation, is behind the "covenant of brotherhood" in Amos 1:9. That our writer was thinking of the brotherhood of men may be confirmed through the parallel with the second rod, "Union". This rod will be broken "annulling the brotherhood between Judah and Israel" (v. 14). The idea of "brotherhood" is one of the technical concepts in treaties.

Deutero-Zechariah seems to be a very important witness of the belief in a covenant between God and all the peoples and thus in a universal covenant.

---

23. M. REHM, "Die Hirtenallegorie Zach. 11:4-14", in *B.Z.*, 4 (1960), pp. 186-208.

THE ETERNAL COVENANT (Sir. 17:12; 44:18)

The book of Jesus Ben Sirach contains several explicit references to prehistory. Two of these texts are of more immediate interest to our study.

Verses 17-18 in chapter 44 belong to the section called "the praises of the Fathers" and recall the story of Noah. The transmission of the text has some problems. The Hebrew text quotes the covenant in v. 17, while the Greek text, on the contrary, has a statement on the covenant in v. 18. But in any case, we have here a clear, explicit reference to the covenant with Noah, often even with the same vocabulary as in Gen. 6:18; 9:1-17. As in the priestly tradition (Gen. 9:16) the covenant is called "everlasting".

The text of Sir. 17:12 is more difficult to interpret. It is part of the section about men in creation (16:24 ff.). Here we are at the level of universalism. Everything that the author says in 17:1 ff. must be applied to men. What is then the "eternal covenant" in v. 12?

The whole paragraph is inspired by prehistory. Someone has called 16:26-30 a midrash commentary of Gen. 1, which belongs to the priestly tradition. But when the author arrives at the creation of men in chapter 17, he seems to be inspired at the same time by the J- and by the P-tradition; 17:1 can be compared with Gen. 2:7; 3:19 J, but 17:2 rather with Gen. 1:28-30 P.[24] The discussion starts in vv. 11-14. We may well ask what the source is that inspired these verses.

Some exegetes continue to see in them allusions to the prehistory: the parallel of "knowledge" and of "life" in v. 11 that could refer to Gen. 2:9; the "law of life" in v. 11 and v. 14 that could refer to Gen. 2:16-17. One can see in this an allusion to the natural laws imposed upon mankind. "Their eyes saw his glorious majesty, and their ears heard the glory of his voice" (v. 13) could well be compared with the attitudes of the first couple towards God (Gen. 2:16-22; 3:8). And thus the "eternal covenant" would then be a covenant concluded by God with mankind right at the beginning. But since the term "eternal covenant" (v. 12a) is the same as in 44:18, where it certainly means the Noah covenant, some exegetes see here, too, a reference to this covenant of Gen. 9:1-17. "The commandments to each of them concerning his neighbour" (v. 14) would confirm their views, since these are precisely the stipulations of the Noah covenant (Gen. 9:5). We would have then a reference to a primitive covenant with Adam or at least with Noah.

But on the other hand, several exegetes believe that vv. 11-14 are more inspired by Mosaic tradition than by prehistory. The preceding verses contain a reference to "natural" laws (e.g. v. 7), but in what follows the "supernatural" revelation is treated. And so "the law of life" (v. 11) could

---

24. B. BRODMANN, "Quid doceat S. Scriptura utriusque Testamenti de indole historica narrationis de paradiso et lapsu, Gen. 2-3", in *Ant.*, 12 (1937), for Ben Sirach, pp. 145-153; J. DE FRAINE, "Het loflied op de menselijke waardigheid in Eccli. 17:1-14", in *Bijdr.*, 11 (1950), pp. 10-22; H. DUESBERG, "La dignité de l'homme. Sir. 16:24-17:14", in *B.V.C.*, n. 82 (1968), pp. 15-21.

be illustrated by Dt. 30:15-30; "their eyes saw his glorious majesty, and their ears heard the glory of his voice" (v. 13) could be compared with the vision and the audition of the divine revelation at Sinai (Ex. 19:11, 16-19; 20:18,22; 24:10-11,16; Dt. 4:12; 5:23-27); and v. 14 would refer to the decalogue (Ex. 20:1-17). Consequently, the "eternal covenant" of v. 12 would mean the Sinai covenant (cf. Sir. 45:5). It is difficult to accept, though, that the author is speaking only about Israel. The whole text from 17:1 ff. treats man simply as creature. Only in v. 17 does he make a difference between Israel and the other nations. If one accepts all these parallels with the Mosaic tradition, then, one must admit that the writer applies all this to describe the destiny of mankind.

It is perhaps not necessary to oppose these two positions. We could well admit that Ben Sirach used the traditions of prehistory and those of the Sinai covenant to speak about mankind. This would then be a very interesting example of another writer whose theology corresponds with the yahwistic tradition. As we have seen, the Yahwist, too, composed his prehistory using the covenant relationship between Yahweh and his people to project this into the past in order to speak about the relationship between God and men. Ben Sirach might have done the same, but went a step further; he even used the term "covenant" which the Yahwist still avoided. Really, God concluded an eternal covenant with mankind.

We now have reviewed most of the texts where the term "covenant" could have a possible reference to a primitive universal covenant. The results we have obtained may perhaps seem poor. Most of these texts, when studied separately, have difficulties. Sometimes the transmission of the texts is discussed, and very often their interpretation, and thus their universalistic dimension, is not accepted. But by bringing all these texts together and comparing them with each other, we obtain richer and more promising results for those who find in them an expression of a universal covenant.

The texts cover the whole biblical period, starting with one of the oldest, namely the Yahwist, and continuing until one of the most recent, namely the Ben Sirach text. The other texts are in between these two extremes, but they become more numerous when we come to the exile. We find them in the three main sections of the Bible: in the "Torah", the "Prophets", and the "Writings". All this proves that it was not just one period or one particular group but several currents of thought that believed in the existence of a universal covenant.

We also find a great divergence in these texts. Sometimes, they contain a direct reference to the covenant concluded in the beginning; sometimes they may refer to future promises described by means of the images of prehistory. Likewise, a great variety of titles exists: "eternal covenant", "covenant of peace", etc. Even with this lack of uniformity, we continue to find the idea of a natural order established by God with his universal promises and demands. One can also see a tendency towards more precision, especially in the priestly tradition, which used previous traditions and made a synthesis in the text on Noah. This text, on the other hand, may have inspired several other authors.

The idea we discover in the yahwistic tradition, therefore, does not remain an isolated case. Its insight did find acceptance, sometimes still imprecise, but Ben Sirach was no longer afraid to say explicitly: God has concluded a primitive universal covenant with mankind.

## Chapter Two

# The Place of the Nations in the Historical Covenant with Israel

This extremely long period in the history of mankind, which we have called the primitive universal covenant, came to a dramatic end with the building of the tower of Babel, or the exile of mankind. But this venture was not the final ending of salvation history. We now come to the second period, which we entitle: the historical covenant with Israel, from the vocation of Abraham to the resurrection of Jesus.

We are not primarily concerned here about its meaning for Israel as such, but rather with the place of the nations. When Yahweh chose Israel, did he reject the nations, or was he indifferent towards them, or were they somehow part of it? And if so, how?

We will see how the first promise of the election of Israel given to the patriarchs already includes the nations. When centuries after these promises had been made, God concluded his covenant with Israel at Sinai, he again acted in the interest of the nations. The practices of the international treaties applied to the covenant between Yahweh and Israel help us to understand some aspects of the attitudes of Israel towards the nations, as well as several other functions of the nations during this second period of salvation history.

### I. THE PROMISES TO ABRAHAM— BLESSING FOR THE NATIONS

The same yahwistic writer, who presented his prehistory as a real covenant between God and mankind, now continues his history. The text

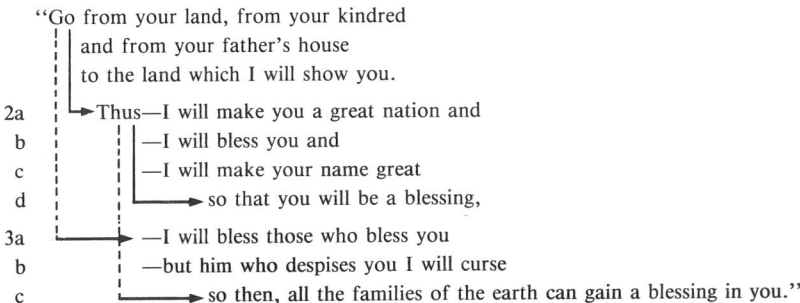

by which he opens this second period is *the call of Abraham* (Gen. 12:1-3).[1]

This translation wants to be as close as possible to the Hebrew text, since there are several difficulties in the text itself. By a schematic presentation of the text as above, we hope to show more clearly the global structure of the text. We shall be able, then, to see how important this structure is to our topic. And finally, we shall reflect upon the meaning of this text in its context.

The *analysis* of the text will not be complete, but will be limited to the theme of universalism. As Adam and Eve were alone in the beginning, and Noah alone after the flood, this second period of salvation history also starts with one person, Abraham, but with this difference: he was chosen from among many. The table of the nations (Gen. 10) has given long lists of the nations. It is from them that one person is predestined for a very precise purpose. To accomplish this, he has to leave: "Go".

Why must Abraham leave? "Thus I..." is a consecutive clause which has the sense of a result as well as the sense of an intention.[2] What God wanted and what the result of Abraham's leaving will be is, first of all, "I will make you a great nation". When the Yahwist wrote, at the time of Solomon, this had become evident. Israel was then a real world empire, with her own land, but this had been unknown to Abraham (v. 1). A small detail in the text might have important consequences. This verse says: "I will make *you* a great nation" and not "from you", or "of you" or the like. So this *you will be* a great nation is interesting and, of course, at the time the Yahwist writes, Israel *is* indeed a great nation. In other words, this "you" plays on Abraham as either being the patriarch or as representing Israel. This concept is common in the Bible and is called "corporate personality". The person represents the group, and the group is

---

1. H. JUNKER, "Segen als heilsgeschichtliches Motivwort im Alten Testament", in *Sacra Pagina* I, Paris-Gembloux, 1959, pp. 548-558; J. SCHREINER, "Segen für die Völker in der Verheissung an die Väter", in *B.Z.*, 6 (1962), pp. 1-31; C. WESTERMANN, "The Way of the Promise through the Old Testament", in *The Old Testament and Christian Faith*, ed. B. W. Anderson, London, 1964, pp. 200-224; J. MUILENBURG, "Abraham and the Nations. Blessing and World History", in *Interpr.*, 19 (1965), pp. 387-398; H. W. WOLFF, "The Kerygma of the Yahwist", in *Interpr.*, 20 (1966), pp. 131-158; I. BLYTHIN, "The Patriarchs and the Promise", in *Scot.J.T.*, 21 (1968), pp. 56-73; O. H. STECK, "Genesis 12:1-3 und die Urgeschichte des Jahwisten", in *Probleme biblischer Theologie, Festschrift G. von Rad*, ed. H. W. Wolff, München, 1971, pp. 525-554; G. LIEDKE, "Israel als Segen für die Völker", in *Frieden-Bibel-Kirche*, ed. G. Liedke, Stuttgart, 1972, pp. 65-74; Th. C. VRIEZEN, "Bemerkungen zu Genesis 12:1-7", in *Symbolae Biblicae et Mesopotamicae F.M.Th. de Liagre* Böhl dedicatae, ed. M. A. Beek et al., Leiden, 1973, pp. 380-392; R. DE TRYON-MONTALEMBERT, "Israël: Une bénédiction pour tous les peuples?", in *Parole et Pain*, 10 (1973), pp. 42-50; G. WEHMEIER, "The Theme 'Blessing for the Nations' in the Promise to the Patriarchs and in Prophetical Literature", in *Bangalore Theological Forum*, 6 (1974), pp. 1-13.

2. H. W. WOLFF, "The Kerygma of the Yahwist", p. 137 note 28, with reference to P. JOÜON, *Grammaire de l'hébreu biblique*, Rome, 1947, § 116 b,h.

represented in the person. If this is correct, then all the following "you"s in the text contain at the same time a reference to Abraham and to Israel.

The same expression appears later in the Bible when God speaks to Moses after the unfaithfulness of Israel in the desert (Ex. 32:10; Num. 14:12; Dt. 9:14). So this expression of making a nation seems to imply a new start. After its unfaithfulness and punishment, a new period in salvation history begins and this is clearly what we have here in this text. We are now at a new beginning, after the complete failure of the primitive covenant.

After a few other promises, we come to the final reason why they were made: "so that you will be a blessing". Several exegetes, just by changing the vowels, translate: "so that *it* may be a blessing", which would mean that the name of Abraham becomes a blessing.[3] His name will be used as a kind of blessing formula: "be blessed like Abraham" (cf. Jer. 29:22). But this change of the traditional writing is not at all necessary. Not the name, but rather "*you* will be a blessing". This corresponds much better with the whole context, in which the "you" is frequently used. The promises are given to the person of Abraham, so he and not his name will be a source of blessing for others. The following verse will confirm this: "those who bless *you*", and not those who bless his name. In other words, the person of Abraham will be a cause of blessing to others. But here this notion of corporate personality becomes very important. In this text the *you* is not only Abraham but also Israel. This means then that Abraham-Israel will be the instrument of the blessing for others. Who could the others be but the nations, as is said explicitly in v. 3. This second verse now becomes extremely rich. It shows the intention behind Abraham's call. He has to leave because God wants to make first of all a nation, which is the theme of the election of Israel. But all of this is now in view of a blessing to the nations, which is the theme of universalism.

More divine promises are added (v. 3) as a result, and likewise the intention behind Abraham's call to leave. God himself will bless or curse, but not independently from men's free will. This blessing or cursing of others depends on their solidarity with Abraham-Israel. "I will bless those who bless you, but him who despises you I will curse". We have a change from the plural to the singular: "those who bless" and "the one who despises". There is a tendency to correct the second part and also to make it a plural, based on the well-known law of parallelism.[4] But again, this correction is not needed. The text, as it stands, is thus very optimistic. Many will receive the blessing because they accept, but only a few will refuse and therefore be cursed.

Finally we come to the conclusion of the text: "so then, all the

---

3. For a discussion on this: J. SCHREINER, "Segen für die Völker", p. 4-5.
4. The Jerusalem Bible, the New American Bible, and The New English Bible change it to a plural, while the Revised Standard Version keeps the singular.

families of the earth...".⁵ The text now becomes very explicit, for in reality the nations are involved. The expression "the families of the earth" is very rare. The only reference to "the families of nations" outside the stories of the patriarchs is in Am. 3:2, where they are mentioned clearly besides Israel, so no doubt they indicate the nations. All nations have a possibility of salvation in relation with Abraham-Israel, but how? Here we come to another and even more difficult problem in the text.⁶

The verb "bless" is in the *nifal* form here and in Gen. 18:18; 28:14. The old Greek translation (LXX) and the Greek text of Ben Sirach (44:21) translated this by a passive "in you all the families of the earth shall be blessed". This has also been the interpretation of some texts in the New Testament (Acts. 3:25; Gal. 3:8), of the Vulgate and of a long tradition. This would give the text a very broad universal perspective. There is a difficulty, however, for even if *nifal* can have a passive meaning, this is not its normal meaning.

Similar promises are found in the stories of the patriarchs, which could be considered as parallel texts: Gen. 22:18; 26:4, which are in the *hitpael* form, and no longer in the *nifal*, can only be translated as: "by your descendants all the nations of the earth shall bless themselves". Some exegetes, starting from these indisputable texts, give the same translation to the three *nifal* texts which are ambiguous. All the texts would then have a reciprocal meaning and not a passive one. In other words, the nations will wish each other the same blessings as Abraham received: "be blessed like Abraham is". But this would mean that Abraham would become an ideal, which would be in line with their interpretation of v. 2 where the name of Abraham is used as a blessing formula. In this interpretation the person of Abraham serves as an example, but not as an instrument, as he is in the passive interpretation.

This reasoning is disputable. Do we have the right to give the same interpretation to these five texts, when we clearly have three in the *nifal* and two in the *hitpael* form? This difference may well be intentional, as we will see later. This interpretation for 12:3 is contrary to the whole context. The subject of all the blessings is God. He is the one who really blesses, the final cause.

We may therefore adopt the following interpretation. We have probably no need to translate this text by a passive; the Yahwist used the *nifal* and not the *pual*, which would have been the normal thing to do, if he had wanted the passive meaning. We do not have to translate by means of a reciprocal, for this is the meaning of the *hitpael* used in two texts, but it is not the meaning of the *nifal*. We give to the *nifal* the mean-

---

5. H. W. WOLFF, "The Kerygma of the Yahwist", p. 137 note 30, with reference to P. JOÜON, *Grammaire de l'hébreu biblique*, § 119 c,i,j.
6. On this question: J. SCHREINER, "Segen für die Völker", pp. 6-7; P.-E. DION, *Dieu universel et peuple élu*, pp. 33-35.

ing of a reflexive form, similar to the Greek middle voice, a kind of procurative concept: "in you, all the families of the earth will acquire for themselves a blessing", whose meaning is in a certain sense very close to the passive. It is really God who will bless through the person of Abraham, who in turn is the mediator of God's blessings. This is in complete harmony with the whole context. God always blesses (v. 2b,3a). Because of their solidarity with the person of Abraham, others receive God's blessing (v. 3a). Abraham is already presented as mediator for the others in v. 2d and again here in v. 3c, where it is now very clear that the others are the nations. But we must remember that this Abraham is Abraham-Israel. God wanted first to make one nation, and when this was done, this nation could then become the mediator of the salvation of the nations, which of course, like any salvation, is ultimately the work of God.

The fact that the entire text is extremely precise and has a well-planned *structure* gives it a special perspective.[7] We have one single imperative, God's order to Abraham: "Go" (v. 1). This is followed by five consecutive clauses indicating the intention and result of this imperative: "I will make" (v. 2a), "I will bless" (v. 2b), "I will make great" (v. 2c), "I will bless" (v. 3a), "I will curse" (v. 3b). These consecutive clauses depend on the initial imperative, and have their own consecutive clauses again containing the intention and result of the promises: the first, as a first stop after the first promises (v. 2d), and finally the one after the two last promises, the consequence of the consequences (v. 3c). This then is the final intention and result of the whole text, the summit, "the salvation of the nations", which was already announced in anticipation in the little summit (v. 2d).

The structure makes clear, then, that the importance of the whole text lies in the final consequence: Go → thus → so then! This could invite us to reflect on the different titles that have been given to this text in most Bibles: "the call of Abraham" (referring to the "go"), or "the promises to Abraham" (because of the "thus"); we could also speak of "the blessing of the nations through Abraham" ("so then").

These few verses become even more meaningful when considered in their *context* and more precisely in connection with prehistory.[8] The last story of the prehistory was the building of the tower of Babel which caused the dispersion of mankind and which represents the end of a period. With the person of Abraham a new beginning starts. Little details in the text show this in a very interesting way.

The purpose of the builders of the tower was very clear: "Let us make a name for ourselves, lest we be scattered abroad upon the face of the whole earth" (11:4). But what they wanted to accomplish by themselves had precisely the opposite effect: "Yahweh scattered them abroad over

---

7. H. W. WOLFF, "The Kerygma of the Yahwist", pp. 138-140.
8. Especially O. H. STECK, "Genesis 12:1-3".

the face of all the earth" (11:9). The primitive universal covenant ended with the exile of mankind, and as we have said before, without any hope!

We have to wait until we come to the person of Abraham to see new hope arise: "I will make your name great" (12:2c). Men had wanted to make their names great through their own initiative; the result we know. But now God will make the name of Abraham-Israel great. All the scattered nations will also be reunited in Abraham-Israel once more. Dispersed mankind must come back from its exile, just as Abraham himself had to leave his country to come to the promised land.

Why does mankind need a "blessing"? This "blessing" is undoubtedly central in the text and is, indeed, repeated five times. The answer is very simple. Mankind needs a blessing because a curse lies upon all men. They became unfaithful to their covenant (Gen. 2-11) and were punished, cursed, and thus are in need of salvation. The word "blessing" is absent from yahwistic prehistory (except in 9:26, where it is not directly used as a blessing for men) but, on the other hand, we have several curses. Some exegetes think that by repeating five times the word "blessing" in Abraham's call (12:1-3) the Yahwist wishes to show the process of restoration following the five curses of the prehistory (3:14,17; 4:11; 5:29; 9:25).[9]

There is again hope for mankind. God will restore the broken universal covenant. These few verses are the bridge between prehistory and this new period which now begins. This first text even says how God will accomplish it. He will first make one nation, bless it, let it grow, and through it a blessing will be given to the others. In other words, this historical covenant of Israel is directed towards a new universal covenant with mankind which will be the final restoration of the primitive one.

The Yahwist who wrote this story at the time of Solomon and who presented the relation between God and mankind in terms of a covenant (without using the term itself to avoid shocking his readers) was reacting perhaps against the popular beliefs of his time, as we have seen. Many of his contemporaries no doubt must have said: "We have conquered all of these nations, because we are the chosen people". The Yahwist tells his people that the nations were conquered as their punishment for their unfaithfulness. But these nations, too, will have another chance. Israel has to share with them her own blessing.

This is not the only biblical text where the promise to Abraham is connected to the salvation of the nations. In the cycle of the patriarchs, the idea is repeated several times,[10] yet we notice some interesting differences. The promise is given three times to Abraham; after him it is transmitted to Isaac, and later passed on to Jacob.

---

9. H. W. WOLFF, "The Kerygma of the Yahwist", pp. 145-146.
10. J. SCHREINER, "Segen für die Völker", pp. 8-12; J. MUILENBURG, "Abraham and the Nations", pp. 393-396; H. W. WOLFF, "The Kerygma of the Yahwist", p. 147 ff.

| | | | | | | |
|---|---|---|---|---|---|---|
| 1. | 12:3 | Abraham | in you | | *nifal* | all the families of the earth |
| 2. | 18:18 | Abraham | in him | | *nifal* | all the nations of the earth |
| 3. | 22:18 | Abraham | in your descendants | | *hitpael* | all the nations of the earth |
| 4. | 26:4 | Isaac | in your descendants | | *hitpael* | all the nations of the earth |
| 5. | 28:14 | Jacob | in you +<br>in your descendants | | *nifal* | all the families of the earth |

Two texts (12:3; 28:14) have exactly the same elements: "bless" in the *nifal*, and "all the families of the earth". This is of course the most universalistic formulation. "All the families", which insists more upon the personal relationship between men, can gain a blessing through Abraham-Israel. Both texts belong to the yahwistic tradition.

Two other texts (22:18; 26:4) are formulated in the *hitpael* form, which is much weaker. The nations will bless themselves by you. So Israel has no real active role to play in it; she is merely used as an example. There is another element, too, which widely differs from the preceding texts. No longer is the reference to "all the families" but to "all the nations". So, the use of this more impersonal (and sometimes even pejorative and contemptuous) term suggests the idea of the pagans. These two texts, while having kept the universalistic idea, have diminished its strength. Many exegetes believe this to be a later development from the deuteronomistic tradition.

One text (18:18) is a mixture of the two different formulations. The verb is still in the *nifal* form, but the word on the other hand is "nations", which can be explained again from a deuteronomistic influence since the following verse (v. 19) belongs probably to this tradition.

Several texts use "in your descendants", a wording which confirms the given interpretation of "you" as a corporate personality. Not only the patriarch, but with him Israel, is the mediator of blessing.

The basic idea that the nations will somehow share in the blessing of Israel is kept in all these different formulations. The Yahwist insisted in his days upon the active role Israel had to play as mediator. In the time of the Deuteronomist, when there was a strong insistence upon Israel's election, Israel is presented more as an example for the nations.

The prophet Jeremiah, who probably was involved, at least for a while, in the deuteronomistic reform, has also adopted the deuteronomistic formula: "the nations will bless themselves *(hitpael)* in him" (Jer. 4:2).

The story of the destruction of Sodom and Gomorrah (Gen. 18-19), in which the formula is quoted, is of very special importance. It is an example and likewise a concrete illustration of how others might share in the blessings of Abraham, for he acts here as a real intercessor and mediator.

Several other biblical texts illustrate the same theme—how others are saved or blessed because of Israel (Gen. 26:28-29; 30:27-30; 39:5; Ex. 12:32; Num. 24:9; Zech. 8:13,23). And so one day, because of this blessing, all nations will also be God's people: "the princes of the peoples gather as the people of the God of Abraham" (Ps. 47:10; cf. Is. 19:24-25, a text which we shall study later in detail).

## II. THE COVENANT—SERVICE TO THE NATIONS

The promises given to Abraham clearly describe how God planned to restore the broken universal covenant. He would first constitute one nation and through it all nations would later share in its blessings. The important moment when Israel was constituted as this very special people was *the covenant at Sinai*. In this mysterious encounter Yahweh took Israel as his covenant partner (Ex. 19:3-8).[11]

3   And Moses went up to God and Yahweh called to him out of the mountain, saying: 'Thus you shall say to the house of Jacob, and tell the sons of Israel:
4   + You have seen what I did to the Egyptians, and how I bore you on eagles' wings and brought you to myself.
5a  + Now therefore, if you will obey my voice and keep my covenant,
 b  + —you shall be my own possession among all peoples; for all the earth is mine,
6      —and you shall be to me a kingdom of priests
       —and a holy nation.
    These are the words which you shall speak to the sons of Israel'.
7   So Moses came and called the elders of the people, and set before them all these words which Yahweh had commanded him.
8   And all the people answered together and said, 'All that Yahweh has spoken we will do'. And Moses reported the words of the people to Yahweh.

This is the well-known text in which Yahweh, through Moses as mediator, offers his covenant to the people who in turn accept it. Several exegetes see in this text the basic structure of the covenant formulary,[12] though this has been rejected by others.[13] We would have in v. 4 the *historical benefits*, recording what Yahweh has done for Israel: "out-into". Yahweh brought Israel out of Egypt, into his intimacy. And, therefore, Yahweh may now ask as gratitude and obedience the *submission* of Israel (v. 5a). "Now therefore ..." is a request for total submission, expressed by two terms which we have already seen in the prehistory as being technical verbs: "obey my voice" (Gen. 3:10) and "keep" (Gen. 2:15). Israel

---

11. R.B.Y. Scott, "A Kingdom of Priests (Ex. 19:6)", in *O.T.S.*, 8 (1950), pp. 213-219; J. Bauer, "Könige und Priester, ein heiliges Volk (Ex. 19:6)", in *B.Z.*, 2 (1958), pp. 283-286; H. Wildberger, *Jahwes Eigentumsvolk*, A.T.A.N.T. 37, Zürich, 1960 (especially pp. 80-95); W. Moran, "A Kingdom of Priests", in *The Bible in Current Catholic Thought*, ed. J. L. McKenzie, New York, 1962, pp. 7-20; G. Fohrer, "Priesterliches Königtum, Ex. 19:6", in *Th.Z.*, 19 (1963), pp. 359-362; R. Van de Walle, "An Administrative Body of Priests and a Consecrated People in Ex. 19:6", in *Ind.J.T.*, 14 (1965), pp. 57-72; L. Perlitt, *Bundestheologie im Alten Testament*, pp. 167-181; W. Zimmerli, "Erwägungen zum 'Bund'. Die Aussagen über die Jahwe-bᵉrît in Ex. 19-34", in *Festschrift W. Eichrodt*, A.T.A.N.T. 59, Zürich, 1970, pp. 171-190; H. Cazelles, "Royaume de prêtres et nation consacrée (Ex. 19:6)", in *Humanisme et foi chrétienne*, Mélanges scientifiques du Centenaire de l'Institut Catholique de Paris, ed. Ch. Kannengiesser and Y. Marchasson, Paris, 1975, pp. 541-545; J. Coppens, "Exode 19:6: Un Royaume ou une Royauté de Prêtres?", in *E.T.L.*, 53 (1977), pp. 185-186.
12. J. Muilenburg, "The Form and Structure of the Covenantal Formulations", in *V.T.*, 9 (1959), pp. 346-365 (for Ex. 19:3-6, pp. 351-357).
13. L. Perlitt, "Bundestheologie", pp. 178-179.

is brought out of her slavery in Egypt into the service of God. This, then, will be the guarantee and the condition of future *blessings* and protection which will be given to her (v. 5b-6).

In this last element of the text the unique position of Israel as a chosen people is made clear by three different expressions which now need further reflection.

Israel is called Yahweh's *segullāh*, God's own possession. The word is used for something very precious, a treasure. Israel is Yahweh's very special people. This term emphasizes strongly the fact of Israel's election. The same word *segullāh* is also used in extra-biblical texts to indicate an intimate relationship between a king and his suzerain or his God. As we have said before, very often in texts speaking about election a reference is made to the nations. Here again, Israel is said to be Yahweh's treasure "among all peoples", and the text goes on: "*for* all the earth is mine". This fact, therefore, makes it possible to reconcile the universal power of God and his special choice of Israel. Everything belongs to Yahweh, but Israel does so in a very special way, if she accepts. The following two terms will further explain what this privilege implies.

The first of these terms involves another title given to Israel: *holy nation*.[14] This does not refer to the moral meaning of holiness. The biblical notion of holiness contains three elements: separation, consecration, service. Israel is taken from among the peoples and put aside. Why? In order that she may be faithfully consecrated to Yahweh for his special service.

The last expression, *mamleket* (kingdom) *kohanîm* (priests), causes greater difficulty. A great variety of explanations have been given and nearly all of them take their arguments from old translations and traditions. The two main interpretations are the following: "royal priesthood" and "priestly kingdom". We can omit minor interpretations such as "kingdom and priests" (Apoc. 5:10), as well as the translation: "you shall be a kingdom, (constituted of) priests and a holy nation", a translation which makes a distinction between the priests and the people. The old Greek translation (LXX), followed by some early Christian writings (1 Pet. 2:5,9), has taken the first position: "royal priesthood". This is understandable. When these Greek translators were at work, Israel was no longer a kingdom. It seems better to translate it by "priestly kingdom" or "kingdom of priests". The parallel expression seems to confirm this. Israel is a *nation*, more precisely a *holy* nation. Israel is also a *kingdom*, a fact which is specified by the word *priestly*.

Thus Israel is called a *kingdom*. Some have understood this to mean that Israel has received royal power to reign over the nations, or that Yahweh reigns as king over Israel. Most probably the term has no specific significant meaning, but is simply used as a parallel with nation (cf.

---

14. H. J. KRAUS, "Das heilige Volk. Zur alttestamentlichen Bezeichnung *'am qādōš*", in *Biblisch-theologische Aufsätze*, Neukirchen, 1972, pp. 37-49.

1 Kgs. 18:10; Ps. 105:13; Is. 60:12). The two terms are here more or less synonymous. Israel is a people, a nation and a kingdom like so many others. What makes her different is that she is a holy nation and a priestly kingdom.

The statement that Israel is a *priestly* kingdom or a kingdom of priests says something special about Israel. To conclude that Israel is a kingdom having priests, or the like, cannot be the right interpretation since all nations at that time had their priests. The meaning, therefore, is that Israel, as a kingdom, is priestly. To understand what this means, we must know what the function of a priest was in the days of the writer. The priest was an intermediary and, therefore, had a mission between God and men. If we apply this concept to Israel as a people, it then suggests that Israel is also an intermediary between God and the nations.

The priest in Israel was consecrated for the service of God. He offered sacrifices. Israel, too, belongs totally to the service of God; she is a consecrated nation. The priests offered these sacrifices not only for themselves, but for the people whom they represented, and they offered sacrifices in atonement for the sins of the people. Israel, as this priestly kingdom, serves God also in the name of others. This function is also stated elsewhere: "You shall be called the priests of Yahweh; men shall speak of you as the ministers of our God" (Is. 61:6).

The priest does not only offer to God; he is, also, mediator between God and men. He brings God to man. He is the man of the torah, and as such he has to transmit instructions and religious traditions, to help people who come to him to consult the divine will. Israel has a similar role to play towards the nations: "You are my witnesses" (Is. 43:10), "a light to the nations" (Is. 42:6; 49:6). Israel's role as intermediary may be accomplished in two different ways: the nations may come to Israel (centripetal universalism) or Israel may go out to the others (centrifugal universalism). This concept will be treated in chapter four of this book. However, we can already quote one of these texts in which it is clearly stated that the torah or the instruction, which was given by the priests to the people, will be given by Israel to the nations: "And all the nations shall flow to it, and many peoples shall come and say: 'Come, let us go up to the mountain of Yahweh, to the house of the God of Jacob; that he may teach us his ways and that we may walk in his paths. For out of Zion shall go forth the torah, and the word of Yahweh from Jerusalem'" (Is. 2:3).

At Sinai, Yahweh makes an overture to Israel, which, if accepted, will make her his covenant partner. God could have chosen whomsoever he wanted, from all the different peoples of the earth, since he is master over all of them. His offer, however, goes to Israel and she becomes his very precious vassal. She is set apart—distinctive from all other nations—to be consecrated to Yahweh, to be in his service, a position which ultimately means service towards the nations. Israel's privilege is one of service. Israel was taken from among the nations to be at the service of the nations. Election and covenant are thus not an end in themselves but a means towards something else.

This text (Ex. 19:3-8) confirms what we have seen before in the promises to Abraham. He would become a people from whom all the nations would one day receive blessings of salvation.

Israel is mediator. She must bring mankind closer to God, pray to God for mankind, and intercede for mankind, as Abraham did. Her service to God is in the name of others. But Israel has also to bring God closer to men, by bringing them God's revelation, his light and the good news of salvation.

Israel's role is well expressed in many of the prayers of Israel. She prays that one day the nations will join her in praises to Yahweh and that he may one day be known by all.

> May God be gracious to us and bless us
> and make his face to shine upon us,
> that thy way be known upon earth,
> thy salvation among all nations.
> Let the peoples praise thee, o God;
> let the peoples together praise thee! (Ps. 67:2-4; cf. Ps. 96; 117).

## III. THE RELATIONS BETWEEN ISRAEL AND THE NATIONS[15]

The idea that Israel has a priestly service towards the nations can now be compared with the real attitudes of Israel. And here of course we face one of the famous "scandals" of the Bible: the repeated killing of enemies, and worse still, the pronouncement sometimes made that God himself will destroy them. This is a real problem. Israel was often very reticent in her relationships with the nations. This can even be said about the attitude of Jesus towards the nations, for he also, during his lifetime, limited himself to Israel. This is why we have found it necessary to include Jesus in this second period called the historical covenant with Israel.

What had been the relationship between Israel and the nations during the time of the historical covenant?[16] To understand this question we

---

15. W. VOGELS, "Covenants between Israel and the Nations", in *Egl.Th.*, 4 (1973), pp. 171-196.
16. H. DONNER, *Israel unter den Völkern. Die Stellung der klassischen Propheten des 8 Jahrhunderts v. Chr. zur Aussenpolitik der Könige von Israel und Juda*, V.T.S., 11 (1964); J. A. THOMPSON, "The Near Eastern Suzerain-Vassal Concept in the Religion of Israel", in *J.R.H.*, 3 (1964), pp. 1-19 (especially "The Secular Treaties of the Old Testament", pp. 5-6); S. MUÑOZ IGLESIAS, "La condenación profética de la politica de pactos, y su vigencia para el pueblo del N.T.", in *Est.Bib.*, 25 (1966), pp. 41-73, or in *Jalones de la Historia de la salvación en el Antiguo y Nuevo Testamento*, XXVI Semana biblica española, coloquio bíblico internacional, Madrid 6-11 Sept. 1965, Madrid, 1970, pp. 357-386; G. FOHRER, "Israels Haltung gegenüber den Kanaanäern und anderen Völkern", in *J.S.S.*, 13 (1968), pp. 64-75; L. PERLITT, "Israel und die Völker", in *Frieden-Bibel-Kirche*, ed. G. Liedke, Stuttgart, 1972, pp. 17-64; J. L'HOUR, "The People of the Covenant encounters the Nations: Israel and Canaan", in *Service and Salvation*, Bangalore, 1973, pp. 71-80; B. VAWTER, "Israel's Encounter with the Nations", *ibid.*, pp. 81-92.

have once more to appeal to the basic covenant which existed between Yahweh and Israel. This relationship was conceived according to the type of vassal treaty well-known in the extra-biblical texts. In such circumstances, too, a suzerain and his vassal were of course not the only kings of the world. There were other kings living as well as them. The behaviour of the two covenant partners towards other kings might well throw light on the problem of the attitude of Yahweh and of Israel towards the nations.

One important aspect of the vassal treaties was the commitment to mutual protection. In other words, the suzerain promised and bound himself to protect and to come to the rescue of his new vassal if he were ever in danger. But in return he demanded total loyalty and protection from the vassal if he himself were attacked. A sentence found in many of these texts, and which can be considered as a technical expression relating to this mutual protection, worked in both ways:

> to my friend thou art friend,
> and to my enemy thou art enemy.

The suzerain promised his protection to the vassal against all possible enemies. This was of course a most encouraging experience for the vassal. He now had nothing to fear from his enemies and could, therefore, hope to live in peace and in prosperity.

We find the same principle clearly affirmed in the biblical tradition. Yahweh promises very strongly to come to the help of his people, if Israel is faithful. "If you listen carefully to his voice and do all that I say, *I shall be enemy to your enemies, foe to your foes*. [Note the technical wording of the extra-biblical treaties.] My angel will go before you and lead you to where the Amorites are and the Hittites, the Perizzites, the Canaanites, the Hivites, the Jebusites; I shall exterminate these" (Ex. 23:22-23). "Observe what I command you this day. Behold, I will drive out before you the Amorites, the Canaanites, the Hittites, the Perizzites, the Hivites, and the Jebusites" (Ex. 34:11). There are many more similar texts which may be understood by this aspect of the covenant. Israel must be able to become a people and live faithfully according to the covenant. Hence these numerous texts in which Yahweh-Suzerain promises victory over all those who would oppose or threaten his vassal Israel.[17]

Biblical tradition was not afraid to make use of this strong, rather strange language to express the conviction that Israel could rely on Yahweh's protection, by stating that he would destroy her enemies. This is, of course, but literature. The problem becomes more real when we reflect upon the concrete attitude of Israel towards the nations.

---

17. F. C. FENSHAM, "Clauses of Protection in Hittite Vassal-Treaties", in *V.T.*, 13 (1963), pp. 133-143; ID., "Covenant, Promise and Expectation in the Bible", in *Th.Z.*, 23 (1967), pp. 305-322; G. E. WRIGHT, "The Nations in Hebrew Prophecy", in *Encounter*, 26 (1965), pp. 225-237.

What about the other side of this mutual protection? What was the suzerain expecting from his vassal in this respect? Here too there were some very clear principles.

The suzerain requested total loyalty from his vassal. He must remain the only suzerain. The vassal might not serve two masters at the same time: "do not acknowledge a second person", "do not set over yourself another king, another lord", "do not turn your eyes to anyone else". Thus the vassal was bound not to choose another suzerain, for this would mean high treason.

Furthermore, the vassal, in dealing with other minor kings of equal power or perhaps even weaker than himself, was bound to observe the same principle: "friend with my friends, enemy with my enemies". This means that the vassal could have relationships, and even conclude treaties with some of these kings, but was forbidden any treaty with an enemy of the suzerain. He could become friendly with friends of the suzerain, but of course not with a view to fomenting a rebellion against his overlord. In other words, any treaty which might constitute a danger for the Great King could not be accepted.

In short, the vassal could never have a treaty with another suzerain but could do so with another minor king if such a treaty would not endanger the basic fundamental treaty by which he was bound to his own suzerain.

These principles are of great assistance in understanding Israel's attitude towards the nations. It would be impossible to study all these relations since Israel was continuously in contact with others. We have, therefore, limited our study to those which are more official and permanent because of a solemn agreement. As was the case with all the other nations, Israel too concluded treaties with other nations. The Bible approves of some of them, while in other cases there is a strong disapproval or interdiction. Why this double judgment on what apparently seems to be the same thing? What are the reasons behind it? Must this be explained by pure political or military opportunism or do we have to look for theological reasons? Did her basic covenant with Yahweh determine when and why a covenant with another nation was acceptable or sinful?

We will analyse the different biblical international treaties, while limiting ourselves to those texts where the technical term $b^e r\hat{\imath}t$ is used. There are, of course, other cases which may constitute a covenant: a marriage of the king with a princess of another country, or trade relations between Israel and another state. By limiting ourselves to the texts which are certainly treaties, we hope to find the answer to our question: Why are some of these treaties acceptable and others sinful according to the Bible?

COVENANT WITH THE MIDIANITES (KENITES) (Ex. 18:1-12)

Even though the term $b^e r\hat{\imath}t$ is not used, we want to examine this case, which is a very interesting example of a treaty between Israel and another nation.

The identification of the father-in-law of Moses causes several problems. He is called by three different names: Reuel (Ex. 2:18), Jethro (Ex. 3:1; 4:18; 18:1-2) or Hobab (Jgs. 1:16; 4:11). Sometimes he is presented as a Midianite but at other times as a Kenite. Are the Kenites perhaps a branch of the Midianites? The answer to these questions is of little importance for our present study.

The text has been understood in various ways, but the general tendency now is to consider it as a real covenant between Israelites and Midianites (Kenites).[18]

Further biblical tradition confirms the existence of such a treaty of friendship between these two groups. The Kenites entered Palestine with the tribe of Judah (Jgs. 1:16). Jael, the wife of Heber the Kenite, felt, according to the legal principles of the treaties at the time, the obligation to kill the enemy of Israel the treaty partner (Jgs. 4:17-22; 5:6,24-27). *Ḥéséd*, which is covenant loyalty, had existed between the Kenites and the Israelites since the departure of Egypt (1 Sam. 15:6).

The two partners act as equals. Jethro takes the initiative (v. 1) but there is a mutual agreement. Jethro goes to Moses (v. 5) and Moses goes to encounter Jethro (v. 7). The type of treaty would thus be a parity treaty of friendship and of mutual non-offensive character.

Nowhere in this text, or anywhere else in the Bible, is there any condemnation or blame expressed about this treaty. Why does the biblical tradition accept this without any restrictions?

Moses tells his father-in-law the whole story of the exodus, how Yahweh has delivered Israel from enslavement by the Egyptians (v. 8). This is exactly what constitutes the *historical prologue* of the well-known covenant formulary. It is the statement of the historical benefit that Yahweh has bestowed on Israel, formulated with the same technical vocabulary.

Because Yahweh freed his people from Egypt, he could request in return her *submission*. Something similar happens also in the case of Jethro. He has already heard about these historical events (v. 1), and after Moses confirms the rumours (v. 8), Jethro rejoices in them (v. 9), and even more, he recognizes in them the mighty hand of Yahweh: "And now I know that Yahweh is greater than all the gods" (v. 11). Some exegetes see in this the proof that Jethro already knew Yahweh and conclude from this fact the Kenite origin of the name "Yahweh". Others think that this

---

18. C.H.W. BREKELMANS, "Exodus 18 and the Origins of Yahwism in Israel", in *O.T.S.*, 10 (1954), pp. 215-224; R. KNIERIM, "Exodus 18 und die Neuordnung der Mosaischen Gerichtsarbeit", in *Z.A.W.*, 73 (1961), pp. 146-171; A.H.J. GUNNEWEG, "Mose in Midian", in *Z.T.K.*, 61 (1964), pp. 1-9; F. C. FENSHAM, "Did a Treaty between the Israelites and the Kenites exist?", in *B.A.S.O.R.*, n. 175 (1964), pp. 51-54; A. CODY, "Exodus 18:12: Jethro accepts a Covenant with the Israelites", in *Bib.*, 49 (1968), pp. 153-166.

verse indicates the conversion of Jethro (cf. 1 Kgs. 17:24; 2 Kgs. 5:15). It may best be understood by the technical juridical vocabulary of the covenant; "and now" is often the conjunction between the historical prologue and the request for submission, (because I have done this... and now...).[19] The verb "to know" is one of those verbs expressing total submission[20] like the verbs "serve", "fear", etc., and can have the meaning of "to recognize". Jethro has seen the power of Yahweh in the events and enters into a covenant relationship with Yahweh.

However, some other details of the texts are of special interest. The whole event takes place at "the mountain of God" (v. 5), which according to Ex. 3:1 is Horeb or Sinai, the mountain of the covenant.

There is also the very significant celebration: "Jethro offered a holocaust and sacrifice to God" (v. 12) which confirms that Jethro now accepts Yahweh; but there is also "a meal in the presence of God" (v. 12) to which he invites the others, symbolically confirming the mutual link between Midian and Israel. The covenant which Israel celebrated at Sinai (Ex. 24:3-11) consisted of similar holocausts and sacrifices (v. 5) and of a communal meal (v. 11).[21]

What happened here could well be compared with the great celebration at Shechem (Jos. 24).[22] This text, composed as a classical covenant formulary, contains the same elements as our text here: a long historical prologue (v. 2-13), followed by the request for submission: "*and now, fear Yahweh...*" (v. 14). Joshua and his family have already chosen Yahweh (v. 15). He now invites others to join him in the covenant with Yahweh, and by doing so the confederation of the tribes is constituted.

We have here, then, something very similar. Moses has already accepted the covenant with Yahweh and is joined now by Jethro. They are now both vassals of the same suzerain. As the covenant of Shechem established peaceful relations between the tribes, here also the two vassals, having the same suzerain, are living in mutual peace of non-aggression, according to the basic principle: "To my friend thou art friend". In other words this parity treaty between Israelites and Midianites (Kenites) does not constitute any danger for Israel's faithfulness to her suzerain, Yahweh.

---

19. A. LAURENTIN, "*We'attah—Kai nun.* Formule caractéristique des textes juridiques et liturgiques (à propos de Jean 17:5)", in *Bib.*, 45 (1964), pp. 168-197, 413-432; H. A. BRONGERS, "Bemerkungen zum Gebrauch des Adverbialen *we'attāh* im Alten Testament", in *V.T.*, 15 (1965), pp. 289-299.
20. H. B. HUFFMON, "The Treaty Background of Hebrew *Yāda'* ", in *B.A.S.O.R.*, n. 181 (1966), pp. 31-37; H. B. HUFFMON and S. B. PARKER, "A Further Note on the Treaty Background of Hebrew *Yāda'* ", in *B.A.S.O.R.*, n. 184 (1966), pp. 36-38.
21. W. VOGELS, "De Viering van het Verbond bij het uitverkoren Volk (Ex. 24:1-11)", in *Catechetische Informatie*, 3 (1975), n. 4, pp. 6-10.
22. J. L'HOUR, "L'Alliance de Sichem", in *R.B.*, 69 (1962), pp. 5-36, 161-184, 350-368.

## Covenant with the "Inhabitants of the Land"
(Ex. 23:32; 34:12,15; Dt. 7:2; Jgs. 2:2)

In four different texts we read about the covenant with the "inhabitants of the land". They have this in common, that all of them forbid Israel to make such covenants.[23]

### Ex. 23:32

The context is very helpful. Ex. 23:20-26 contains many elements of the covenant formulary; Yahweh requests total submission from Israel: "if you listen attentively to his voice..." (v. 22a), but he promises protection, expressed by the technical language known from the extra-biblical texts: "I shall be enemy to your enemies, foe to your foes" (v. 22b). He will therefore exterminate the inhabitants of the land, who are enumerated for us in a long list (v. 23). Yahweh promises to give the land to Israel, his covenant partner, and thus, all those who oppose Israel will also become his enemies.

The loyal submission asked from Israel is the absolute service to Yahweh as suzerain (v. 25), and consequently it prohibits service to other gods (v. 24). This now is the reason why no covenant with those gods can be tolerated, not even with the inhabitants of the land (v. 32). Their idolatry could constitute a real temptation for Israel to become unfaithful to Yahweh and thus to commit high treason (v. 33).

It is important to note that the text refers only to the "inhabitants of the land". These are the peoples living close to Israel, and who represent a daily danger of idolatry. Nothing is said here about possible treaties with other peoples.

### Ex. 34:12,15[24]

These verses again are in a context of covenant and, according to some exegetes, express the covenant formulary itself. It is said explicitly that Yahweh concludes a covenant with Israel (v. 10). This involves the total submission of Israel (v. 11a), but she can count on Yahweh's protection, for he will fight her enemies (v. 11b). The submission of Israel, therefore, means that she will recognize only Yahweh as her suzerain (v. 14), and, as a logical consequence, will not accept any other god, or even make any

---

23. G. Schmitt, *Du sollst keinen Frieden schliessen mit den Bewohnern des Landes. Die Weisungen gegen die Kanaanäer in Israels Geschichte und Geschichtsschreibung*, B.W.A.N.T. 11, Stuttgart, 1970; R. Smend, "Das Gesetz und die Völker. Ein Beitrag zur deuteronomistischen Redaktionsgeschichte", in *Probleme biblischer Theologie, Festschrift G. von Rad*, ed. H. W. Wolff, München, 1971, pp. 494-509.
24. F. Langlamet, "Israël et 'l'habitant du pays'. Vocabulaire et formules d'Ex. 34: 11-16", in *R.B.*, 76 (1969), pp. 321-350, 481-507; F. E. Wilms, "Das jahwistische Bundesbuch in Ex. 34", in *B.Z.*, 16 (1972), pp. 24-53.

covenant with any of the inhabitants of the land (v. 12,15), who might lead her into idolatry. Israel is aware that such a covenant would be a direct rejection of Yahweh and thus be high treason. We have here exactly the same principles as in the first text.

## Dt. 7:2

The context of this verse is also very significant. It belongs to the preaching of the covenant. Yahweh promises victory over the enemies who would oppose Israel entering into the land (v. 1), but he asserts to Israel: "You shall make no covenant with them" (v. 2-3). Relationships with these peoples must be avoided. Two reasons are given for this. The first is a negative one: "because they would turn away your sons from following me..." (v. 4-5); in other words, they are a proximate danger of idolatry, of unfaithfulness to Yahweh. The second reason is a positive one: "because you are a people holy to Yahweh your God..." (v. 6 ff.). Israel as the vassal belongs to Yahweh who is her only suzerain.

## Jgs. 2:2

This text is another well-known structure of covenant theology. It is a lawsuit or Rîb after the unfaithfulness of Israel. Yahweh brought Israel out of Egypt into the promised land (v. 1a) and concluded a covenant with his people (v. 1b). What Yahweh expected from Israel was her total loyalty, which necessitated that she refrain from making any covenant with the peoples of the land, who through their idolatry could endanger her faithfulness (v. 2). Since Israel has not obeyed Yahweh's demand, Yahweh no longer promises his protection; in other words, he will no longer be "the enemy to their enemies": "I will not drive them out before you; but they shall become adversaries to you..." (v. 3).

It is important to note how those four texts which forbid the contracting of a covenant with the inhabitants of the land are all in a covenant context. In other words, the fundamental covenant between Yahweh and Israel has priority. This relationship determines relationships with the others.

Yahweh-Suzerain promises protection to his vassal Israel. He wants to give the land to Israel and those who oppose this will be exterminated.

Israel is obliged to render absolute service to her suzerain and as a consequence cannot serve other gods. Linked with this, as an unavoidable consequence, no covenant is permitted with the inhabitants of the land. Such an arrangement could indeed constitute a daily danger for Israel to accept their gods and so to fall into idolatry, and thus become unfaithful to Yahweh.

These four texts concern only those peoples living with Israel in the land. Nothing is said about relations with the nations as such.

## Covenant with the Gibeonites (Jos. 9)

A clear example of a covenant between Israel and another nation is described in Jos. 9.[25] Several elements in the text indicate the ratification of a real treaty. The term "b$^e$rît" is used several times (v. 6,7,11,15,16) with the juridical terminology: "So now make a covenant with us" (v. 6).[26] A covenant implies a real binding oath (v. 15,18,19,20). There is also the covenant meal (v. 14), the description of the condition of the food (v. 4-5, 12-13) which clearly shows that if the Israelites accept this kind of food, it is certainly not as a present nor for a banquet, but for a common meal, one of the elements which accompanies a treaty.

It is quite easy to determine the kind of treaty that is concluded. The Gibeonites take the initiative from fear (v. 3). They consider Israel to be much superior to them and more powerful. It is, therefore, not a parity treaty between equals, but a vassal treaty. Gibeon becomes Israel's vassal: "we are your *servants*" (v. 8,11,23,24), which is a technical term in this type of treaty, confirmed also by the text: "Now, see, we are in your hands" (v. 25). The service which the vassal has to render to his suzerain is also mentioned: "Let them be woodcutters and watercarriers in the service of the whole community" (v. 21,23,27), which is perhaps a stereotyped expression for slave labour (Dt. 29:10). On the other hand, the suzerain is now expected to protect his new vassal. He has first of all to respect the life of his vassal: "guaranteeing their lives" (v. 15; v. 18,19; "let them live", v. 21,26), and also to come to the rescue of the vassal in case the latter is attacked by his enemies. All this is according to the well-known principle: "enemy of your enemies...". This is why the Gibeonites, while under attack, appeal for the promised help according to the arrangements of the treaty (Jos. 10): "Do not desert your servants: come up here quickly to save us and help us, because all the Amorite kings

---

25. J. Liver, "The Literary History of Joshua IX", in *J.S.S.*, 8 (1963), pp. 227-243; F. C. Fensham, "The Treaty between Israel and the Gibeonites", in *B.A.*, 27 (1964), pp. 96-100; J. M. Grintz, "The Treaty of Joshua with the Gibeonites", in *J.A.O.S.*, 86 (1966), pp. 113-126; J. Blenkinsopp, "Are there traces of the Gibeonite Covenant in Deuteronomy?", in *C.B.Q.*, 28 (1966), pp. 207-219; Id., *Gibeon and Israel. The Role of Gibeon and the Gibeonites in the Political and Religious History of Early Israel*, Cambridge, 1972; A. Ibañez Arana, "El pacto con los gabaonitas (Jos. 9) como narración etiológica", in *Est.Bib.*, 30 (1971), pp. 161-175; P. J. Kearney, "The Role of the Gibeonites in the Deuteronomic History", in *C.B.Q.*, 35 (1973), pp. 1-19; B. Halpern, "Gibeon:Israelite Diplomacy in the Conquest Era", in *C.B.Q.*, 37 (1975), pp. 303-316; J. Halbe, "Gibeon und Israel. Art, Veranlassung und Ort der Deutung ihres Verhältnisses in Jos IX", in *V.T.*, 25 (1975), pp. 613-641.
26. W. F. Albright, "The Hebrew Expression for 'making a covenant' in Pre-Israelite Documents", in *B.A.S.O.R.*, n. 121 (1951), pp. 21-22; M. Noth, "Das Alttestamentliche Bundschliessen im Lichte eines Mari-Textes", in *Gesammelte Studien zum Alten Testament*, München, 1960, pp. 142-154; J. A. Soggin, "Akkadisch *TAR BERITI* und Hebraïsch *krt b$^e$rît*", in *V.T.*, 18 (1968), pp. 210-215.

living in the mountains have allied themselves against us" (v. 6). In other words, this is a peace treaty (v. 15).[27]

The Israelites and the Gibeonites thus contracted a vassal treaty. We hear about this same covenant much later, at the time of David, when it appears that Saul has been unfaithful and has broken the covenant (2 Sam. 21:1-14).

How are we to understand that Israel accepted this treaty, which is contrary to the four texts we have just studied forbidding any treaty with the "inhabitants of the land"? One might answer that the Gibeonites do not belong to the "inhabitants of the land", since their name is never mentioned in any of the many lists of these peoples. They are absent also from the list in the beginning of this same chapter (v. 1). But, on the other hand, the name "Gibeonites" seems to be a collective name referring to a confederation of four cities, with the first or the most important city giving the name to the group (v. 17). It is, thus, more a territorial name. Ethnologically they belong to the Hivites according to the text (v. 7; also Jos. 11:19). The Septuagint translates 9:7 by "Horites" and some manuscripts of the LXX have "Hittites". In 2 Sam. 21:2, they are said to be Amorites. But whoever they were, all these names appear in the lists of the "inhabitants of the land". So the "Gibeonites" were no exception and the prohibition of making a covenant with the inhabitants of the land applied to them. Two explanations, however, may show why the Israelites accepted this treaty.

First of all, the Gibeonites present themselves by trickery (v. 3-5) as people living far and hence not belonging to the inhabitants of the land. As such they dare to ask for a treaty: "We come from a distant country, so make a treaty with us" (v. 6). The whole subsequent discussion serves to verify this (v. 7-13). Consequently, the Israelites did not endanger their fundamental covenant with Yahweh by accepting the request for a covenant with a people they believed to live far away. Israel is not looking for another suzerain. On the contrary, the Gibeonites are the weaker partner. To accept a treaty with a vassal living far away would not constitute a danger of contamination from idolatry, a condition which is fundamental to the four preceding texts' prohibition. We have here the same principle as proposed in Dt. 20:10-18: to offer "peace" (v. 10) to "the far-distant towns not belonging to the nations near you" (v. 15).

There is a second reason why this treaty could be accepted. The Gibeonites, as in the covenant with Jethro but less explicitly, proclaim the *magnalia Dei*: "because of the name of Yahweh your God" (v. 9), the historical benefits Yahweh has given Israel, the exodus (v. 9) and the conquest (v. 10), formulated with the technical covenant language. Without speaking clearly of a conversion, the Gibeonites seem to accept

---

27. A. G. LAMADRID, "Pax et bonum, 'Shālôm' y 'ṭôb' en relación con 'bᵉrît'", in *Est.Bib.*, 28 (1969), pp. 61-77, or in *Ant.*, 44 (1969), pp. 161-181.

the power of Yahweh (v. 24), so that the Israelites do not hesitate to make them servants of the "altar of Yahweh" (v. 23,27) and finally to assimilate them.

Evidently the covenant asked for by the Gibeonites did not constitute, in the eyes of Israel, a danger to her faithfulness to the main covenant with Yahweh.

COVENANT WITH THE TYRIANS (1 Kgs. 5:15-26)

We have another explicit reference to a covenant between the Israelites and a foreign nation, the Tyrians, at the end of the story in 1 Kgs. 5:15-26.[28] The term "b$^e$rît" is used (v. 26), and several other indications in the text prove that it is a report on political and trade relations between the two states.

Hiram, king of Tyre, was always the "friend" of David (v. 15b). This could very well be a technical term belonging to treaty language and refer to an existing covenant between David and Hiram, and such seems to be presupposed in the text of 2 Sam. 5:11. When Solomon succeeded David, Hiram, according to international policy, sent an embassy to the new king to renew the existing treaty between the two countries (v. 15a).

Solomon, in his answer, uses technical covenant language: "You know David, my father. Lo, he was not able to build" (v. 17), with the technical verb "to know" for covenantal relationship. Typical also is the text: "my servants with your servants" (v. 20), and the final conclusion of the text: "and there was peace between Hiram and Solomon; and both of them made a treaty" (v. 26). All is formulated clearly in technical juridical treaty language. And this proves that there is here not simply a good relationship between two kings, but much more—a real political agreement.

The stipulations of this treaty are specified: Hiram offers materials for the building of the temple (v. 24), Solomon gives wheat and oil (v. 25). Other points of the mutual obligations are given in the following chapters. Hiram also offers the architect or workman (1 Kgs. 7:13-14) "cedar wood, juniper wood and gold" (1 Kgs. 9:11-14), as well as co-operation in navigation (1 Kgs. 9:27-28; 10:11,22). Solomon gives in return twenty cities (1 Kgs. 9:11-14).[29]

Such mutual advantages seem to suggest a parity treaty between Israel and Tyre. This is confirmed by the title Hiram gives to Solomon: "my brother" (1 Kgs. 9:13), a title which is the technical term used in parity treaties, rather than "servant", the usual title for a vassal.

---

28. F. C. FENSHAM, "The Treaty between the Israelites and Tyrians", in *V.T.S.*, 17 (1969), pp. 71-87.

29. F. C. FENSHAM, "The Treaty between Solomon and Hiram and the Alalakh Tablets", in *J.B.L.*, 79 (1960), pp. 59-60; F. VATTIONI, "Il trattato tra Salomone e Hiram e le tavolette di Alalakh", in *Riv.Bib.It.*, 8 (1960), pp. 273-276.

Some exegetes believe that there is another biblical text which attests the existence of this treaty. Amos accuses Tyre of inhuman behaviour and of having thus broken a covenant: "They have not remembered the covenant of brotherhood" (Am. 1:9). Such an expression refers to this parity treaty between the Israelites and the Tyrians. We saw earlier that there is yet another possible interpretation for this text.[30]

Nowhere does the biblical text blame David or Solomon for concluding this covenant. The fact that it is a parity treaty is clearly one of the reasons why it was acceptable. By such an agreement Israel does not show a lack of confidence in Yahweh, her only possible suzerain.

Furthermore, the Tyrians do not belong to the "inhabitants of the land" since they are never mentioned in any of the lists. They live at a distance and thus do not constitute a daily danger of idolatry. And, moreover, Hiram also proclaims the greatness of Yahweh and his people: "Now blessed be Yahweh who has given David a wise son to rule over this great people" (v. 21). There is, of course, no question of a "conversion" of Hiram, but there is at least a real acceptance that Yahweh is guiding the history of Israel. This seems to imply that Hiram respects the fact that Yahweh is the God (and should remain the God) of Solomon. This is even clearer in the parallel text of the Chronicles where Hiram goes a step further. He recognizes Yahweh as creator: "'Because Yahweh loves his people he has made you king. Blessed be Yahweh, the God of Israel'. Hiram went on to say: 'He has made the heavens and the earth, and gives King David a wise son...'" (2 Chr. 2:10-11).

Solomon is later blamed, however, for not observing the covenant of Yahweh and his law because of his idolatrous worship (1 Kgs. 11:9-11) of the gods which his many foreign wives had brought with them (1 Kgs. 11:1 ff.). This text speaks about foreign peoples and refers even to Dt. 7:3-4, one of the four texts which forbid covenants with the inhabitants of the land. Some of these wives were from Sidon, and their marriages also constituted perhaps some kind of treaty, but with a great difference. These wives brought with them their gods and thus idolatry (1 Kgs. 11:4 ff.), whereas in the treaty with Tyre, each partner could remain faithful to his own god.

In the same manner we understand how this treaty, which was accepted without blame, was condemned by the prophet Elijah when Ahab, king of Israel, renewed this covenant through his marriage with Jezebel, daughter of Ethbaal, king of Tyre (1 Kgs. 16:31). Now by marrying a woman from Tyre and bringing her to Israel, idolatry had been brought into the land, thus endangering the faithfulness of Israel to Yahweh.

COVENANT WITH THE ARAMAEANS
(1 Kgs. 15:19 = 2 Chr. 16:3; 1 Kgs. 20:34)

The story of the rivalrous relationship between Damascus and Israel

---

30. *Supra*, p. 30, note 19.

is very complex. Many texts speak about this. We limit ourselves here, for our purpose, to those texts where the word "b$^e$rît" is used explicitly. Treaties with the Aramaeans are mentioned for the northern kingdom, Israel, and likewise for the southern kingdom, Judah.

1. Two texts refer to an existing treaty between the North and Damascus. First Asa, king of Judah, asks Ben-Hadad, king of Damascus, to break his covenant with Baasha, king of Israel: "Come break off your alliance with Baasha, king of Israel" (1 Kgs. 15:19 = 2 Chr. 16:3). So, indirectly, we learn of the existence of a covenant between the North and Damascus which must have been a non-offensive treaty of mutual peace.[31] This can be seen from the following verses, where Ben-Hadad agrees to break his covenant and as a consequence attacks the cities of Israel (v. 20).

The second case is that of the relationship between Ahab and Ben-Hadad, which was more to the disadvantage of Ahab (1 Kgs. 20:3 ff.). When, later, circumstances change in favour of Ahab, the servants of Ben-Hadad most probably refer to this prior relationship when they say: "We have heard that the kings of the house of Israel are *héséd*" (v. 31), which is the technical word for loyalty to a treaty; and so they dare to intercede for the life of their master calling him: "Your *servant* Ben-Hadad" (v. 32). In other words, the king of Damascus accepts his defeat and presents himself with the title of a vassal: "servant". But Ahab in his answer, on the contrary, says of Ben-Hadad: "He is my *brother*" (v. 32), the title for equal kings in a parity treaty. This favourable implication was understood by the servants of Ben-Hadad (v. 33), and a treaty was concluded with mutual obligations and advantages: "Ahab concluded a treaty with him" (v. 34).

These two cases would, therefore, appear to be parity treaties between Israel (northern kingdom) and a people who do not belong to the inhabitants of the land. So the same principles apply as for the preceding treaty between Israel and Tyre.

2. The treaty between Judah and Aram is of another type. Asa, king of Judah, takes the initiative himself, by addressing himself to Ben-Hadad, king of Damascus: "An alliance between myself and you, as between my father and your father! With this I send you a gift of silver and gold" (1 Kgs. 15:19 = 2 Chr. 16:3). Asa uses for this gift the treasures of the temple and of the palace (v. 18). He intends to protect himself against Baasha, the king of Israel (v. 16,17). In other words, Asa requests help and protection from Aram. This is the demand from a weaker king to a stronger one. Such an agreement would be a vassal treaty.

This type of situation becomes very clear if we compare it with what king Ahaz of Judah later did with Tiglath-pileser, king of Assyria

---

31. W. THIEL, "*Hēfēr B$^e$rît*. Zum Bundbrechen im Alten Testament", in *V.T.*, 20 (1970), pp. 214-229.

(2 Kgs. 16:7-9). Ahaz asks the king of Assyria for help against the kings of Israel and Aram. For this he, too, takes the treasures of the temple and of the palace. But the text is even more explicit. Ahaz says clearly to Tiglath-pileser: "I am your *servant* and your *son*" (v. 7), thereby using the technical titles of a vassal in relation to his suzerain.

Such a comparison leaves no doubt that king Asa presents himself as the vassal of Ben-Hadad. The only true suzerain of Israel is Yahweh, and a vassal cannot take another suzerain without becoming unfaithful to his first overlord. This understanding then is the reason why the initiative of Asa is strongly condemned by the prophet Hanani: "Since you have relied on the king of Aram and not on Yahweh your God, the army of the king of Aram will slip through your fingers" (2 Chr. 16:7). The king has shown a lack of confidence in the power of Yahweh, who has proved his faithfulness in the past under similar and even worse circumstances with the Cushites and the Lybians (2 Chr. 16:8 = 14:8 ff.). This, indeed, is the first of several similar condemnations by the prophets of the covenant policies of some of the kings. Yahweh's covenant people have and can have only one suzerain.

## Covenant with Assyria (Hos. 12:2)

In several circumstances Judah and Israel tried to conclude a treaty with Assyria, but in only one text is the word "b$^e$rît" used. Hosea condemns Ephraim for "making a treaty with Assyria" (Hos. 12:2). This policy of covenants is also condemned in a very general way (Hos. 10:4 with the term "b$^e$rît").

This fact applies to the northern as well as to the southern kingdom. We have just mentioned how king Ahaz of Judah became the vassal of Tiglath-pileser (2 Kgs. 16:7-9), to whom Hosea refers in a very clear text: "Judah has appealed to the Great King" (Hos. 5:13).

The relationship between Assyria and Judah or Israel is evidently always a relation of suzerain to vassal. Since Israel has Yahweh as her suzerain, this seeking of a new overlord is always high treason for a vassal. Several prophets, therefore, unanimously condemn this policy of putting confidence in Assyria (Hos. 7:11; 8:9; 14:4; Is. 7:1 ff.; Jer. 2:18; Ezek. 16:28; 23).

Assyria is really considered as a possible competitor of Yahweh. Assyria was believed indeed to be a God and to be as powerful or even more powerful than Yahweh. The temptation was very strong for Israel to put her confidence in Assyria in dangerous situations. An interesting text is 2 Kgs. 18:17 ff. (= Is. 36:1 ff.) where the king of Assyria pretends that neither confidence in Egypt nor confidence in Yahweh can help.

The reason, then, why the covenants with Assyria are condemned is very simply that they represent an act of high treason to the suzerain, Yahweh.

## Covenant with Egypt (Hos. 12:2)

As in the preceding case, several treaties with Egypt were concluded, though the term "bᵉrît" is never used. But in the same text of Hosea, there is an explicit reference to a rite connected with covenant making, "sending oil to Egypt" (Hos. 12:2), which is confirmed by the parallelism "making a treaty with Assyria" (Hos. 12:2).[32]

Hosea and all other prophets have always condemned such a treaty with Egypt (Hos. 7:11; Is. 20; 30:1-7; 31:1-3; 36:6 ff. (= 2 Kgs. 18:21 ff.); Jer. 2:18; Ezek. 16:26; 17:7,15; 29:6-7,16) and this for the same reason. Egypt is another possible overlord and therefore Israel is committing high treason. Egypt considers herself as God: "The Egyptian is a man, not a god" (Is. 31:3), as creator and as powerful as Yahweh: "My Niles are mine, I made them" (Ezek. 29:3,9).

So, for the same reason as was the case for Assyria, no treaty with Egypt can be accepted.

## Covenant with Babylon (Ezek. 17:13,14,15,16,18)

A real "bᵉrît" existed between Zedekiah, king of Israel, and Nebuchadnezzar of Babylon (Ezek. 17:13).[33] This certainly was a vassal treaty, Babylon being the suzerain and Israel the vassal (v. 14). Like Assyria and Egypt, Babylon also presents herself as equal to Yahweh (Is. 47:8), but nevertheless the prophet does not condemn this treaty. Even worse, when Zedekiah sends messengers to Egypt for help, this initiative is condemned by Ezekiel—who is the only prophet to do so—as infidelity on the part of the king to his commitment to his Babylonian overlord (v. 15; cf. 2 Chr. 36:13): "He has ignored the oath and broken the covenant by which he was bound" (v. 18) and therefore, he shall be punished (v. 16,18).

Why then is there such a difference here as compared to the other vassal treaties studied above? It is simply that the situation is not at all the same. In the case of Aram, Assyria or Egypt, it is the king of Israel who takes the initiative, who submits himself voluntarily as vassal. But here, Nebuchadnezzar imposes his treaty upon Israel (v. 13; cf. 2 Kgs. 24:17). This is according to one of the principles of the foreign policy of Babylon, by which the conquered land becomes a vassal state governed by a national ruler, or simply a Babylonian province administered by a governor.

More surprising still is the reason why Zedekiah is condemned: "And so, the Lord Yahweh says this: As I live, I swear: *my* oath which he has

---

32. D. J. McCarthy, "Hosea 12:2: Covenant by Oil", in *V.T.*, 14 (1964), pp. 215-221; K. Deller, "*šmn bll* (Hosea 12:2). Additional Evidence", in *Bib.*, 46 (1965), pp. 349-352.
33. M. Tsevat, "The Neo-assyrian and Neo-babylonian Vassal Oaths and the Prophet Ezekiel", in *J.B.L.*, 78 (1959), pp. 199-204.

ignored, *my* covenant which he has broken, I will make them both recoil on his own head" (v. 19; compare the use of the same vocabulary as in v. 18). Zedekiah, who became unfaithful to his suzerain, Nebuchadnezzar, is accused of being unfaithful to Yahweh!

This is generally explained by the juridical procedures of the treaties. The vassals swore loyalty to their suzerain not only by means of the Babylonian gods but also by their own gods. Zedekiah, by pledging faithfulness to Nebuchadnezzar, must have done so by invoking the name of his God, Yahweh, as witness and guarantee. This covenant then becomes in a certain sense also the covenant of Yahweh. Unfaithfulness to the $b^e r\hat{\imath}t$ with Nebuchadnezzar is unfaithfulness to the $b^e r\hat{\imath}t$ of Yahweh.

On the other hand, this is the only example in the Bible where "*my* covenant" has this meaning. Normally, "my covenant", "your covenant", "his covenant", when applied to Yahweh, refer always to Yahweh as the active partner of the covenant and not to him as the witness. When Israel is called unfaithful to "my covenant", this refers to her covenant with Yahweh. We would do well to keep this meaning also for this text. Zedekiah asks Egypt for help; he wants thus to conclude a treaty with Egypt. He, therefore, becomes thereby unfaithful to Nebuchadnezzar. What is even worse, Israel again takes the initiative to become a vassal of Egypt which thereby becomes Israel's suzerain. We have seen that this is in opposition to the fundamental covenant with Yahweh, the only real suzerain of Israel.

In this last interpretation, the attitude of Ezekiel is basically the same as that of the other prophets. He condemns Israel whenever she wants to become a vassal of a human suzerain, through asking help from a worldly power, rather than putting her total confidence in her only suzerain, Yahweh. But Ezekiel must accept reality. He cannot condemn Israel for a covenant which has been imposed upon her by Babylon.

After studying these different texts where the Bible speaks explicitly of a $b^e r\hat{\imath}t$ between Israel and another nation, we come to some general principles on which the prophets based their condemnation or acceptance of such a treaty.

An important distinction must be made between a treaty which is imposed and one which is freely concluded. In the case of the treaty with Babylon, there was no choice. It is only when Israel, on her own initiative, asks for a treaty, or when she accepts the request for a treaty by one of the nations, that the prophets can judge her.

In such situations, the principles we have seen before in the extrabiblical international treaties are applied.

The vassal is obliged to give total loyalty to his suzerain; he can never look for another overlord. Israel's only suzerain is Yahweh. Hence, treaties with such nations as Aram (as in the case of Judah), Assyria and Egypt, which present themselves as equal to Yahweh, are considered acts of high treason. They constitute a direct rejection of Yahweh by Israel. She no longer puts her confidence in him but places it in a human power. By becoming the vassal of a new suzerain there is the danger that the latter will also impose his gods.

As regards the parity treaties between Israel and a nation, or the vassal treaties, when Israel accepts the suzerainty of one of the nations as a vassal, we can apply the principle: "To my friend thou art friend, and to my enemy thou art enemy". It is because of this principle, therefore, that all covenants (whether of parity or vassalage) with the "inhabitants of the land" are condemned. The reason for such a condemnation is that these people oppose the plan of Yahweh to give the promised land to Israel and that they also oppose Yahweh by adoring other gods. Such an attitude constitutes a daily danger of idolatry for Israel. On the other hand, in the case of the nations who are not the inhabitants of the land, and especially when they recognize the greatness of Yahweh in some way, a parity treaty can be accepted, e.g. Midianites (Kenites), Tyrians, Aramaeans (as in the case of Israel North). Also a vassal treaty, which is even less dangerous, can be accepted, as in the case of the Gibeonites, who pretended not to be inhabitants of the land, and who recognized the works of Yahweh.

In this third section we have tried to understand a very difficult problem which appears during this period of the historical covenant with Israel. We have also endeavoured to suggest the reason for this rather negative and sometimes violent attitude of Israel towards nations, and why it is that Yahweh himself is said to desire the destruction of some of these nations. In order to consider these problems we have limited ourselves and have analysed only those texts in which Israel is in a more formal relation with a nation and where a treaty is concluded with one of them.

The principles of international treaties seem to supply the answer for Yahweh's and Israel's attitude towards the nations. It could be summarized as follows: the nations are treated according to their own attitude towards the two partners of the covenant: Yahweh (suzerain) and Israel (vassal).

At the beginning of this second period in salvation history the covenant between Yahweh and Israel had to be consolidated. Henceforth Yahweh will protect Israel against all those who endanger her existence; Israel must oppose all those who might be a source of danger to her fidelity to her suzerain, Yahweh. One must be fortified by strong personal convictions before one can risk facing others.

We have considered the relationship of Israel with other nations, and not with individual foreigners. This is a completely different problem. Many individuals have been in a certain sense assimilated, integrated into Israel: Rahab (Jos. 2:6), Ruth, the widow of Zarephath (1 Kgs. 17), Naaman (2 Kgs. 5).

## IV. THE NATIONS, WITNESSES OF THE COVENANT

A comparison of extra-biblical treaties also helps us to see another and more positive role of the nations in this period of the historical covenant with Israel. To be valid, any treaty needs witnesses. In international treaties the gods of the two partners are invited as witnesses, as is deified nature: heaven–earth–mountains–hills.

Biblical tradition similarly called upon nature as witness to the covenant between Yahweh and Israel (Dt. 4:26; 30:19; 31:28).[34] In the lawsuits as well, Yahweh assembled these same witnesses in order to testify against his unfaithful covenant partner: "Give ear, O heavens, and I will speak; and let the earth hear the words of my mouth" (Dt. 32:1); "Arise, plead your case before the mountains, and let the hills hear your voice. Hear, you mountains, the controversy of Yahweh, and you enduring foundations of the earth; for Yahweh has a controversy with his people, and he will contend with Israel" (Mic. 6:1-2; cf. Is. 1:2; Jer. 2:12).

Further, in a few of these texts something new appears. The nations are called to witness between Yahweh and his people. "Proclaim to the strongholds in Assyria (or Ashdod), and to the strongholds in the land of Egypt, and say, 'Assemble yourselves upon the mountains of Samaria, and see the great tumults within her, and the oppressions in her midst'" (Am. 3:9). Such a text expresses, of course, a rather surprising and very strong concept, namely, two major world powers are invited when Yahweh convokes his own people for trial.

Sometimes the two, nature and the nations, are called together to be the witnesses: "Hear, you peoples, all of you; hearken, O earth, and all that is in it" (Mic. 1:2; cf. also Jer. 6:18-19). We have here the "earth", which is nature, and "all that is in it", which could be her inhabitants, men, confirmed by the parallel, "you peoples".

This might, therefore, suggest that whenever the Bible calls nature, it no longer refers to deified nature, as in the extra-biblical texts, but rather to the inhabitants of heaven and earth.

Yahweh can only call the nations to witness his trial against Israel, if they have been witnesses of Yahweh's covenant with Israel. And indeed, the nations have seen what Yahweh has done for his people; they have also witnessed the answer of Israel. The Bible uses a very technical expression for this. Everything happened *"in the eyes of the nations"*.[35]

The formula, "in the eyes of...", when used in a juridical context, means an action done before legal witnesses. For instance, when Jeremiah buys his house, everything is done perfectly according to legal procedures: "In the eyes of Hanamel my cousin, in the eyes of the witnesses who signed the deed of purchase, and in the eyes of all the Jews who were sitting in the court of the guard" (Jer. 32:12). In some texts those before whom

---

34. M. Delcor, "Les attaches littéraires, l'origine et la signification de l'expression biblique 'prendre à témoin le ciel et la terre'", in *V.T.*, 16 (1966), pp. 8-25; G. M. Tucker, "'Witnesses' and 'Dates' in Israelite Contracts", in *C.B.Q.*, 28 (1966), pp. 42-45.
35. H. G. Reventlow, "Die Völker als Jahwes Zeugen bei Ezechiel", in *Z.A.W.*, 71 (1959), pp. 33-43; Id., *Wächter über Israel. Ezechiel und seine Tradition*, B.Z.A.W. 82, Berlin, 1962, especially p. 134 ff.

something happens are not merely spectators, but witnesses, who are supposed to take a position as well (Dt. 31:7; Jer. 28:1,5,11).

It is often said that Yahweh has bestowed his benefits in favour of Israel in the eyes of the nations. In other words, the nations are witnesses, but at the same time they are invited to take a personal stand. These texts are mostly to be found in two sections of the Bible: first in Exodus, which is understandable since "I brought you out of Egypt" is *the* historical benefit and the basis of the covenant; but often, too, in the book of Ezekiel, which describes Israel's restoration after the exile as a new exodus and conquest.

The nations have seen how Yahweh has delivered his people from Egypt: "Moses and Aaron did as Yahweh commanded; in the eyes of Pharaoh and in the eyes of his servants..." (Ex. 7:20). The Egyptians are witnessing Yahweh's power. But this divine action is also a call to them to make a personal decision: "So Pharaoh's heart remained hardened, and he would not listen to them" (Ex. 7:22; cf. also Ex. 9:8,12). We can quote some other explicit texts such as: "They set out from Rameses in the first month, on the fifteenth day of the first month; on the day after the passover the people of Israel went out triumphantly in the eyes of all the Egyptians" (Num. 33:3), and "but I will for their sake remember the covenant with their forefathers, whom I brought forth out of the land of Egypt in the eyes of the nations, that I might be their God" (Lev. 26:45). Thus the nations also have to reflect upon these events (Ex. 9:14,16,29), as was the case with the signs done in the eyes of Israel, which were an invitation for her to discern Yahweh's power (Ex. 17:6; Dt. 34:12).

The nations have not only witnessed Yahweh's benefits, but also his request for submission. Israel was asked to answer with gratitude and obedience to Yahweh's gifts. The nations will then be impressed if Israel is faithful: "Keep them and do them [i.e. the statutes and the ordinances]; for that will be your wisdom and your understanding in the eyes of the peoples, who, when they hear all these statutes, will say, 'Surely this great nation is a wise and understanding people'" (Dt. 4:6).

This mutual agreement between Yahweh and Israel, based upon divine historical actions and the human answer, is lived out in the eyes of the nations. They are not pure spectators but real witnesses, who are invited to take a position. They could come to realize the power of Yahweh and the human wisdom this service of God brings.

The same expression "in the eyes of..." is often used by Ezekiel. He is one of the most interesting prophets in this respect. Because Yahweh wants to manifest himself to others, he acts in the eyes of the nations and does not permit that his name be profaned by Israel in the eyes of the nations: "But I acted for the sake of my name, that it should not be profaned in the eyes of the nations among whom they dwelt, in whose eyes I made myself known to them in bringing them out of the land of Egypt" (Ezek. 20:9,14,22).

When Israel has become unfaithful, Yahweh then decides to execute his punishment in the eyes of the nations. "I will execute judgment in the midst of you in the eyes of the nations" (Ezek. 5:8; cf. 5:14; 22:16).

But the curse is not the final word of Yahweh. He will restore Israel again in the eyes of the nations. "It is not for your sake, O house of Israel, that I am about to act, but for the sake of my Holy name, which you have profaned among the nations to which you came. And I will vindicate the Holiness of my great name, which has been profaned among the nations, and which you have profaned among them; and the nations will know that I am Yahweh, says Yahweh God, when through you I vindicate my Holiness before their eyes. For I will take you from the nations, and gather you from all the countries and bring you into your own land... Then the nations that are left round about you shall know that I am Yahweh; I have rebuilt the ruined places and replanted that which was desolate; I, Yahweh, have spoken, and I will do it" (Ezek. 36:22-36; cf. also 20:41; 28:25; 39:27). Yahweh will accomplish the restoration of his people, which is presented as a renewal of the first exodus and conquest, in the eyes of the nations. They are again witnesses and not pure spectators.

Just as the signs accomplished at the time of Exodus were invitations for reflection, this marvellous restoration, too, is accomplished so that the nations "will know that I am Yahweh" (36:23,36).

The expression *"they will know that I am Yahweh"* is a technical formula very often used by Ezekiel while speaking about Israel (6:7,10, 13,14; 7:4,9, etc.).[36] It is normally in a very precise context. In most cases a divine salvific action precedes this formula of recognition. God acts, intervenes in the history of Israel, and so Israel "will know that I am Yahweh". Divine action and human recognition is a basic movement in covenant theology. And indeed the verb "to know" is one of those technical verbs used to express the total submission of the covenant partner. Israel has to accept Yahweh.

In the above quoted text (36:23,36) Ezekiel applies the same formula to the nations as he uses in some other texts: "So I will show my greatness and my holiness and make myself known in the eyes of many nations. Then they will know that I am Yahweh" (Ezek. 38:23; cf. also 37:28; 38:16; 39:7,23). This clearly then shows that the salvific actions of God were also in view of the nations. God has basically the same intention with the nations as he had with Israel because both "will know that I am Yahweh". Far from being pure spectators of something which concerns only Yahweh and Israel, the nations are witnesses, who are directly involved.

The whole historical covenant between Yahweh and Israel had from the beginning a universal dimension. The nations are real witnesses. Yahweh's saving actions, the punishment, and the restoration which he

---

36. W. ZIMMERLI, "Ich bin Jahwe", in *Geschichte und Altes Testament, Festschrift A. Alt.* Tübingen, 1953, pp. 179-209; ID., *Erkenntnis Gottes nach dem Buche Ezechiel. Eine theologische Studie*, A.T.A.N.T. 27, Zürich, 1954; ID., "Das Wort des göttlichen Selbstverweises (Erweiswort). Eine prophetische Gattung", in *Mélanges A. Robert*, Paris, 1957, pp. 154-164.

imposed upon Israel, were at the same time a preaching to the nations. They could discern in these historical events that it is Yahweh who acts. Israel's response to such benefits was also witnessed by the nations who could see that Israel's faithfulness brought her happiness, but her unfaithfulness brought disaster.

This is clearly expressed in a few texts which could be called "the question of the nations": "And many nations will pass by this city, and every man will say to his neighbour, 'Why has Yahweh dealt thus with this great city?' And they will answer, 'Because they forsook the covenant of Yahweh their God, and worshipped other gods and served them'" (Jer. 22:8-9; cf. also Dt. 29:21-28).[37]

## V. THE NATIONS, YAHWEH'S INSTRUMENT OF THE CURSES AND BLESSINGS OF THE COVENANT

The last element of the covenant formulary is the blessings and curses according to the faithfulness or unfaithfulness of the vassal. Among the great variety of curses, war and destruction are very frequently mentioned. In the extra-biblical treaties the gods normally bestow these curses and grant the blessings.[38] In other words, those who were the witnesses of the contract are also the executors of the curses and the blessings.

This practice of a witness becoming an executor was not limited to international juridical procedures, but was also employed in the case of domestic laws. A witness at a trial had an important role to play in the execution of the judgment: "The hand of the witnesses shall be first against him to put him to death" (Dt. 17:7).

All this explains, then, why the nations who were the witnesses of the covenant between Yahweh and Israel are also the instruments in God's hand for the execution of curses and blessings.[39] Israel is judged by the world.

Since examples of *curses* are abundant, it may suffice to give just a few. Israel, because of her unfaithfulness to Yahweh, will be punished by invasions, wars, destructions, which are all typical examples of covenant curses: "For behold, I will raise up against you a nation...and they shall oppress you..." (Am. 6:14); "I will come against the wayward people to chastise them; and nations shall be gathered against them when

---

37. D. E. Skweres, "Das Motiv des Strafgrunderfragung in biblischen und neuassyrischen Texten", in *B.Z.*, 14 (1970), pp. 181-197; B. O. Long, "Two Question and Answer Schemata in the Prophets", in *J.B.L.*, 90 (1971), pp. 129-139.
38. F. C. Fensham, "Malediction and Benediction in Ancient Near Eastern Vassal-Treaties and the O.T.", in *Z.A.W.*, 74 (1962), pp. 1-19; Id., "Common Trends in Curses of the Near Eastern Treaties and Kudurru-Inscriptions compared with Maledictions of Amos and Isaiah", in *Z.A.W.*, 75 (1963), pp. 155-175; D. R. Hillers, *Treaty-Curses and the O.T. Prophets*, Biblica et Orientalia 16, Rome, 1964.
39. F. Huber, *Jahwe, Juda und die anderen Völker beim Propheten Jesaja*, B.Z.A.W. 137, Berlin, 1976, "Andere Völker als Jahwes Gerichtsvollstrecker", pp. 161-173.

they are chastised for their double iniquity" (Hos. 10:10; cf. also Is. 5: 26 ff.; 7:18 ff.).

Nearly all the nations which endangered Israel at any time are named: "The *Syrians* on the east and the *Philistines* on the west devour Israel with open mouth" (Is. 9:11); "In that day Yahweh will whistle for the fly which is at the sources of the streams of *Egypt*, and for the bee which is in the land of *Assyria*" (Is. 7:18); "The *Babylonians* and all the *Chaldeans*, Pekod and Shoa and Koa, and all the Assyrians with them..." (Ezek. 23:23).

Sometimes the kings, as leaders of these nations, are mentioned as executors of the curse: Nebuchadnezzar, king of Babylon (Jer. 25:9; 27:6); Gog (Ezek. 38:16: "In the latter days I will bring you against my land, that the nations may know me, when through you, O Gog, I vindicate my holiness before their eyes").

Some images illustrate how the nations are instruments in God's hand. They are called a razor (Is. 7:20), or a rod, a staff (Is. 10:5), and their king, Yahweh's "servant" (Jer. 25:9; 27:6; 43:10).[40]

Nearly all prophets repeat that the nations are Yahweh's instrument for the execution of the curses, but there are fewer texts which indicate the nations as Yahweh's instrument for the *blessings*. One case, however, is that of Cyrus who is called by Yahweh to be the instrument for Israel's restoration. "I stirred up one from the north, and he has come, from the rising of the sun, and he shall call on my name..." (Is. 41:25); "Thus says Yahweh to his anointed, to Cyrus, whose right hand I have grasped, to subdue nations before him and ungird the loins of kings, to open doors before him that gates may not be closed..." (Is. 45:1).[41] Noteworthy is the title given to Cyrus: "his anointed".

This function of the nations as executors of punishment in particular becomes even more meaningful when compared with what we have studied in section three. There we saw how the nations were treated according to their attitude towards the two partners of the covenant. Yahweh protected Israel and gave her victory over the nations who were opposing her. The texts which we have just quoted, on the other hand, say something nearly the opposite. These same nations became an instrument in God's hand to punish Israel, the unfaithful covenant partner.

This chapter is concerned with the second period of salvation history: the historical covenant with Israel. We have examined this period in order to answer the question: Were the nations somehow part of the covenant, and if they were, in what manner?

The covenant seeks, finally, to serve the nations. Therefore they should

---

40. Z. ZEVIT, "The Use of *'ebed* as a Diplomatic Term in Jeremiah", in *J.B.L.*, 88 (1969), pp. 74-77.
41. P. AUVRAY, "Cyrus, instrument du Dieu unique", in *B.V.C.*, n. 50 (1963), pp. 17-23; H. LEENE, "Universalism or Nationalism? Isaiah 45:9-13 and its Context", in *Bijdr.*, 35 (1974), pp. 309-334.

respect this covenant and allow Israel to live out her experience. The nations which witness to her conduct are not purely spectators because what they see invites them to come to some kind of understanding. Since the nations are witnesses, they also are the instruments of God's curses and of the blessings which he bestows upon Israel.

Chapter Three

# Parallel Covenants with the Nations?

The nations are not totally forgotten during this second period of salvation history, which we entitled the historical covenant with Israel. They are really part of it in different ways, but at the same time they always keep what we could call a secondary position. The emphasis is, undoubtedly, upon the two covenant partners Yahweh and Israel.

Of special interest, therefore, are some particular texts where Yahweh acts directly on nations which, therefore, no longer play a secondary role, but are in direct relationship with Yahweh. Some of these texts even use vocabulary, structure and theology similar to the covenant language the Yahwist used to describe the relation between God and mankind in his prehistory.

We might thus ask ourselves whether Yahweh concluded a special covenant with other nations? Mankind, after the failure of its primitive universal covenant, was in need of salvation. Just as Yahweh offered a covenant to Israel to bring his salvation to her, he perhaps offered the same to other individual nations. In other words, we would then have several parallel divine covenants with different nations.

We will now study in detail some of the texts involved. In the past, these texts have not received the attention they deserve, although they are of the utmost importance. We face here an important existential question: Is there only one revelation, one salvation history, or are there several different ones, parallel to each other? It is only by a very rigorous analysis of these texts that we shall see whether Yahweh, during this second period of salvation history, acts exactly in the same way with the nations as he does with Israel, whether he acts towards them in a totally different way, or whether he acts towards them in a way which is neither exactly the same nor totally different.

These texts will show that Yahweh's relationship with the nations is very similar to his relationship with Israel. He intervenes directly in their history, and thereby they belong to him and are responsible before him. If the nations refuse to accept Yahweh's relationship, they will experience punishment like that of Israel, but there is also always hope. It is easy to see in all this the great moments of Israel's own experience. We will go through it step by step, but at each level we will always notice one important difference: the nations' lack of knowledge of Yahweh's revelation. Therefore, in the strict sense, we can speak only of a covenant with Israel, but not of a covenant with other nations, since a covenant presupposes mutual knowledge.

## I. THE "EXODUS EXPERIENCE" OF THE NATIONS AND THEIR BELONGING TO YAHWEH

One of these exceptional texts is the oracle of the prophet Amos (Am. 9:7):[1]

> Are you not mine, sons of Israel,
>   as the Cushites (are mine)? Oracle of Yahweh.
> For is it not true, that I made Israel come here from the land of Egypt, but also the Philistines from Caphtor, and the Aramaeans from Kir?

There is no doubt that the people must have been greatly surprised and deeply shocked while listening to this statement. Amos does not only establish a comparison between the elected people and one of the nations, but he even compares Israel's salvation history with the history of other peoples. The prophet does not refer to just any event of Israel's history, but to her exodus experience, an incident which immediately must have recalled to the minds of his listeners their covenant. How could the prophet dare to make such a parallel?

The modern reader is still puzzled and surprised by those words of Amos. The text sounds so different from what we are used to in most of the biblical texts. For this reason Amos's verse has been given many different interpretations and translations. This oracle, according to the majority of the exegetes, puts Israel at the same level as the other nations, a situation which suggests equality and a consequent loss of privilege. We can classify authors according to their insistence upon one of two possible aspects in such an interpretation: the more positive aspect is the equality of all nations; the negative aspect is the rejection of Israel. These two aspects are closely interrelated so it is more a question of insistence.

A first group of exegetes, each one portraying some personal minor difference of opinion, believes that Amos teaches here the equality of all nations: "Are you not like the Cushites to me, sons of Israel?" Such an interpretation implies that Israel has no special privilege, nothing more than that of the Cushites, because Yahweh is concerned about the history of all peoples. It also implies that Yahweh takes care of everybody. This is a highly advanced concept of universalism, a high point not only of

---

1. W. VOGELS, "Invitation à revenir à l'alliance et universalisme en Amos 9:7", in *V.T.*, 22 (1972), pp. 223-239.

the book of Amos, but of the entire Old Testament.[2]

A second group, on the contrary, insists that Amos preaches the rejection of Israel: "You are just like the Cushites, sons of Israel". These interpreters suggest that because Israel has become unfaithful to Yahweh, the prophet is here announcing the end of the covenant. They conclude that Israel has been rejected from Yahweh's predilection. Some even see a note of disdain in this comparison with the Cushites because the latter are blacks. So they see Israel rejected at the lowest level.[3]

Though these two hypotheses are considerably different from one another, they do have something in common. They both ultimately consider that an equality between Israel and the nations may be achieved by raising the nations up to the level of Israel or by lowering Israel to the level of the nations. But in either case, how will they combine the idea of such an equality with the fundamental teaching of the whole biblical tradition, namely, Israel's election and her covenant with Yahweh? Can one say that there is no longer any difference between the elected people and the nations? Amos himself, following the orthodox tradition, leaves no doubt; he strongly affirms Israel's special place: "You, only, have I known of all the families of the earth" (Am. 3:2). Such a sentence contradicts the preceding interpretations. Even if a prophet, and especially someone like Amos who likes popular language and shock effects (4:1; 5:18), may "contradict" himself, we wonder if we should not search for another interpretation which will establish more harmony between this text and the other oracles of Amos and the rest of biblical theology.

Recent studies on the covenant have given us precisely this possibility for a better understanding of this truly surprising text.

The text of Amos 9:7 contains two questions, each of which is introduced by the particle *hălô'*. This permits one to divide the verse into two distinct parts: v. 7a and v. 7b. The well-known "oracle of Yahweh" in between the two questions confirms this clearcut division. But they are not completely parallel. The first (v. 7a) is addressed to the "sons of Israel" and formulated in the second person. In other words, we have a real question directly compelling some people to react by way of an expected answer. The second question (v. 7b), on the contrary, is impersonal, formulated in the third person, and speaks about "Israel" in a more collective sense. Nobody is constrained directly; this question is rather a rhetorical one.

---

2. A typical example of this approach to the text is the following commentary: "It is the verse which appears to be the climax of the book, that astounding verse in which Amos seems for the moment to take back all that he has said about the unique position of Israel in the plan of Yahweh (9:7). It is a verse which noticeably expands the horizons of the world of Amos... There can be no doubt of the importance of this verse. Yahweh not only regards all the nations as similar in his sight but extends his concern to the whole history of peoples...", N. K. GOTTWALD, *All the Kingdoms of the Earth. Israelite Prophecy and International Relations in the Ancient Near East*, New York, 1964. p. 112.
3. E.g. E. FLORIVAL, "Le Jour du Jugement. Amos 9:7-15", in *B.V.C.*, n. 8 (1954/55), pp. 61-75; R.B.Y. SCOTT, *The Relevance of the Prophets*, New York, 1968, p. 133.

So, no doubt, the first is the main question to which the second is subordinated. The latter serves as a theological justification of the first one.

The interrogative particle *halô'* normally introduces a question which calls for a positive answer, which is the case in v. 7a; but the particle sometimes loses its interrogative value and then introduces something which is self-evident, as it does in v. 7b.[4] The main question of v. 7a becomes thus: "*Are you not...?*" with its justification in v. 7b: "*for is it not true that...?*" The rhetorical question of v. 7b, which is evident, should help people to find the answer to the real question they are asked in v. 7a.

We, therefore, begin the analysis with the theological justification (v. 7b), which is clear and evident and which will help us to understand the main question, whose meaning is quite frequently discussed among exegetes, as we have seen.

We have here a truly typical formula of the Old Testament,[5] composed of four elements: the subject, "Yahweh" (sometimes his mediator, Moses); the verb expressing the idea of bringing out; the object, "Israel"; and the determination, "from Egypt". We really can call this a technical formula for the salvific action accomplished by God in favour of Israel by bringing her out of the land of Egypt. There is a variety of such formulas because of the use of different verbs. The verb in this text of Amos is one of the best known; as a matter of fact it is the second most frequently used.[6] The verb has a more geographic and military connotation, and does not only refer to the "bringing out", but at the same time to "the arrival". It is thus a very interesting formula to express simultaneously exodus and conquest. One could translate: "I made you come (here) out of Egypt".

It is very enlightening for the understanding of this text to note how this technical formula and its parallel formulas are nearly always in a covenant context. In our introduction we have given different structures corresponding to the different moments of the covenant relationship between Yahweh and his people. The formula is used in these literary structures to recall the historical acts whereby Yahweh has benefitted Israel. These acts become the basis and motivation for Israel to belong to Yahweh. This belonging has to be expressed by the observation of the covenant stipulations. In the structure of the promise of the future covenant, the formula corresponds to the promise of the salvific action: "I will bring you up out of Egypt..." from which the future submission will follow (Ex. 3:8,17; Jer. 16:14; 23:7). In the formulary of the conclu-

---

4. P. Joüon, *Grammaire de l'hébreu biblique*, Rome, 147, § 161 c.; § 164 d.
5. P. Humbert, "Dieu fait sortir. Hiphil de *yāṣā'* avec Dieu comme sujet", in *Th.Z.*, 18 (1962), pp. 357-361; Id., "Dieu fait sortir. Note complémentaire", in *Th.Z.*, 18 (1962), p. 433-436; J. J. Wijngaards, "*Hôṣî' and he'ĕlāh*. A Twofold Approach to the Exodus", in *V.T.*, 15 (1965), pp. 91-102.
6. J. J. Wijngaards, *The Formulas of the Deuteronomic Creed*, Tilburg, 1963, "The Exodus Formulas", pp. 22-27.

sion of the covenant, the formula is used in the historical prologue: "I brought you up out of Egypt..." and now you have to serve Yahweh (Jos. 24:17; 1 Sam. 12:6). In the covenant lawsuit or trial after Israel has broken the covenant, the same formula appears again in the historical inquiry to recall the benefits Yahweh had given to Israel: "did not I bring you up out of Egypt..." but you did not serve me (Jgs. 2:1; 6:8; Am. 2:10; Mic. 6:4; Jer. 2:6).

The rhetorical question of Amos, *"Is it not true, that I made Israel come here from the land of Egypt?"*, is thus clearly formulated and borrowed from technical covenant language. He, undoubtedly, must have called to the minds of his auditors the great reality of the covenant between Yahweh and his people.

But the prophet does not stop there, and this is what is unusual. He extends this sacred formula in speaking about other peoples. Amos uses one single verb, "I made come here", to speak equally in the same sentence about the history of Israel and about the history of the Philistines and the Aramaeans. These two peoples had been dangerous enemies of Israel, the Philistines especially at the time of Saul and the Aramaeans in the period preceding the preaching of Amos. The link between the two parts of the sentence can be translated differently. It may be a very simple and weak connection: *"and* the Philistines...". A better translation would be "like" which would introduce a comparison: *"like* the Philistines...". But the most adequate meaning here is *"but also..."*, with the sense of a very emphatic affirmation. This last interpretation best renders the strength of Amos's statement, and also the paradox of putting Philistines and Aramaeans side by side with Israel. This constituted putting the elected people with two enemies for whom she had little love: *"Is it not true, that I made Israel come here from the land of Egypt, but also the Philistines from Caphtor and the Aramaeans from Kir?"*

The Philistines had left Caphtor, generally identified with Crete,[7] to migrate to Egypt but were expelled from there by Rameses around 1191 and 1188, and finally landed and settled along the coast of Palestine. They had been a continual threat to Israel until they were conquered by David (2 Sam. 5:17 ff.). Their presence had always troubled the minds of the Israelites. How is it possible to explain that these Philistines were there with them in the land which had been promised to Israel? The text of Gen. 9:25-27 reflects perhaps upon this preoccupation and explains why Israel could conquer Canaan (v. 25) and why she has to share the land with Japheth (v. 27), who is sometimes identified with the Philistines.[8] In this sentence Amos gives a very surprising answer. The Philistines are here because Yahweh wanted it that way. He has guided their history,

---

7. G. A. WAINWRIGHT, "Caphtor–Cappadocia", in *V.T.*, 6 (1956), pp. 199-210.
8. D. NEIMAN, "The Date and Circumstances of the Cursing of Canaan", in *Biblical Motifs. Origins and Transformations*, ed. A. Altmann, Cambridge, 1960, pp. 113-134.

their departure and their arrival in the promised land. Yahweh made the Philistines come *here* from Caphtor.

The Aramaeans had come from the desert of Arabia. Amos states that they came from Kir. Its localization still remains uncertain but the region of Elam or the city of Ur have been suggested. The Aramaeans had founded several kingdoms, such as Damascus, around 1100. They had threatened Israel, the northern kingdom, and occupied several regions of the promised land, but at the time of Amos, Israel had recovered her territory (2 Kgs. 13:25; 14:25). The migration and the settlement of this people, too, was the work of Yahweh as in the case of Israel and the Philistines.

Amos has chosen the example of two peoples who influenced the political situation in Palestine for a long time—two very dangerous nations, who are even judged first in his oracles against the nations (Damascus: 1:3-5; Philistines: 1:6-8). Nevertheless, Yahweh has guided their history. They also had their "exodus experience". This choice of Amos is very significant. Their migrations happened more or less at the same period as Israel's own exodus, around 1200. The exodus of the Philistines, expelled from Egypt and settled in Palestine, did recall Israel's leaving Egypt to go to the promised land. Furthermore, the migration of the Aramaeans should have reminded Israel of the migration of their own ancestors with Abraham.

But we have to note something which will be important in the interpretation of the whole verse. The histories of these three peoples have several points in common. We can even say that their histories are very similar without being identical. The history of one nation is never exactly the same as the history of any other nation.

After this analysis of v. 7b, we can now return to the main question of v. 7a. As we have seen before, the formula "I brought you up out of Egypt" in the different structures belonging to the covenant theology always refers to the historical benefits which Yahweh had given to Israel. This history constitutes the basis and the justification of the bond which now unites Israel and Yahweh and becomes a claim on Israel's obedience and observance of the covenant stipulations. Since the historical benefit is so automatically linked with mutual belonging, verse 7a should be understood in the same way. "Are you not mine (Do not you belong to me), sons of Israel?"

Amos, as God's messenger, asks his listeners in this main question: "Do not you belong to me, sons of Israel?" (v. 7a). And of course he is expecting a positive answer. To make this evident, and so that no escape nor excuse is possible, he adds this rhetorical question as a theological justification: "For is it not true, that I made Israel come here from the land of Egypt?" (v. 7b).

The structure and the content of this verse suggest this interpretation. There is no verb in the Hebrew text of v. 7a; it is simply "you to me". Such an expression is a "formula of belonging", as can be seen in similar cases: the adoption of the two sons of Joseph by Jacob: "they to me" = they are mine (Gen. 48:5); marriage: "to him two wives" = he had two wives (1 Sam. 1:2); "My beloved (is) mine and I (am) his" (Ct. 2:16; 6:3);[9] relationships with Yahweh: "you (are) mine" (Is. 43:1), "I (am) to Yahweh" (Is. 44:5); and finally and above all the formula of the covenant itself, which expresses so clearly this mutual belonging: "You are my people, I am your God" (Ex. 6:7; Lev. 26:12; Dt. 26:16-19; 29:12; 2 Sam. 7:24 etc.).

What we find in Amos 9:7 is thus clearly technical covenant language, "*You belong to me*", (v. 7a) and the reason is very simple: "*because I made Israel come here out of Egypt*" (v. 7b). We have only one half of the complete formula of mutual belonging: "you to me, I to you". But precisely this "I to you" is missing at the time of the prophet. Yahweh is master over Israel, "you to me", because he has delivered her, but the Israelites do not recognize Yahweh any more; they do not live according to the stipulations of the covenant. The question that Yahweh addresses to them is a real lawsuit, a kind of accusation, a reproach, which invites Israel to recognize her guilt and to convert.[10] Israel still *says* that Yahweh is with her, but the word has become an empty one without any meaning in life: "Seek good, and not evil, that you may live; and so Yahweh, the God of hosts will be with you, *as you have said*" (Am. 5:14). In other words, Amos says: "Do not you belong to me, sons of Israel?", and implicitly, "and consequently do you not owe me recognition and submission?".

But again the prophet does not stop here. As in v. 7b where he uses one verb to express Yahweh's action not only in the history of Israel, but also in that of the Philistines and the Aramaeans, here again in v. 7a he associates the Cushites with the Israelites in their belonging to Yahweh: "*Are you not mine, sons of Israel, as the sons of the Cushites?*"

This does not at all imply total equality between Israel and the Cushites as the first group of exegetes suggests. Where we translate by "as", "like", we introduce a comparison which may be perfect (equality) or imperfect (similarity). Unlike the second group of exegetes, we do not believe that the sentence contains any idea of disdain. It has been said that the Cushites, because they were black, were considered inferior; the following text is often invoked to support this viewpoint: "Can the Ethiopian change his skin?" (Jer. 13:23), and the same verse goes on: "or the leopard his spots?". This text does not indicate any contempt; they are simply two examples of things that are impossible. Israel apparently did not practise colour discrimination. Cush has a normal place in the table of the nations (Gen. 10:6 ff.; 1 Chr. 1:8-9); Moses married a Cushite woman

---

9. A. FEUILLET, "La formule d'appartenance mutuelle (2:16) et les interprétations divergentes du Cantique des Cantiques", in *R.B.*, 68 (1961), pp. 5-38.
10. A. SINCLAIR, "The Courtroom Motif in the Book of Amos", in *J.B.L.*, 85 (1966), pp. 351-353.

(Num. 12:1); the Cushites could aspire to more or less important positions at the royal court (Jer. 38:7 ff.); they were rather admired and feared for their wealth (Is. 43:3; 45:14; Job. 28:19) and for their power (Is. 18:1-2; Jer. 46:9; Ezek. 38:5).

But one question remains: why did Amos compare the Israelites with the Cushites? If it is God who intervenes in the history of peoples and this gives him a right over them, we should then expect a comparison with the Philistines and Aramaeans who also had their exodus experience. Several reflections could be made on this. It would have been difficult to present the Philistines and Aramaeans as examples of conduct, since they are condemned by the prophet for their crimes (Aramaeans 1:3-5; Philistines 1:6-8); but the Cushites are not mentioned in Amos's oracles against the nations (Am. 1:3-2:16). What appears to be the most obvious reason is that Amos indicates, in this way, Yahweh's universal power over mankind. Of all the known peoples of that time, the Cushites were the most distant in the *south* (Esth. 1:1; 8:9). The Philistines symbolized the *west*. The movement of the Aramaeans from Kir (Ur?) to Damascus covered the *east* and the *north*. Symbolically, all the nations are thus represented. Yahweh guides their history and, therefore, they all belong to him.

"Do not you belong to me, sons of Israel, as the Cushites also belong to me?" Amos does not speak about total equality, neither is there any connotation of disdain, but rather the belonging of each people to Yahweh, each one on its own level. God guides the history of each people. Even if the histories of Israel, the Philistines and the Aramaeans are very similar, they are not exactly the same or identical. Thus these benefits which remain different create a bond of belonging which will also be different. We touch here upon God's freedom; nobody is left aside, but at the same time, "you only have I known of all the families of the earth" (Am. 3:2).

The essential difference between Israel and the nations is evident. They may have viewed the exodus as just another historical event, but for Israel it had a special meaning. Only Israel knew that Yahweh was guiding her history because God had revealed himself as Yahweh at that moment of her history: "but if they ask me what his name is..." (Ex. 3:13). Thus there was a real mutual belonging: "you to me, I to you". Israel belonged to Yahweh as his special "people", and Israel had the knowledge of who Yahweh was.

The Philistines and the Aramaeans were ignorant of the real meaning of their own migrations and unaware that Yahweh was guiding their history, since he did not reveal himself to them. So for the nations, up to now, it has been only "you to me", and they have not yet been called his "people". Consequently their responsibility and their answer to God will be different from that of Israel's.

Amos has, therefore, addressed his question to the sons of Israel inviting them to recognize Yahweh. He points out that they have the possibility of accepting or of refusing, but: *"Behold, the eyes of the Lord Yahweh are upon the sinful kingdom"* (v. 8a). The expression "sinful kingdom" is unique in the whole biblical tradition and is likewise extremely strong. Its meaning is remarkable when compared with another unique expression. When Yahweh concludes his covenant with Israel at Mount Sinai, she is called a "priestly kingdom" (Ex. 19:6). Israel is commissioned with a priestly function between God and the nations. But Israel, through her conduct, is far from being this light to the nations. Amos says here that, on the contrary, the nations are giving a lesson to Israel. From "priestly kingdom" Israel became a "sinful kingdom". Under these circumstances Yahweh reiterates the terms of punishment: *"I will destroy it from the surface of the ground"* (Am. 9:8b; also *"shake among all the nations"*, 9:9). But for those who accept the invitation to repent, salvation remains possible: *"except that I will not utterly destroy the house of Jacob"* (Am. 9:8c).

This oracle of Amos is without doubt an invitation addressed to unfaithful Israel to return to the covenant. It is to the sons of Israel that the prophet speaks.

But the text has another aspect which remains subordinated to the first intention of the text, namely, that Amos teaches here a very rich form of universalism. But universalism does not mean necessarily equality. Each nation receives benefits from Yahweh, each one has its "exodus experience", and each thereby enters into the relationship of belonging to God which must manifest itself by recognition and submission. Since the benefits are not identical the degree of belonging will be different and thus also the demands that flow from it will be different.[11]

This interpretation is more in accord with the meaning of all the texts of Amos (thus 9:7 is not at all in contradiction with 3:2), and is in better harmony with the whole biblical tradition which teaches at the same time the election and covenant of Israel and universalism.

We have analysed this particular text of Amos in detail because of its exceptional strength. We could quote other texts where Yahweh guides the history of the nations (cf. 2 Kgs. 5:1), such as the different texts we have already mentioned where Yahweh uses the nations as instruments and in which we see that their victory over Israel is part of Yahweh's plan. But in the text of Amos the most basic historical event is applied to the nations—not only the deliverance from Egypt, but also the entry into Palestine: the exodus and the conquest. Other texts develop to a greater extent the theme of landgiving for the nations. Yahweh has given a land to the Edomites: "You are about to pass through the territory of your brethren the sons of Esau, who live in Seir; ... do not contend with them; for I will not give you any of their land, no, not so much as for the sole of the foot to tread on, because I have given Mount Seir to Esau as a possession" (Dt. 2:4-5); to the Moabites (Dt. 2:9); and to the Ammonites (Dt. 2:19).

---

11. R. L. HONEYCUTT, *Amos and his Message*, Nashville, 1963, p. 20.

## II. THE JUDGMENT OF THE NATIONS

Since the nations, too, have their "exodus experience" and as a consequence belong to God, they are thereby responsible before him. If they refuse to serve, they also will be judged and punished. The prophets especially speak about this quite often in what have been called "the oracles against the nations". We find long series in the following texts: Am. 1-2; Is. 13-23; Jer. 46-51; Ezek. 25-32.[12]

ORACLES AGAINST NEIGHBOURING NATIONS (Am. 1:3-2:16)[13]

The same Amos who preached the exceptional text 9:7 also presents a long list of oracles against several of the nations. Yahweh will judge and punish Damascus (1:3-5), the Philistines (1:6-8), Tyre (1:9-10), Edom (1:11-12), Ammon (1:13-15), Moab (2:1-3), as well as Judah (2:4-5) and Israel (2:6-16). This text is of special interest, because this list includes not only the neighbouring "nations" but also the "elected people", and this, therefore, makes a good comparison possible. We can easily find out whether the sins and the punishment of the two are different or identical.

One of the many problems with these oracles is their authenticity. For many reasons the oracle of Judah is generally considered as an addition and some others are also open to discussion. We shall take the text as it stands, because even the later additions have respected the total structure and ideas.

Each individual oracle is composed of the same elements:

1 *Formula of introduction:*

Thus says Yahweh.

The same Yahweh has something to say about each of these nations, not only about the elected people.

---

12. J. H. HAYES, "The Usage of Oracles against Foreign Nations in Ancient Israel", in *J.B.L.*, 87 (1968), pp. 81-92; G. FOHRER, "Vollmacht über Völker und Königreiche. Beobachtungen zu den prophetischen Fremdvölkersprüchen anhand von Jer. 46-51", in *Festschrift J. Ziegler*, ed. J. Schreiner, Würzburg, 1972, pp. 145-153; T. H. MCALPINE, "The Word against the Nations", in *Studia Biblica et Theologica*, 5 (1975), pp. 3-14; D. L. CHRISTENSEN, *Transformations of the War Oracle in Old Testament Prophecy. Studies in the Oracles against the Nations*, Missoula, 1975.
13. A. BENTZEN, "The Ritual Background of Amos 1:2-2:16", in *O.T.S.*, 8 (1950), pp. 85-99; A. FEUILLET, "L'Universalisme dans la religion d'Amos", in *B.V.C.*, n. 17 (1957), pp. 17-29; M. HARAN, "Observations on the Historical Background of Amos 1:2-2:6", in *Isr.E.J.*, 18 (1968), pp. 201-213; S. M. PAUL, "Amos 1:3-2:3: A Concatenous Literary Pattern", in *J.B.L.*, 90 (1971), pp. 397-403; K. N. SCHOVILLE, "A Note on the Oracles of Amos against Gaza, Tyre and Edom", in *V.T.S.*, 26 (1974), pp. 55-63; G. PFEIFER, "Denkformenanalyse als exegetische Methode erläutert an Am. 1:2-2:16", in *Z.A.W.*, 88 (1976), pp. 56-71.

## 2 General motivation:

> For three transgressions of X
> and for four, I will not revoke the punishment.

Yahweh decides now to punish each nation for its unfaithfulness. "Three" and "four" which together make "seven" (which is a perfect number) constitute a fullness of sins and Yahweh's patience is exhausted. Or perhaps a better explanation might be that "three" crimes (three is itself a perfect number) could still be acceptable, but an additional crime would make four and then the measure overflows.[14]

Of rather particular interest is the word "transgression".[15] It expresses the rebellion of an inferior against his superior for not respecting his demands (Gen. 31:36; 50:17; 1 Kgs. 21:19; 2 Kgs. 1:1). It is very often used when Israel does not observe Yahweh's commandments (Am. 3:14; 4:4; 5:12; Hos. 8:1; Jer. 2:29). Amos here uses this same term, "transgression", for the nations as he does for Israel. He thus suggests that the nations too have rejected an order established by Yahweh. Since they have been unfaithful, Yahweh will punish all of them: "I will not revoke the punishment".

## 3 Specific motivation:

> because they have...

One particular transgression of these numerous transgressions is now specified for each nation. Since each case is different, we shall study the situation in more detail, asking precisely why it happened and of what crime each is guilty.

## 4 Punishment:

> So I will...

A concrete punishment is predicted with different images. Each individual nation will be ruined by war and destruction. The following formula occurs very frequently: "So I will send a fire upon the house of X, and it shall devour the strongholds of X" (1:4,7,10,12,14; 2.2,5). Interesting also is the reference to a possible exile, so well-known in the biblical tradition, which at the same time leaves open the possibility of return and restoration: "and the people of X shall go into exile" (1:5,15).

It is always Yahweh who punishes all nations: "*I* will send a fire... *I* will break... *I* will cut off..." (1:4-5; etc.).

---

14. M. WEISS, "The Pattern of Numerical Sequence in Amos 1-2, a Re-examination", in *J.B.L.*, 86 (1967), pp. 416-423.
15. E. BEAUCAMP, "Amos I-II: Le pèsha' d'Israël et celui des Nations", in *Sc. Espr.*, 21 (1969), pp. 435-441.

5 *Final conclusion* (in several of the oracles):

Oracle of Yahweh.

These oracles thus show very clearly that all the nations are responsible before Yahweh. They all have committed "transgressions" and have not respected an order established by God. Yahweh, therefore, will punish each one of them. This punishment will have the same severity for the nations as for the elected people because there are no exceptions and no privileges.

But for what specific reason are they condemned? In each oracle we find a concrete motive, an example of their evil. And here something very interesting appears which distinguishes the "nations" from the "elected people".

*All the foreign neighbouring nations* have something in common: they have not respected their fellowmen. Their crime is always inhuman behaviour towards another nation—"war crimes". Damascus has committed cruelty towards Gilead: "because they have threshed Gilead with threshing sledges of iron" (1:3); the Philistines have deprived people of their freedom: "because they carried into exile a whole people to deliver them up to Edom" (1:6) and so has Tyre: "because they delivered up a whole people to Edom" (1:9); Edom has hated his brother: "because he pursued his brother with the sword, and cast off all pity, and his anger tore perpetually, and he kept his wrath for ever" (1:11). Ammon has not respected harmless pregnant women: "because they have ripped up women with child in Gilead, that they might enlarge their border" (1:13). And Moab has dishonoured even the dead: "because he burned to lime the bones of the king of Edom" (2:1).

If it is not always clear who the people are that suffered, at least in the case of Moab it is certain that his crime is not against Israel. On the contrary, it is against Edom, one of the long-standing enemies of Israel. In other words, all of these nations are accused of the crime of not respecting their fellowmen as human beings, and not of having wronged the chosen people.

Against Tyre it is charged that because of cruelty it "did not remember the covenant of brotherhood" (1:9).[16] This has been interpreted in different ways, as we have seen. Some interpret this as an allusion to a treaty between Tyre and Israel (1 Kgs. 5:15-26). Tyre is then blamed for unfaithfulness to its given word. Others think of the Noah covenant which constituted a brotherhood between all men (Gen. 9:1-17). The sin of Edom, too, seems worse because it is against his "brother" (1:11).[17]

---

16. *Supra*, p. 30, note 19.
17. *Supra*, p. 30, note 20.

The crimes of the chosen people are also cited. First of all *Judah* is condemned: "because they have rejected the law of Yahweh and have not kept his statutes" (2:4). The southern kingdom has been unfaithful by rejecting the stipulations of the covenant. This is a rejection of Yahweh as a covenant partner (1 Sam. 8:7; 10:19; 15:23,26). We have the well-known vocabulary used to exhort Israel to total submission (Lev. 18:5, 30; Dt. 4:2; 5:1; Is. 5:24). "But their lies have led them astray, after which their fathers walked" (2:4); like their ancestors they have followed other gods and have committed idolatry (Dt. 4:3; 6:14; Jgs. 2:12; 2 Kgs. 17:15). It is very easy then to see the difference between Judah and the other nations: Judah has rejected Yahweh and the law he has given her.

The oracle against *Israel* is the longest one. It has the same structure as those of the other nations, but some new elements have been added which make it a real lawsuit or trial. The specific motivation is more developed ("because..." v. 6b-8); their crime is worse since it is a refusal after all the historical benefits Yahweh has bestowed upon them: the exodus, the conquest and the prophets ("yet..." v. 9-12); and thus Yahweh will execute his punishment ("Behold..." v. 13-16).[18]

Many commentaries have shown parallels between the accusations and several lawtexts.[19] In other words, Israel did not observe the stipulations of the covenant: "They sell the righteous..." (v. 6b). The law did not permit a person to be made one's slave or to be sold in a trifling manner (Ex. 22:1-3; Dt. 24:7). Oppression of the poor and injustices towards little people (v. 7a) were completely contrary to the law, which protected in a special way widows, orphans and the poor (Ex. 23:6; Dt. 16:19).[20] Sacred prostitution or the abuse of a girl by a man and his father (v. 7b) was also prohibited (Dt. 23:18-19 or Lev. 18:8,15,17; 20:11,12,14). And Israel did not respect the special provision of the law regarding the pledge of some of the poor man's belongings (v. 8; cf. Ex. 22:25-26; Dt. 24:12-13,17). Not only was this law not observed but there was even intermingling with an impious cult.

Israel is condemned because she does not observe these different stipulations of the law; she has not respected men nor has she celebrated the right cult. And this, as Amos says: "so that my holy name is profaned" (2:7). Every human action against the law profanes Yahweh's name (cf. Lev. 18:21; 19:12; 20:3 etc.; Ezek. 20:39; 36:20 etc.). The "nations",

---

18. R. Rendtorff, "Zu Amos 2:14-16", in *Z.A.W.*, 85 (1973), pp. 226-227.
19. R. Bach, "Gottesrecht und weltliches Recht in der Verkündigung des Propheten Amos", in *Festschrift G. Dehn*, Neukirchen, 1957, pp. 23-34; P.-E. Dion, "Le message moral du prophète Amos s'inspirait-il du 'droit de l'alliance'?", in *Sc.Espr.*, 27 (1975), pp. 5-34.
20. F. C. Fensham, "Widow, Orphan and the Poor in Ancient Near Eastern Legal and Wisdom Literature", in *J.N.E.S.*, 21 (1962), pp. 129-139.

too, do not respect men, as is the case with Israel. But for her, the unfaithfulness is worse because she is consciously dishonouring Yahweh. Israel by her crimes has not only broken the "covenant of brotherhood" but at the same time has broken the "covenant with Yahweh".

The sin of Israel consists of a greater ingratitude because of all she has received (v. 9-12). The different biblical lawsuits very often recall the historical benefits of the exodus and conquest, but Amos adds here another favour for Israel: the prophets Yahweh has sent to her (cf. Jgs. 6:8-10; 2 Kgs. 17:7-14; Jer. 7:22-26). This is again important in this context of a universal judgment. Amos proclaimed that the nations also had an exodus experience (9:7), but, as we have seen, were unconscious of it. Only Israel had understood the meaning of her history. It was the special function of the prophets to interpret history and to transmit Yahweh's revelation: "And I raised up some of your sons for prophets..." (2:11); but Israel refused the light: "you commanded the prophets, saying, 'You shall not prophesy'" (2:12).

Judah and Israel, then, have something in common. They both have rejected Yahweh's law and thus have consciously rebelled against Yahweh himself.

Thus Amos makes a clear distinction between what the "nations" are guilty of, and that of which "the chosen people" are guilty. Both have rebelled against Yahweh, they have committed "transgressions", they are responsible before him, but each one at the level of his belonging to God. The "nations" are condemned because they did not respect men. Everybody is conscious of the value of a human being. We could call this "the law of the human conscience", or "natural law", or "natural order", or the like—a law that God has put in the hearts of men. But the "chosen people" are condemned for something more: they did not respect "the law of Yahweh", the "revealed law", the "revealed order". They had received Yahweh's law, his revelation, and it is this which they rejected.

## THE CONDEMNATION OF EGYPT (Ezek. 29:1-12)[21]

It is not only the minor kingdoms and neighbours of Israel that are under Yahweh's judgment; the great world empires are also responsible before him. Ezekiel, like so many of the prophets, has a series of oracles against the nations (25-32) in which Egypt occupies an important place (29-32). We will analyse only the first of his oracles against Egypt (29:1-12) because of its particular interest to our topic.

---

21. W. VOGELS, "Restauration de l'Egypte et universalisme en Ez. 29:13-16", in *Bib.*, 53 (1972), pp. 473-494, on the condemnation of Egypt, pp. 473-480.

We have already seen that Ezekiel uses covenant language in referring to the first exodus and to the new exodus, to the first covenant and to the new covenant. According to the prophet, the nations are witnessing all this and, finally, "they will know that I am Yahweh" and they will proclaim: "these are the people of Yahweh" (Ezek. 36:20). He certainly likes to use the characteristic and technical vocabulary of the covenant to speak about salvation history.

The text (29:1-12) can be divided into three sections, each constructed according to a well-known pattern: accusation of guilt, announcement of punishment, formula of recognition.

1) v. 1-6a: —you said... (v. 3)
         —I will... (v. 4-5)
         —then all the inhabitants of Egypt shall know that I am Yahweh (v. 6a)

2) v. 6b-9a: —because you... (v. 6b-7)
         —therefore... (v. 8)
         —then they will know that I am Yahweh (v. 9a)

3) v. 9b-12: —because you said... (v. 9b)
         —therefore... (v. 10-12)

— This oracle changes then into a perspective of restoration (to be studied in our next section) before reaching the final formula of recognition (v. 16).

The structure itself is already very enlightening: because Egypt has done something wrong, Yahweh will punish her and so she will come to the recognition of Yahweh.

The announcement of the *punishment* of Egypt contains several stereotyped images, which are typical of Ezekiel himself, but are also used by other prophets to predict the curse of Israel after she has broken the covenant. We find the same images in the fundamental text of the covenant curses in Lev. 26, and in the extra-biblical texts for the treaty curses.[22]

"Behold, I am against you" (29:3,10), addressed here to Egypt, is exactly the same expression that Ezekiel uses against Israel: "Behold I, even I, am against you; and I will execute judgments in the midst of you in the eyes of the nations" (5:8; 13:8,20 etc.).[23] This thus means a breaking off of a relationship and a consequent chastisement.

The text contains many of the most characteristic curses for the unfaithfulness of the covenant partner.

---

22. *Supra*, p. 68, note 38.
23. P. HUMBERT, "Die Herausforderungsformel 'hinnenî êlékâ'", in *Z.A.W.*, 52 (1933), pp. 101-108.

|  | Egypt | Israel | |
|---|---|---|---|
|  | *Ezek. 29:1-12* | *Ezekiel* | *Lev. 26* |
| sword[24] | v. 8 | 5:2,12,17; 6:3,11,12; 7:15; 11:8,10; 14:17; 33:2; 39:23 | v. 25,33,36,37 |
| wild beasts | 5 | 5:17; 14:15,21; 33:27 | 22 |
| the land becomes desolation | 9,10 | 5:14; 35:4; 36:4,10,33; 38:8,12 | 31,33 |
| and desert | 9,10,12 | 6:14; 12:20; 14:15,16; 15:8; 33:28,29; 35:3,4, 7,9,14,15 | 33 |
| no tomb | 5 | 35:8; 37 (the story of the bones); 39:11 ff. | 30 (cf. Dt. 28:26) |
| no passers-by | 11 (cf. 32:13) | 5:14; 14:15; 33:38; 36:34 (cf. Jer. 9:9,11) |  |

But the most interesting formula is without doubt: "I will scatter the Egyptians among the nations, and disperse them among the countries" (29:12). This is repeated further on against Egypt (30:23,26; 32:9). This is the well-known formula for the announcement of the exile of Israel, her supreme punishment (11:16; 12:15; 20:23; 22:15; 36:19; and partly in Lev. 26:33). We have exactly the same expression for Egypt as we have for Israel. This expression of punishment may also remind us of the exile of mankind at the end of the broken primitive universal covenant when the people were "scattered" (Gen. 11:4,8,9).

Here, then, we clearly have a series of curses for the unfaithful partner of a covenant. Since both Egypt and Israel have the same punishment we may well ask: did they commit the same crimes? Are they condemned for the same reason?

In the accusations presented in three sections of the text we find out why Egypt is condemned and what her *sins* are. The same reason is given in the first and in the third section, namely, that the king of Egypt has declared: "The Nile is mine, I made it" (v. 3,9). The sin of Egypt is her pride, her hubris. The implication of this becomes even clearer if one compares the words of Pharaoh with some statements of Yahweh in the book of Ezekiel: "I, Yahweh, have spoken, and I will do (make) it" (12:25,28; 17:24; 22:14; 24:14; 36:36; 37:14). The Pharaoh has indicated that he believes himself to be God and creator. It is interesting to compare this attitude with a similar attitude on the part of the king of Tyre: "Because

---

24. O. EISSFELDT, "Schwerterschlagene bei Hesekiel", in *Studies in Old Testament Prophecy, Festschrift T. H. Robinson*, Edinburgh, 1950, pp. 73-81; or in *Kleine Schriften* III, Tübingen, 1966, pp. 1-8.

your heart is proud, and you have said, 'I am a god, I sit in the seat of the gods, in the heart of the seas', yet you are but a man, and no god, though you consider yourself as wise as a god" (Ezek. 28:2). On the other hand, the sins of which Israel is declared guilty are very often summarized with the traditional formula: "you have not walked in my statutes, nor executed my ordinances". These two terms, "statutes" and "ordinances" are very frequently put together in the book of Ezekiel (5:6 ff.; 11:12,20; 18:9,17; 20:11,13,16,18,19,21,24,25; 36:27; 37:24) and elsewhere in the Bible, for instance in Leviticus and Deuteronomy, where they refer to the demands of the whole law.[25] The difference is now again very clear and important. Israel has become unfaithful to the demands of the "revealed law of Yahweh", that is, to the stipulations of the covenant. In the case of Egypt the sin is not against a revealed law but against something fundamental in human conscience. Man is capable of coming to some knowledge of a god above him who is the creator and thus Egypt's sin is against a kind of "natural law".

In the second section of the text proud Egypt is condemned for another reason (v. 6b-7). She has been a continual temptation for Israel. In times of danger Israel has often looked for help from Egypt, instead of putting her trust in Yahweh, her only suzerain. Egypt has thus been a danger for this covenant relationship between Israel and Yahweh. And as we have seen before, the nations are judged according to their attitude towards the mutual partners of this covenant.

Ezekiel here clearly uses covenant language to condemn Egypt for her unfaithfulness. Destruction and exile are the result. But this is not the end and new hope will arise.

We have chosen these two texts (Am. 1:3-2:16; Ezek. 29:1-12) from among the "oracles against the nations" because they permit a very clear comparison between Israel and the nations. All peoples, both the "nations" and the "chosen people", are responsible before the same God who will apply the same punishment for their unfaithfulness. But the reasons for this judgment are different: Israel is guilty of rejecting the "revealed law", the nations, of not observing the "natural law".

## III. THE RESTORATION OF THE NATIONS

The nations have had their "exodus experience" and thus belong to Yahweh. This implies that they are henceforth responsible to him. If they become unfaithful, they will be punished by God. But the curse is not the final word of God. He desires to restore them. Several biblical texts contain such a promise of restoration for the nations: the nations in general (Jer. 12:14-16; Is. 66:18-23); Egypt (Is. 19:16-25; Jer. 46:26; Ezek. 29:13-16); Tyre (Is. 23:17-18); Moab (Jer. 48:47); Ammon

---

25. N. LOHFINK, *Das Hauptgebot*, pp. 56-67.

(Jer. 49:6); Elam (Jer. 49:39); Sodom and Samaria (Ezek. 16:53).[26] Most of these promises are, surprisingly enough, in the "oracles against the nations". God's message is that of justice and mercy, death and life, destruction and hope.

THE RESTORATION OF EGYPT (Ezek. 29:13-16)[27]

In Ezekiel's oracle of doom against Egypt (29:1-12), which we have just analysed, we now suddenly discover a turn towards a perspective of salvation (29:13-16). This rather surprising change explains why the authenticity of this promise is very much discussed. But on the other hand, many other reasons are in favour of the unity of the whole passage.

To understand the richness of this promise given to Egypt, it is necessary for us to compare it with a series of very similar texts by the same prophet where he expresses promises of the restoration of Israel (Ezek. 11:17-20; 16:59-63; 20:39-44; 28:23-26; 34 (especially v. 11 ff.); 36 (especially v. 22 ff.); 37 (especially v. 11 ff. and v. 21 ff.); 39:25-29).

After the condemnation of Egypt we have the formula: "For thus says the Lord Yahweh" (29:13) followed by the oracle of restoration. Often after a severe oracle of doom against Israel, Ezekiel introduces a hope of restoration for Israel by the same formula: "for thus says the Lord Yahweh" (11:17; 16:59; 20:39; 36:22; 39:25). So in a certain sense, without any interruption, we see that after doom hope naturally follows.[28] All these promises to Israel are built according to a well-known structure: "the promise of the future covenant". But since it is a promise of restoration for Israel, who has been punished for her unfaithfulness to the covenant, all these texts have the more precise structure of "the promise of the new covenant" which we mentioned earlier.[29]

This promise is composed of three elements: (I) A cry for help, which in the promise of the new covenant is conversion; (II) A promise of salvific actions; (III) A request for future submission.

What Ezekiel does is again extremely important to our topic. As he did for the punishment of Egypt (29:1-12), he now does for her restoration (29:13-16). He uses the same vocabulary, the same literary formulas

---

26. H. M. ORLINSKY, "Nationalism–Universalism in the Book of Jeremiah", in *Essays in Biblical Culture and Bible Translation*, New York, 1974, pp. 117-143. P. HÖFFKEN, "Zu den Heilszusätzen in der Völkerorakelsammlung des Jeremiabuches. Zugleich ein Beitrag zur Frage nach den Überlieferungsinteressen an den Völkerorakelsammlungen der Prophetenbücher.", in *V.T.*, 27 (1977), pp. 398-412.
27. W. VOGELS, "Restauration de l'Egypte et universalisme en Ez. 29:13-16", in *Bib.*, 53 (1972), pp. 473-494.
28. W. ZIMMERLI, "'Leben' und 'Tod' im Buche des Propheten Ezechiel", in *Th. Z.*, 13 (1957), pp. 494-508; ID., "Planungen für den Wiederaufbau nach der Katastrophe von 587", in *V.T.*, 18 (1968), pp. 229-255; A. W. BLACKWOOD, *Ezechiel: Prophecy of Hope*, Grand Rapids, 1965: J. ALONSO DIAZ, "Ezequiel, el profeta de ruina y de esperanza", in *Cu.Bib.*, 25 (1968), pp. 290-299.
29. W. VOGELS, *La promesse royale de Yahweh préparatoire à l'alliance*.

and structures, and the same theology of the covenant, which he used for the chosen people to describe the promise of the restoration of Egypt. We shall study the parallel between the two of them and search for evidence not only of the great similarities between them but also of some important differences. This evidence will show, as in the case of the preceding texts, the extensive universalism of this text and at the same time what it is exactly which still distinguishes Israel from the other nations.

(1) *The "conversion" of Egypt* (v. 13a)

The restoration of Egypt will take place "at the end of forty years" (v. 13). This number has already been mentioned in the preceding punishment (v. 11-12).

The number "forty", which is the length of time of one generation, has a very strong connotation in biblical tradition of the period in the desert. Israel's punishment for her infidelity lasted indeed forty years: "According to the number of the days in which you spied out the land, forty days, for every day a year, you shall bear your iniquity, forty years, and you shall know my displeasure" (Num. 14:34; cf. Ex. 16:35; Num. 13:25; 14:33-34; 32:13; Dt. 2:7; 8:4; 29:4; Jos. 5:6; Neh. 9:21; Ps. 95:10; Am. 2:10; 5:25).[30]

We have seen before how Ezekiel likes to use images of the first exodus and covenant to speak about the events of his own time. He announces that Israel will be sent to "the desert of the peoples" (20:35) as their fathers were "in the desert of the land of Egypt" (20:36; cf. 20: 10 ff.).[31] He is the only prophet to apply to Judah the number "forty" to describe the new punishment which the chosen people will undergo because of their new infidelities: "...you shall lie down a second time, but on your right side, and bear the punishment of the house of Judah; forty days I assign you, a day for each year" (4:6). By applying to Egypt a similar punishment of forty years (29:11,12) the prophet once more underlines the parallel between Israel and Egypt.

But the period in the desert was not only a time of punishment for Israel, it was also the time of her betrothal, of the education of her people, of her preparation to enter the promised land. In biblical tradition a return to the desert has often the meaning of a purification, a call to conversion. And thus the number "forty" is linked with the desert and is, therefore, a number associated with preparation, conversion (Ex. 24:18; 34:28; Dt. 9:9,11,18) or renewal (1 Kgs. 19:8). And this is also what Ezekiel implies by this period of forty years for Egypt: it is not the end,

---

30. R. POELMAN, *Le signe biblique des quarante jours*, Paris, 1961.
31. W. ZIMMERLI, "Der 'neue Exodus' in der Verkündigung der beiden grossen Exilspropheten", in *Maqqél Shâqédh. La Branche d'Amandier, Festschrift W. Vischer*, Montpellier, 1960, pp. 216-227, or in *Gottes Offenbarung. Gesammelte Aufsätze zum Alten Testament*, München, 1963, pp. 192-204.

the total destruction, but a preparation for restoration (v. 13), a time of purification and of conversion. The great, proud nation of Egypt will be humbled and become powerless; then she will finally call for help to him who can restore her. It is through conversion that Ezekiel believes in the possibility of life after death, of restoration after condemnation (14:6; 16:61; 18:21; 33:10 ff.).[32] Now this has become possible also for a foreign nation.

Just as the old sinful generation of Israel had first to die in the desert (Num. 32:13) so that a new people could enter the promised land, so also the proud old people of Egypt had to disappear and a new people, whose characteristics are described later, would enter.

Ezekiel is not the only biblical writer to apply the number "forty" to the nations. The Yahwist, whose writing is strongly universalist in thought and who has composed his prehistory from the viewpoint of a covenant between Yahweh and mankind, uses the number "forty" in describing the punishment of unfaithful mankind by means of the flood (Gen. 7:4,12,17). He also shows a new world emerging "at the end of forty days" (Gen. 8:6). The prophet Jonah announces to the inhabitants of Nineveh that they have yet "forty" days before the destruction of the city, a period of purification and conversion (Jon. 3:4).

(II) *The promise of salvific actions of Yahweh* (v. 13-14)

> I will gather the Egyptians from the peoples
> among whom they were scattered.

Ezekiel continues to apply to Egypt Yahweh's conduct towards his own people. We now have a promise of salvation: "I will gather you from the peoples" (11:17; 20:34,41; 28:25; 34:13; 36:24; 37:21; 39:27). This formula with the verb "gather" became a stereotype through its use in the Bible to denote return from exile, the gathering after dispersion. It belongs to the technical language used in the texts of the new covenant. It is one of the several "exodus formulas".[33] Just as Yahweh once brought Israel out of Egypt, he will also bring Israel back from exile.

At Mount Sinai, when Yahweh concluded his covenant with Israel, he chose her to be his "own possession among all the peoples" (Ex. 19:5). When he gathers Israel "from the peoples" it is to make her again his people through a new covenant (Ezek. 11:17,20). But now, Egypt similarly is chosen as a people "from the peoples"; she also will have a special place and function, as the rest of the text confirms (v. 15-16).

Very often, as in the present instance, we find, following the promise

---

32. J. DELORME, "Conversion et pardon selon le prophète Ézéchiel", in *Mémorial J. Chaine*, Lyon 1950, pp. 115-144.
33. J. J. WIJNGAARDS, *The Formulas of the Deuteronomic Creed*, pp. 22-27; G. WIDENGREN, "The Gathering of the Dispersed", in *Svensk Exegetisk Årsbok*, 41-42 (1976-77), pp. 224-234.

of return, the formula "among whom they were scattered" (11:17; 20:34, 41; 37:21). This formula recalls the punishment of the exile by using the verb "scatter" (v. 12). The whole sentence, thus, means that restoration will take place after a punishment, and thereby stresses God's mercy and goodness.

> I will bring back the captives of Egypt.

In discussing the translation of this Hebrew formula[34] some emphasize the root of the verb "to capture". Others emphasize the root of the verb "to return". In the first translation the text would read: "I will bring back the captives of Egypt" (to turn the captivity). In the second translation we would have: "I will restore the fortunes of Egypt" (to accomplish a change). But in any case, the restoration of Egypt entails the return of Egyptian captives. It is another technical expression, very frequently used in the Bible to speak about the restoration of Israel (Dt. 30:3; Ps. 14:7; 53:7; 85:2; 126:4; Jer. 29:14; 30:3,18; 31:23; 32:44; 33:7,11,26 etc.). Ezekiel, too, uses it elsewhere in his book (16:53 (three times, Jerusalem, Sodom, Samaria); 39:25 (Jacob)).

So after the gathering of the Egyptians (v. 13), there will follow their return (v. 14) through one single salvific action of Yahweh.

> I will reinstall them in the land of Pathros,
> the land of their origin, and there they shall
> be a lowly kingdom.

The restoration of Israel is not only her gathering and return, but it comprises a second salvific action of Yahweh: "I will give you the land of Israel" (11:17; cf. 20:42; 34:13; 36:24; 37:12,21). Several technical formulas are used in the Bible to express the return ("exodus formulas"), while others are used for this second action: the gift of the land ("landgiving formulas"). Ezekiel now applies one of these "landgiving formulas"[35] to speak about Egypt.

The two great salvific actions of Yahweh in the history of Israel are undoubtedly the deliverance from Egypt and the gift of the promised land (Exodus and Landgiving). Her restoration is presented as a renewal of this first experience by a gathering and return and a new gift of the land (new Exodus and Landgiving). This double action restores the double punishment of the exile, that is, dispersion of the people and loss of the land. This whole history is now applied in identical terms to Egypt.

Israel, at the moment of her restoration, gets back "the land of Israel" (11:17) and is brought back "to the land of Israel, the country which I

---

34. E. L. Dietrich, *Sûb s$^e$bût. Die endzeitliche Wiederherstellung bei den Propheten*, B.Z.A.W. 40, Berlin, 1925; E. Baumann, "*Šûb š$^e$bût*. Eine exegetische Untersuchung", in *Z.A.W.*, 47 (1929), pp. 17-44.
35. J. J. Wijngaards, *The Formulas of the Deuteronomic Creed*, pp. 28-34.

swore to give to your fathers" (20:42; 28:25). It was the land, the heritage, the possession, that Yahweh had destined for her (Ex. 6:8; Ezek. 33:24).[36] The nations were guilty of desiring to take this promised land as "their possession" (Ezek. 36:2 ff.). In a similar way the Egyptians are brought back to "the land of Pathros, the land of their origin" (compare with Ezek. 16:3). Each nation has that part of land that Yahweh destined to it. "When the Most High gave to the nations their inheritance, when he separated the sons of men, he fixed the bounds of the peoples according to the number of the sons of God" (Dt. 32:8; cf. Gen. 10; Am. 9:7; Jer. 12:15; Ezek. 16:55). Yahweh wants to restore Israel and Egypt to what they were in his original plan, but with some purification; for Israel, "I will let you go in by small number" (20:37), and for Egypt a reduction to her real proportions at Pathros in southern Egypt.

In this place the Egyptians will constitute "a lowly kingdom". At Sinai, Yahweh elected Israel from among all the peoples to make her "a priestly kingdom" (Ex. 19:6). Egypt is now chosen from among the peoples and is re-established as a "kingdom" whose characteristics are to be "lowly" and humble. This is a condition which seems indispensable for man and which constitutes his richness: "exalt that which is low, and abase that which is high" (Ezek. 21:31; cf. 17:6,14,24). God prefers the weak: "It was not because you were more in number than any other people that Yahweh set his love upon you and chose you, for you were the fewest of all peoples" (Dt. 7:7). And so, reduced to these humble dimensions, Egypt can receive the divine blessings and finally be capable of recognizing God.

(III) *The submission of Egypt* (v. 15-16)

This restoration of Egypt to the limits of the original divine plan has some effects upon the attitude of Egypt. She now responds with submission to the salvific actions of Yahweh.

> It shall never again exalt itself above the nations...
> it shall never again rule over the nations.

Egypt, having been reduced to the proportions of a lowly kingdom, no longer has any reason to "exalt" herself above the others. She no longer will succumb to the temptation to believe herself to be the "creator", an attitude which constituted her sin and was the reason for her punishment (29:3,9). She will lose the desire to "rule" over others and she will respect them, as was requested in the Noah covenant (Gen. 9:5) and as is expected from nations in the covenant of brotherhood (Am. 1:9,11). In other words, Egypt will now observe the two fundamental aspects of what we have called "natural law", laid down in man's conscience: to recognize the one above

---

36. W. BRUEGGEMANN, *The Land: Place as Gift, Promise, and Challenge in Biblical Faith*, Philadelphia, 1977; J. I. ALFARO, "The Land—Stewardship", in *B.T.B.*, 8 (1978), pp. 51-61.

you and to respect your fellowmen. This behaviour is precisely that on which the nations were judged, as we have seen in the texts we analysed above:

> it shall never again be the reliance of the house of Israel.

But Egypt was judged and condemned for still another reason, namely, because of her power she was a continual temptation for the chosen people. Israel often lacked confidence in Yahweh and relied more on Egypt, concluded treaties with her and thus became unfaithful to her covenant with Yahweh. Egypt was condemned for this (29:6b-7). Now that Egypt has lost her power, she is no longer a real danger to the covenant between Israel and Yahweh. The second reason for Egypt's condemnation is thus also removed.

The restoration of Egypt is not purely geographical; it removes the basis of the sins which caused her to be punished.

We have seen in the preceding chapter how the nations in this period of history are treated according to their attitude towards the two covenant partners: Yahweh and Israel. Yahweh, on his part, promised to protect his people against those who endangered their existence (Ex. 23:22-23). Egypt no longer constitutes a danger because she has no power to rule over others including Israel (v. 15). Israel, in return, promises Yahweh that she will oppose everything which might endanger her faithfulness to her suzerain (Ex. 34:14-17). Since Egypt is so weak, Israel is no longer tempted to turn to her for help instead of relying upon Yahweh (v. 16). If a nation acts in such a way with regard to Yahweh and Israel, the two partners of the covenant, she, too, may be saved. This is what we then see in the rest of the text:

> and they will know that I am the Lord Yahweh.

Finally, Ezekiel describes the personal and direct attitude of Egypt towards Yahweh. This "formula of recognition" concludes the three sections of the entire passage (Ezek. 29:1-16; v. 6a,9a,16b). In v. 6a it is said explicitly that "all the inhabitants of Egypt shall know that I am Yahweh". So, no doubt, "they" in our sentence are the Egyptians.

This technical formula, which we have studied before, is very frequently used by Ezekiel, but also by others. The formula has its origin in the language and the theology of the covenant. The verb "to know" in the covenant context implies the recognition of Yahweh as the one God, the recognition of his benefits in history and the decision to submit to his demands. The Egyptians, instructed by historical events in which Yahweh manifests himself, finally recognize him and submit to him. But this is accomplished by each according to his abilities and according to the degree that God wants to reveal himself to men. Therefore, for instance, in the "formula of recognition" as applied to Israel, one reads sometimes: "and you shall know that I am *Yahweh, your God*" (Ex. 6:7; cf. Ezek. 28:26); in other words, Israel will recognize Yahweh as her covenant partner. The Egyptians, too, will recognize Yahweh, but as Ezekiel says, as their master: "they will know that I am the *Lord Yahweh*". They will recognize that Yahweh is great and powerful and that he is the master, the Lord.

God has a plan for each people. It consists of harmonious order in which each one has his place and his land where he can live in peace. None will rule over the other and all will recognize Yahweh.

Egypt thus will act according to the norms of the Noah-covenant, or the covenant of brotherhood between the nations (v. 15). She will respect the covenant between Yahweh and Israel (v. 16a) and will enter into some relation of belonging to Yahweh (v. 16b).

This text (Ezek. 29:13-16) is clearly composed of the vocabulary, the formulas, the theology of the covenant and the structure of the "promise of the future covenant". Ezekiel uses all this in his promises of the new covenant to Israel. We see once more the importance of a text like this for the concept of universalism. Ezekiel does not only apply a judgment, comparable to the one of Israel, to Egypt but promises a restoration which is also very similar.

But as always, even if there are many similarities between the promises to Israel and the one given to Egypt, important differences remain, especially in elements (II) and (III) of the structure. To show this we will put this promise to Egypt into parallel schema with one of the many texts for Israel. Of all the texts in Ezekiel that we have quoted above (and to which we have referred often in our analysis) we take, for reasons of clarity, only one (11:17-20). But this analysis could be done with all of them and even with some other texts such as Dt. 30:3-5.

| **Egypt** (Ezek. 29:13-16) | **Israel** (Ezek. 11:17-20) |
|---|---|
| II) *Promise of salvific actions:* | |
| I will gather the Egyptians from the peoples among whom they were scattered. | I will gather you from the peoples. |
| I will bring back the captives of Egypt. | I will assemble you out of the countries where you have been scattered. |
| I will reinstall them in the land of Pathros. | I will give you the land of Israel. |

We have in these two cases the expressions of the gathering and return (Exodus formula) and of the gift of the land (Landgiving formula). These are also found in the promise to Israel of the first covenant (Ex. 3:8,17; 6:6,8). But in the promise to Israel of the new covenant, and only here, a new promise is added.

| | |
|---|---|
| | I will give them one heart. |
| | I will put a new spirit within them. |
| | I will give them a heart of flesh. |

This is a promise of an interior renewal, of a new heart, so that what was not obtained in the first covenant may be obtained in the new. Similar formulas are found in other texts: cleaning of the heart (Jer. 4:14;

Ps. 51:12); circumcision of the heart (Jer. 4:4; 9:25; Ezek. 44:7,9; Dt. 30:6); humiliation of the heart (Lev. 26:41); the law in the heart (Jer. 31:33); a heart (Jer. 24:7); one heart (Jer. 32:39); a new heart (Ezek. 18:31; 36:26); a heart of flesh (Ezek. 11:19; 36:26); and many others concerning a new spirit. We can really consider them as stereotyped formulas of the new covenant, along with the Exodus and Landgiving formulas. Since Israel failed in her first call, something has to be changed in her in order for her to come to a real faithfulness.

III) *Request for submission:*

| They will know that I am Yahweh. | That they may walk in my statutes and keep my ordinances and obey them. |

The submission is different. Yahweh expects from Egypt the recognition of a global submission. Of Israel he requests, besides total submission, the observance of the specific stipulations of the covenant which only Israel knows, since they were revealed only to her. As we have seen earlier, Israel was punished because she had refused to observe these stipulations of the "revealed law"; Egypt was punished for not observing the "natural law".

| | They shall be my people, and I will be their God. |

This is the well-known covenant formula,[37] expressing mutual belonging. Finally, in this new covenant, because of the interior renewal, Israel will be God's faithful people, and what did not succeed the first time will now become a reality. This situation does not yet apply to Egypt and for the same reason. Egypt did not receive the revelation. Yahweh is not yet their God. Egypt is not yet called his people as in another text, which we will now analyse.

EGYPT MY PEOPLE (Is. 19:16-25)[38]

Most commentators of Is. 19:16-25 agree on at least one point, that it has an exceptional richness as far as the biblical concept of universalism is concerned.[39] When it comes to the interpretation of the text, however, many divergences arise.

---

37. N. LOHFINK, "Dt. 26:17-19 und die 'Bundesformel'," in *Z.K.T.*, 91 (1969), pp. 517-553.
38. W. VOGELS, "L'Égypte mon peuple—L'universalisme d'Is. 19:16-25", in *Bib.*, 57 (1976), pp. 494-514.
39. A. FEUILLET, "Un sommet religieux de l'Ancien Testament. L'oracle d'Isaïe XIX (vv. 16-25) sur la conversion de l'Égypte", in *R.S.R.*, 39 (1951), pp. 65-87; J. SCHREINER, "Segen für die Völker in die Verheissung an die Väter", in *B.Z.*, 6 (1962), pp. 1-31, for Is. 19, pp. 20-26; J. WILSON, "In that Day. From Text to Sermon on Isaiah 19:23-25", in *Interpr.*, 21 (1967), pp. 66-86. But see H. M. ORLINSKY, "Nationalism—Universalism and Internationalism in Ancient Israel", in *Essays in Biblical Culture and Bible Translation*, New York, 1974, pp. 78-116.

It appears that its understanding remains hopeless as long as one tries to find precise historical allusions or realizations in its oracles. Certain verses, especially towards the end of the passage, escape all possible historical realization. The key expression, which is repeated six times, "in that day", also suggests that the oracles refer to a vague future and that they, like others of the same genre, are expressive of a hope and an ideal that is to come.[40]

When the prophets predicted the restoration of Israel after the exile, they used the well-known images of exodus and conquest. There will be a new exodus, a new conquest, a new covenant. To describe the future, they took images from the past. The author of Is. 19:16-25 made a similar transposition. He chose images of the experience of his own people to depict the salvation offered to the nations. The experiences of Israel's history are applied to the history of the nations. He does what the Yahwist did to compose his prehistory, and what all the texts which we have studied in this chapter have done. He, too, dared to apply to other nations what Israel believed to be her privilege. If we approach this text in such a manner, many problems may disappear.

This oracle, like many such promises of restoration of the nations, is within the section of the "oracles against the nations" (Is. 13-23). As in the preceding text of Ezekiel (29:1-16) which we have just analysed, we have first the condemnation of Egypt (Is. 19:1-15) which suddenly changes into a promise of salvation (Is. 19:16-25). The beginning of this second section still contains a punishment (v. 16-17), but these verses nevertheless seem to belong to the second part because of the formula "in that day". The repetition of the expression "in that day" (v. 16,18,19, 21,23,24) clearly divides the whole passage into six oracles.

*1st Oracle* (v. 16-17)

Egypt will first be humiliated: "*...the Egyptians will... tremble with fear before the hand which Yahweh Sabaot stretches out against them*" (v. 16). The image of an outstretched hand reminds us of the outstretched hand of Moses over the sea, saving Israel and drowning the Egyptians (Ex. 14:26-28; cf. Dt. 5:15; Is. 51:9-10) or according to a different tradition, the hand of Yahweh: "Thou didst stretch out thy right hand, the earth swallowed them" (Ex. 15:12). This salvific event of the past is sometimes projected into the future to describe Israel's restoration: "In that day the Lord will extend his hand yet a second time..." (Is. 11:11); "And Yahweh will utterly destroy the tongue of the sea of Egypt; and will wave his hand over the River..." (Is. 11:15-16; cf. Is. 13:2; Zech. 2:13).

The text says concretely what instrument in the hand of God will cause this terror: "*the land of Judah will become a terror to the Egyptians*"

---

40. A. LEFÈVRE, "L'expression 'en ce jour-là' dans le livre d'Isaïe", in *Mélanges Bibliques rédigés en l'honneur de André Robert*, Paris, 1957, pp. 174-179.

(v. 17). At the time of the exodus and the conquest, Israel had been, through divine intervention, the terror of Egypt: "Terror and dread fall upon them..." (Ex. 15:16); "Egypt was glad when they departed, for dread of them had fallen upon it" (Ps. 105:38; cf. Dt. 2:25; 11:25; Jos. 2: 9 ff.). The restoration of Israel will cause a similar recurring fear (Mic. 7:17; Jer. 33:9).

Several biblical writers represent the restoration of Israel as a new exodus but our author describes the future humiliation of Egypt as a renewal of the first.

The Egyptians will be *"like women"* (v. 16). This expression is a typical stereotype for covenant curses in the extra-biblical treaties and in the Bible (Jer. 50:37; 51:30; Nah. 3:13).[41] It is interesting to note that the author uses covenant language to describe the humiliation of Egypt.

*"Everyone to whom it is mentioned (remembered) will fear..."* (v. 17). The verb "to remember" in the *hifil* form has often a juridical connotation: to report a fact in a trial.[42] It also belongs to covenant language. The prophets often ask Israel to remember the benefits of God in order to remember the demands of fidelity. Egypt will now remember the events, and this time, she will come to the understanding of their meaning. She will consider this as a punishment and will convert to Yahweh, as the rest of the text shows. This contrasts with the hardened attitude of Egypt at the time of the exodus.

An interesting comparison could be made between our text and Dt. 28:47-68, which speaks about the curses on Israel because of her unfaithfulness to the covenant. Yahweh will punish unfaithful Israel through the instrumentality of a nation from afar (v. 49) just as, in our text, Israel became the terror of Egypt. The plagues of Egypt will be repeated, but will now be directed against Israel: "He will bring upon you again all the diseases of Egypt, which you were afraid of; and they shall cleave to you" (v. 60). There will be dread and fear (v. 66,67); Israel will be powerless (this concept is expressed with other images (v. 62,65) similar to the expression "like women"). Such a comparison shows how the writer of Is. 19:16-17 portrays the humiliation of Egypt in terms similar to the curse of Israel for her unfaithfulness to the covenant.

But just as there is always hope of restoration for Israel, "if you call them to mind... and return to Yahweh..." (Dt. 30:1 ff.), so Egypt, too, will receive salvation if she "remembers". Fear can be the beginning of

---

41. K. J. CATHCART, "Treaty-curses and the Book of Nahum", in *C.B.Q.*, 35 (1973), pp. 179-187, for Nah. 3:13, p. 185; ID., *Nahum in the Light of Northwest Semitic*, Biblica et Orientalia 26, Rome, 1973, p. 140.
42. H. G. REVENTLOW, "Das Amt des Mazkir. Zur Rechtsstruktur des öffentlichen Lebens in Israel", in *Th.Z.*, 15 (1959), pp. 161-175; H. J. BOECKER, "Erwägungen zum Amt des Mazkir", in *Th.Z.*, 17 (1961), pp. 212-216; B. S. CHILDS, *Memory and Tradition in Israel*, S.B.T. 37, London, 1962; W. SCHOTTROFF, *"Gedenken" im Alten Orient und im Alten Testament*, W.M.A.N.T. 15, Neukirchen, 1964. But see H. GROSS, "Zur Wurzel *zkr*", in *B.Z.*, 9 (1960), pp. 227-237.

salvation. The plagues of Egypt will achieve these results in the future. This is *"the design of Yahweh Sabaot"* (v. 17) concerning Egypt. The design or the purpose of God is humiliation (Jer. 49:20; 50:45; Mic. 4:12) but it is also salvation (Is. 46:10 ff.; Ps. 73:24; 106:13).

*2nd Oracle* (v. 18)

*"There will be five cities in the land of Egypt which speak the language of Canaan"* (v. 18). That the different nations all speak their own language is evident and accepted as normal (Gen. 10:5,20,31; Esth. 1:22; 3:12; 8:9). But often people speaking a different language are considered enemies (Dt. 28:49; Is. 28:11; 33:19; Jer. 5:15; Ezek. 3:5-6). The story of the tower of Babel (Gen. 11:1-9) also develops this theme. At one point the people no longer understood each other, but in the ideal world everybody spoke the same language (v. 1). To express the hope that one day there will again be human understanding, the image of people who will all speak the same language is used. Peoples with different languages will be united (Zech. 8:23; Is. 66:18). The Jewish writer like anybody else is proud of his own language (Neh. 13:24) and he describes this hope, now, by saying that Hebrew will be spoken in Egypt. He, however, says discreetly "the language of Canaan". When this has occurred and people understand each other again, there will be no divisions nor war.

Hebrew will be spoken in *"five cities"* of Egypt. Those who interpret this text in an historical perspective try to identify these five cities. In our symbolic interpretation, one has to conclude that this number also has a symbolic meaning. And indeed, five, like other numbers such as seven or three, can have a merely symbolic significance. The description of the richness of Job plays precisely on these numbers: "There were born to him seven sons and three daughters. He had seven thousand sheep, three thousand camels, five hundred yoke of oxen, and five hundred she-asses..." (Job. 1:2-3). Five sometimes represents a small number (Gen. 18:28; Is. 17:6), but it often expresses the abundance of richness and of a gift (Gen. 43:34; 45:22; 1 Sam. 21:4; 25:18,42) or a perfect restitution (Ex. 21:37; 1 Sam. 6:4). Its use in certain texts of the conquest is enlightening. Five is enough to obtain a victory (Jgs. 18:2 ff.; 1 Sam. 17:40; 2 Sam. 13:19) and in this sense is the significant text of the blessings of the covenant: "And you shall chase your enemies, and they shall fall before you by the sword. Five of you shall chase a hundred, and a hundred of you shall chase ten thousand; and your enemies shall fall before you by the sword" (Lev. 26:7-8; cf. Is. 30:17). With five, one is capable of accomplishing great things (cf. also Jn. 6:9; Lk. 12:6; 1 Cor. 14:19).

It would seem that this is the meaning expressed here by Isaiah. In the second oracle, the conversion of Egypt is only beginning, but it will be more and more complete as the text progresses. The five cities signify only the start of the total spiritual "conquest". The symbolic value of five may have had its origin in the five fingers of the hand, for in verse 16 we see a precise reference to the outstretched hand of Yahweh.

Certain exegetes even go a step further. Since the writer is using images of exodus and conquest, they see in the five cities an allusion to one particular story of the conquest (Jos. 10:1-27) where Joshua had to fight a coalition of five Canaanite kings (the text insists upon the number five: v. 5,16,17,22,23,26). This was the beginning of the total conquest of Canaan.[43]

Only one of the five cities is named: *"Ir Hahèrès"*. Because of the great variety of ways by which the text has been transmitted, as well as the number of corrections and identifications which have been suggested for this city, we are faced with an insoluble problem.[44] In view of these facts we limit ourselves here to the two most important traditions. In the Hebrew masoretic text, the name of the city is Ir hahèrès, which means: "city of destruction". This suggests clearly that it is a name with a symbolic meaning rather than one to be located geographically. It means, thus, that this good understanding, expressed through the imagery of the language, will exist even where there is "destruction". The place itself, which is a symbol of destruction, will now enjoy peace. A second important tradition is to be found in the old Greek translation, the LXX, where a different name is used: "city Asedek". This word is undoubtedly Hebrew and proves that the Greek translators just kept the Hebrew term they had before them (which is, of course, a precious indication of the value of this tradition). One of the five cities is thus named "city of justice", a title which corresponds perfectly with the context. One of these cities, even though we are only at the beginning of the total conversion of Egypt, has a name which expresses an ideal yet to be realized: "city of justice". The prophet Isaiah gives a similar name to the Jerusalem of the future: "Afterward you shall be called the city of righteousness, the faithful city" (Is. 1:26). The writer perhaps alludes to a kind of "Jerusalem" in Egypt because of the presence of an altar (v. 19) (even if it is not said that this altar is in this city). Those who see these five cities as a reminder of the five Canaanite kings also note that one of these kings was the king of Jerusalem (Jos. 10:1). "Sedek" in the biblical tradition is often related to Jerusalem. Thus we find such names as Melchisedek, king of Salem (Gen. 14:18) and likewise Adonisedek, king of Jerusalem (Jos. 10:1).

Once good understanding between all men is restored on the horizontal level, one may hope for faithfulness of man towards God to follow: *"they will swear allegiance to Yahweh Sabaot"* (v. 18; cf. Dt. 10:20; Is. 45:23; 2 Chr. 15:14). This is the normal path of reconciliation in biblical tradition. Man has first to reconcile himself with his fellowmen before he can recover peace with God.

---

43. A. FEUILLET, "Un sommet religieux de l'Ancien Testament", p. 70.
44. W. VOGELS, "L'Égypte mon peuple", pp. 501-503.

*3rd Oracle* (v. 19-21a)

The preceding oracle suggests that the five cities were only the beginning of marvellous things to come. This is now fulfilled: *"In that day there will be an altar to Yahweh in the midst of the land of Egypt, and a pillar to Yahweh at its border. It will be a sign and a witness..."* (v. 19-20). The whole land of Egypt is now concerned, as indicated by the altar *"in the midst of the land"* and the pillar *"at its border"*.

The Egyptians will have in their own land an *altar* to Yahweh. This corresponds with an idea expressed in some other biblical texts. The nations can offer sacrifice to Yahweh in their own land (Jon. 1:16; Mal. 1:11). A *pillar* is sometimes built as a commemorative monument.

In a few texts we also find the simultaneous presence of an altar and a pillar. These examples are most enlightening for an understanding of our text. A first example is the treaty between Jacob and Laban (Gen. 31:43-54): the two concluded "a covenant" (v. 44). Jacob sets up a "pillar" (v. 45), a "heap" is made (v. 46) on which they "ate" (v. 46), and there is also a "sacrifice" (v. 54). This suggests that the heap is a kind of altar. The text notes several times that this heap and this pillar are "witnesses" (v. 48,52) and that Jacob "swore" (v. 53). It is easy to see the number of elements which are present in Is. 19: the "altar" and the "pillar" (v. 19), "witness" (v. 20), "sacrifices" and "vows" (v. 21). One may well compare them with the tradition of Jacob at Bethel, where God revealed himself to him. Jacob set up a "pillar" (Gen. 28:18,22; 35:14), he made a "vow" (28:20), he built an "altar" (35:1,3,7) and he invited his family to abandon foreign gods (35:2).

Another significant text is the description of the covenant celebration at Sinai (Ex. 24). Moses builds an "altar" (v. 4) and twelve "pillars" (v. 4), there are "sacrifices" (v. 5 ff.), and there is a commitment on the part of the people (v. 3). In a similar context of covenant, at the great celebration at Shechem (Jos. 24), Joshua invites the people to commit themselves to the true God (v. 14 ff.); there is also a "stone" (v. 26,27) which serves as a "witness" (v. 27), and if one adds to this Jos. 8:30-35, there is an "altar" (v. 31), with "sacrifices" (v. 31). When Israel is rejected because of her unfaithfulness, there will be no altar nor pillar: "For the children of Israel shall dwell many days... without sacrifices or pillar" (Hos. 3:4).

These comparisons suggest that the text of Isaiah should be equally interpreted in the light of the theology of the covenant and this is confirmed by the rest of the text. Everything now is prepared so that the Egyptians can celebrate the covenant with Yahweh.

This third oracle is composed according to the structure of "the promise of the future covenant" which the Bible uses for the promise of the Sinai covenant and its restoration in the new covenant. We have already seen how in Ezek. 29:13-16 this same structure is applied to Egypt. This is also what the writer of Is. 19 does. In order to see very clearly that the author ascribes to Egypt the experience of Israel, we will put in parallel schema, just as we did for Ezekiel, the text of Isaiah with the two texts of the promise of the future covenant to Israel (Ex. 2:23b-25; 6:2-8 (P), and Ex. 3:7-8,12,16-18 (JE)).[45]

| Egypt | Israel |
|---|---|
| (I) *A cry for help:* When they *cry* to Yahweh because of *oppressors*... (v. 20b). | And the people of Israel groaned under their bondage, and *cried* out for help, and their *cry* under bondage came up to God (Ex. 2:23). And now, behold, the *cry* of the people of Israel has come to me, and I have seen the *oppression* with which the Egyptian *oppress* them (Ex. 3:9). |

As in Israel's case when she was under oppression and in slavery in Egypt and crying out for help to God, we now witness Egypt in terror because of Judah (v. 16-17) and therefore crying for help to Yahweh. It is interesting to note that the vocabulary is identical in both cases: "cry" and "oppress".

| | |
|---|---|
| (II) *The promise of salvific actions:* he will send them a saviour, and will defend and *deliver* them (v. 20c). | I will *deliver* you from their bondage, and I will redeem you with an outstretched arm and with great acts of judgment (Ex. 6:6). I have come down to *deliver* them out of the hand of the Egyptians... (Ex. 3:8). |

In these two situations we have the same idea, Yahweh will *deliver*, expressed by the same verb. Yahweh will also *defend* the Egyptians, a verb whose meaning is often juridical in treaty texts.[46] This juridical defense is comparable with the "great acts of judgment" of Exodus. As Yahweh has saved Israel through a mediator, Moses, so also he will send a saviour to Egypt, like a new Moses.

Another covenant text (1 Sam. 12) also provides an interesting comparison: "...and the Egyptians oppressed them (in the Greek text); then your fathers cried to Yahweh, and Yahweh sent Moses and Aaron, who brought forth your fathers out of Egypt" (v. 8; cf. Num. 20:15-16).[47]

The elements (I) and (II) of this structure can also be compared with the formulas of the deuteronomistic framework of the Book of Judges. The Israelites were unfaithful to the covenant and consequently underwent punishment: "...and the people of Israel served Cushan-rishathaim... But when the people of Israel cried to Yahweh, Yahweh raised up a saviour

---

45. W. Vogels, *La promesse royale de Yahweh*, pp. 45-75.
46. J. Limburg, "The Root *Rîb* and the Prophetic Lawsuit Speeches", in *J.B.L.*, 88 (1969), pp. 291-304.
47. R. J. Sklba, "The Redeemer of Israel", in *C.B.Q.*, 34 (1972), pp. 1-18.

for the people of Israel, who delivered them..." (Jgs. 3:8-9; the same formulas are repeated over and over again in the same book for each judge).[48]

| And Yahweh will make himself known to the Egyptians (v. 21). | ‖ |

It is not enough that God guides the history of the peoples; the people ought to be conscious of this guidance. In the texts of Exodus where we discovered the promise of the future covenant to Israel, there is also the revelation of the name of Yahweh. When Moses is sent to the people, he has a problem: "If they ask me, 'What is his name?' what shall I say to them?" (Ex. 3:13). Then God reveals himself as Yahweh (v. 14-15). We have the same revelation of Yahweh in the second text (Ex. 6:2 ff.). Now Yahweh will reveal himself to the Egyptians, and this is, of course, something new and extremely important if compared with the other texts we have studied in this chapter.

(III) *Submission:*

| And the Egyptians will *know* Yahweh (v. 21). | ‖ | you will *know* that I am Yahweh (Ex. 6:7). |

The salvific action of Yahweh by which he delivers the oppressed and reveals himself should provoke an answer. As Israel submitted herself, so also will the Egyptians. And this again is expressed in the two cases with the same verb, "to know". This verb expresses, as we have seen before, recognition demanding a total life involvement.

The parallel between the text of Isaiah and these two texts with their promise of a future covenant with Israel shows us that they have the same structure and the same typical covenant vocabulary. We may, therefore, conclude that the meaning of our text is a promise that "in that day" Yahweh will make a covenant with the Egyptians.

### 4th Oracle (v. 21b-22)

The fourth oracle is closely linked with the third through the formula "in that day" which simultaneously closes the third and opens the fourth oracle. This expression really constitutes the turning point for the entire text. The oracle is so composed that it has the same structure as the preceding one, yet the sequence of its three elements is inverted. It contains the same ideas but it is more interiorized than the third oracle.

(III) *Submission:*
They will serve with sacrifice and burnt offering.
They will make vows to Yahweh and perform them (v. 21b).

---

48. W. RICHTER, *Die Bearbeitungen des "Retterbuches" in der deuteronomischen Epoche*, B.B.B. 21, Bonn, 1964.

Total submission in the covenant is often expressed by the verb "serve", as we saw earlier, and this service may be sacramentally celebrated by sacrifices. The same expressions are found in the promise of the future covenant with Israel (Ex. 3:12,18b). The Egyptians will pay moral and cultural homage to Yahweh and they will pledge themselves to Yahweh, but what is even more important, they will fulfill their promises. They will keep their commitment faithfully, a condition which is absolutely essential for a covenant partner—so essential in fact, that the prophets over and over again accuse Israel particularly of this kind of unfaithfulness (Am. 2:11-12).

As we have seen in the third oracle there will be "an altar to Yahweh in the midst of the land of Egypt" (v. 19) upon which the Egyptians can thus offer their sacrifices, and "a pillar to Yahweh at its border" (v. 19) which is the witness of their irrevocable commitment to Yahweh.

The fact that mention is made of these sacrifices and vows at the same time is a very clear indication of the right-mindedness of the Egyptians (Jon. 1:16; 2:10; Ps. 50:14; 66:13).

(II) *The promise of salvific actions:*
And Yahweh will smite Egypt, smiting and healing (v. 22a).

The first oracle predicted that Yahweh will "smite" the Egyptians (v. 16). Sickness is often considered to be a punishment upon an individual and, in relation to a people, it is considered the punishment for unfaithfulness. That is why in the covenant (Lev. 26:16; Dt. 28:21,22,27), wounds and other sicknesses are characteristic curses. We may, therefore, conclude that Egypt is punished for her unfaithfulness.

But Yahweh also cures the sick (Job 5:18) or heals his unfaithful people who have been struck by sickness.[49] It would seem, then, that Yahweh is ready to restore Israel through a renewal of his covenant with her. Two texts, which certainly have covenant overtones, combine the two images of "smiting" and "healing": Hos. 6:1 and Dt. 32:39.[50] The text of Hosea is very helpful in the understanding of our text. Israel was struck with sickness because of her unfaithfulness (Hos. 5:13a), yet she hoped for healing by concluding a treaty with another nation. But it is in vain: "Then Ephraim went to Assyria, and Judah sent messengers to the great king. But he is not able to cure you or heal your wound" (Hos. 5:13b). Only Yahweh can cure and restore the covenant (Hos. 6:1-3).

---

49. H. W. Wolff, *Anthropology of the Old Testament*, London, 1974, pp. 143-148.
50. E. M. Good, "Hosea 5:8-6:6: An Alternative to Alt", in *J.B.L.*, 85 (1966), pp. 273-286; J. J. Wijngaards, "Death and Resurrection in Covenantal Context (Hos. 6:2)", in *V.T.*, 17 (1967), pp. 226-239; M. L. Barré, "New Light on the Interpretation of Hosea 6:2", in *V.T.*, 28 (1978), pp. 129-141; G. E. Wright, "The Lawsuit of God: A Formcritical Study of Deuteronomy 32", in *Israel's Prophetic Heritage, Festschrift J. Muilenburg*, ed. B. W. Anderson and W. Harrelson, New York, 1968, pp. 26-67.

Conversion is needed before God can accomplish such a reversal (Ex. 15:26; Jer. 18:7-8; Hos. 6:1). This is what the rest of this oracle says.

(I) *A cry for help—conversion:*
They will return to Yahweh, and he will heed
their supplication and heal them (v. 22b).

The first element in the structure of the promise of a future covenant is a "cry for help". This cry becomes a "conversion" when it is a promise of a renewal of a covenant. That Yahweh has struck Egypt is an indication that she has been unfaithful. In order to be restored, Egypt has to be converted. The writer once more uses exactly the same verb which so often expresses the conversion of Israel before her restoration,[51] and Yahweh accepts this cry.

The fourth oracle clearly has the same structure as the third but it is inverted. The whole process shows a kind of crescendo, a deepening and interiorization. Egypt now will undergo sincere conversion and commit herself faithfully.

*5th Oracle* (v. 23)

"*In that day there will be a highway from Egypt to Assyria*". The image of a highway is often applied to Israel. As at the time of the exodus when Yahweh made a road through the dried sea (Is. 51:10; cf. Ex. 14:10), so on the return from exile the same image of a road prepared by God is evident: "And Yahweh will utterly destroy the tongue of the sea of Egypt; and will wave his hand over the River with his scorching wind, and smite it into seven channels that men may cross dryshod. And there will be a *highway* from *Assyria* for the remnant which is left of his people, as there was for Israel when they came up from the land of *Egypt*" (Is. 11:15-16; cf. Is. 35:8; 40:3; 49:11; 57:14; 62:10; Jer. 31:21). The road leads to freedom.

But the highway is often also the place of combat (Is. 59:7; Joel 2:8). Israel encountered several obstacles on her way to the promised land. Edom, for instance, refused passage to her (Num. 20:19). Here now, there are no longer any obstacles, no wars: "*And the Assyrian will come into Egypt and the Egyptian into Assyria*". There will no longer be hostility between these two peoples, who are the traditional symbols of world powers (Zech. 10:11; interesting to note, they are both mentioned in the text of Is. 11:16).

The prophets always condemned Israel when she contracted treaties with Assyria or Egypt, thereby forgetting the fundamental covenant by which she was committed to Yahweh alone (Hos. 7:11; 12:2; Is. 18:1-7; 28:14-15; 30:1-7; 31:1-3). This is no longer a cause of concern, because

---

51. W. L. HOLLADAY, *The Root sûbh in the Old Testament with Particular Reference to its Usages in the Covenantal Contexts*, Leiden, 1958.

now *"the Egyptians will serve with the Assyrians (Yahweh)"*. We have the technical term to "serve" which expresses total submission: Egypt with Assyria will submit to Yahweh (Zeph. 3:9; cf. 2:11). After peace is restored between the peoples, harmony will also be restored between mankind and God.

In many other universalistic texts (e.g. Is. 2:2-4) the nations have to come to the centre, to Zion, as we will see in the following chapter. In this text the highway between Egypt and Assyria passes through Palestine, through the promised land, and serves as a place of passage, of transit. In the first oracle, the land of Judah is a terror to the Egyptians (v. 17) but now everything is at peace. Is Israel seen here as a possible bridge between the nations?

*6th Oracle* (v. 24-25)

*"In that day Israel will be the third with Egypt and Assyria"* (v. 24a). Israel occupies an equal position with these world powers. She will no longer be subjected to their conquests or to their rivalry or have to submit to any one of them. The fundamental brotherhood among men is re-established.

But there is something more. Israel will be *"a blessing in the midst of the earth"* (v. 24b). It is said in the third oracle that Yahweh will make himself known (v. 21). The "how" of this revelation becomes very clear here and it is in conformity with the whole of biblical tradition. It will be through Israel. She occupies a central position in this unified world (Ezek. 38:12) and, therefore, the highway passes through her territory. Israel will also be the instrumental cause of blessing. This expression seems to refer directly to the text of the promises to Abraham (Gen. 12:3; 18:18; 22:18; 26:4; 28:14; cf. Zech. 8:13). Abraham-Israel will be used as an instrument for the blessing of the nations. But the real source of blessing is always Yahweh, as in Gen. 12:3: "I will bless". He alone blesses: *"whom Yahweh Sabaot has blessed, saying, 'Blessed be Egypt my people, and Assyria the work of my hands, and Israel my heritage'"* (v. 25). This "whom" corresponds to a singular in Hebrew, by which the unity of all those who are blessed by Yahweh is underlined.

We have now completed the whole text. Egypt, Assyria and Israel are not only equal as peoples (v. 24) but, since others have received, through Israel, God's blessing, all are at the same level in their relationship with God. Egypt and Assyria symbolize the whole world which will participate in God's blessing (Ps. 47:10).

Everywhere else the title *"my people"* is reserved for Israel and is a typical designation of the people of the covenant. It is often used in the covenant formula (Ex. 6:7; Hos. 1:9; 2:1,3,25; Jer. 24:7; 30:22; Ezek. 11:20 etc.). Now it also becomes the title for Egypt. Another term attributed to Israel: *"the work of my hands"* (Is. 60:21; 64:7), which in the two texts is parallel to the title "my people", is now given to Assyria. Israel keeps a third title: *"my heritage"* (Dt. 9:26,29; 32:9; 1 Sam. 10:1;

1 Kgs. 8:51; Is. 47:6; Ps. 28:9), which in all these texts is a parallel to "my people". Evidently, the words "people", "work of my hands" and "heritage" are often used in parallel. This proves that there is no longer any difference among these three peoples. Since Yahweh has revealed himself to others, there is now a relationship of mutual belonging which is an indispensable condition for a covenant relationship.

The analysis of the whole text (Is. 19:16-25) suggests that its structure is extremely well-planned. The redactor used a procedure of composition which is very frequently found in biblical writings. He arranges the different sections of the text symmetrically and, more precisely, in *crossed symmetry* or *chiasmus*.

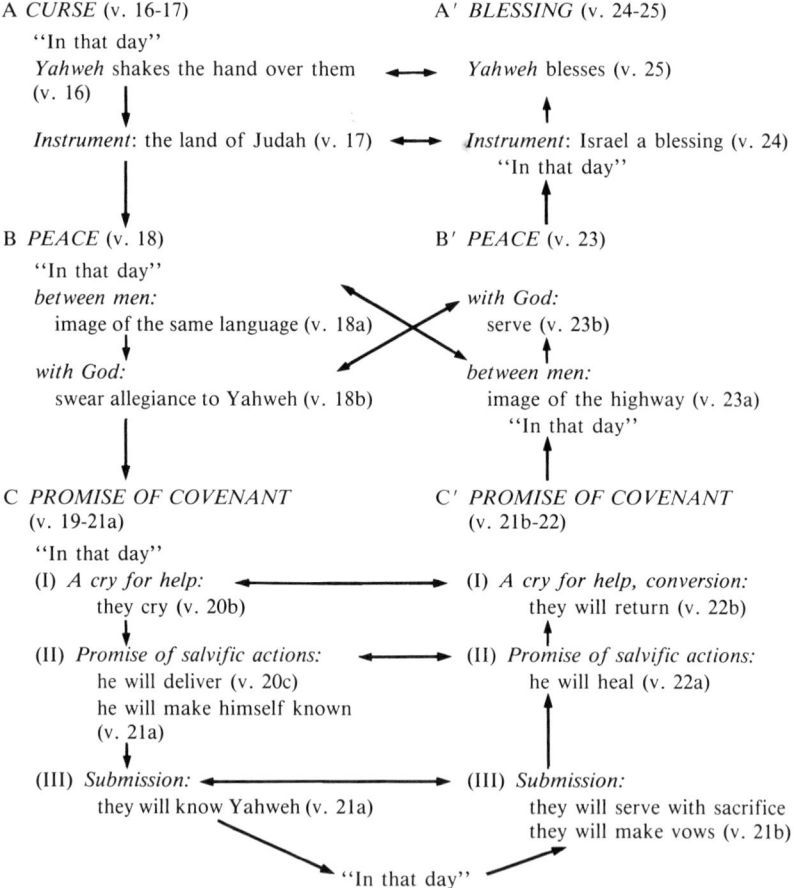

The whole development starts with the curse of Egypt because of her unfaithfulness. God inflicts his punishment by means of a human instrument, Israel. When the Bible says that the nations are unfaithful to Yahweh and therefore deserve his punishment, it is because of their pride, since they believe themselves to be God, and also because of their lack of respect for their fellowmen. These two attitudes are contrary to what is most fundamental to human conscience. They have broken "the everlasting covenant" (Is. 24:5) (= 1st oracle). This breach, then, must be repaired. Men must first be reconciled among themselves and then submit to God. Only then will there again be complete harmony (= 2nd oracle). When men once again live according to their consciences, they will be capable of receiving the revelation of God and enter into a covenant relationship (= 3rd oracle). This is what the author develops in A, B and C.

The writer now repeats his ideas but in inverted order and moves from C' and B' to A', where Egypt is blessed as a people of God and receives this blessing but through the instrumentality of Israel.

The exceptional value of Is. 19:16-25 is that it suppresses all differences between Israel and the nations. This is because Yahweh has revealed himself to the nations.

\* \* \*

In this chapter we have studied a few very interesting texts relating to our topic. They all have technical language, structures and teaching borrowed from covenant theology. Their writers have applied to the nations what was Israel's privilege. We have drawn parallels between texts speaking of the nations and texts referring to Israel. In this way the impressive similarities have appeared more clearly. But we may also observe from such parallels one very important difference: only Israel received the revelation. This difference disappears only in the last text.

We can then schematically summarize the results of our investigation as follows.

| **Nations** | **Israel** |
|---|---|

*Exodus experience* (Am. 9:7b)

| unconscious | ‖ conscious |
|---|---|

Yahweh guides the history of all peoples. Only Israel is conscious of who is guiding her history, because Yahweh has revealed himself to her.

*Belonging to Yahweh* (Am. 9:7a)

| you are mine | ‖ you are mine, |
|---|---|
|  | I am yours |

Since Yahweh acts in favour of all peoples, they all belong to him. But this is unilateral in the case of the nations. Israel knows Yahweh, and thus only for her is there a mutual belonging or a real covenant.

*Responsible before Yahweh and judged* (Am. 1-2; Ezek. 29:1-12)

"natural law"    ||    "revealed law"

Belonging creates responsibilities within the measure of one's knowledge. The nations can only be judged on their faithfulness to the natural law. Israel, on the contrary, is questioned about her faithfulness to revealed law.

*Punishment* (Am. 1-2; Ezek. 29:1-12)

No difference is seen here. All undergo the same divine punishment. But just as for the exodus experience, we can also say that Israel alone is conscious of who it is who is punishing her.

*Restoration* (Ezek. 29:13-16)

In this text we again see how the restoration of Egypt differs from the restoration of Israel (cf. Ezek. 11:17-20). One is restored to what one was before. Only in Israel's case is it said that she will observe the revealed law and be re-established as the people of Yahweh.

So on each level, we see another instance of the same fundamental difference: only Israel received Yahweh's revelation.

*Is. 19:16-25*

In this text this difference disappears. Yahweh says he will reveal himself to the nations and therefore there will be a mutual belonging. Israel has a special role to play in this revelation. Only when all have become recipients of this same knowledge will there be complete similarity. There will be one single covenant, one in which Yahweh will call all nations "my people" just as he did earlier for Israel.

In the beginning of this chapter we asked ourselves if one could speak about different parallel covenants or different salvation histories, or whether only one existed. During the period in which Yahweh concluded his historical covenant with Israel, did he do the same thing with others? Our answer now is very simple. God acted upon these nations directly and he really cared for them but he did not make a covenant, since a covenant presupposes mutual belonging and mutual knowledge. The nations did not yet have these necessary qualifications.

So there will be only one covenant, one in which the nations will share. The text of Is. 19:16-25 has already made it clear that Israel has a responsibility in this respect. We came to the same conclusion in chapter two: Israel was elected to be a priestly kingdom in the service of others. In the following chapter we shall study what is asked of Israel in order that this universal covenant of mankind may be initiated.

We may now conclude that the biblical perspective is not only universalistic but unitarian.[52] All peoples are called by one God through Israel to know the same God and to form one single people of God. Then Yahweh will call all nations "my people" and the nations will say to Yahweh "my God". "Many nations shall join themselves to Yahweh in that day, and shall be my people" (Zech. 2:15).

---

52. P. Rossano, "Le Religioni non Cristiane alle luce del Concilio e della Bibbia", in *Riv.Bib.It.*, 15 (1967), pp. 113-130; Id., "Y a-t-il une révélation authentique en dehors de la révélation judéo-chrétienne?", in *Riv.Bib.It.*, 16 (1968), pp. 225-228; J. A. Izco, "Las religiones de las naciones a la luz del Antiguo Testamento", in *Misiones Extranjeras*, n. 4-5 (1971), pp. 7-38 and the same article J. A. Izco Ilundain, "El conocimiento de Dios entre los Gentiles según el Antiguo Testamento", in *E.T.L.*, 49 (1973), pp. 36-75; L. Ruppert, "Jahwe und die Götter. Zur religionskritischen Funktion des Jahweglaubens", in *T.T.Z.*, 84 (1975), pp. 1-13; J. Van Der Veken, "Can the True God be the God of one Book? The Particularity of Religion and the Universality of Reason", in *E.T.L.*, 51 (1975), pp. 35-48; C. J. Labuschagne, "De godsdienst van Israel en de andere godsdiensten. Op zoek naar een bijbelse fundering van de theologia religionum" in *Wereld en Zending*, 4 (1975), pp. 4-16; R. R. De Ridder, "God and the Gods: Reviewing the Biblical Roots", in *Missiology*, 6 (1978), pp. 11-28.

Chapter Four

# The New Universal Covenant

We have seen that, to restore the broken primitive universal covenant with mankind, Yahweh chose first one particular people, Israel, with whom he concluded a covenant and to whom he revealed himself gradually during this second period of salvation history. He also cared about the nations, but they lacked the knowledge of Yahweh and his revelation and could not therefore have a real covenant relationship with Yahweh. Israel's special role and mission is to communicate this knowledge to the nations. The salvation of the nations will be accomplished only "in" and "through" Israel.

But the question is, how? Two possibilities are open to Israel. She may behave in such an exemplary way that she becomes a light which attracts the nations to her. This is called *centripetal universalism*. Or Israel may go out to the nations to bring them revelation. This is called *centrifugal universalism*.

The manner in which the salvation of the nations is brought about may be found in numerous texts, all of which are the well-known texts treated in books about universalism. We shall not repeat all this material here, since this is not the purpose of this book. We shall take only a few clear texts which show how the nations will receive the revelation.

We have now reached the third period of salvation history: the new universal covenant between God and mankind. Many of the prophets promised that it would come. It was instituted by Jesus at the end of his life and will last until the end of time.

## I. CENTRIPETAL UNIVERSALISM

We have seen before how the nations are the witnesses of the covenant between Yahweh and Israel. They are eye-witnesses of God's benefits in favour of Israel and also of Israel's answer. In other words, Israel lives as a sign in the world[1] and therefore she is capable of attracting others. She is a living witness in the sight of others. This is stated explicitly in

---

1. W. BULST, "Israel als 'signum elevatum in nationes'", in *Z.K.T.*, 74 (1952), pp. 167-204.

Is. 55:3b-5;[2] just as David was a witness to the peoples: "I made him a witness to the peoples..." (v. 4), so is Israel: "Behold, you shall call nations that you know not, and nations that knew you not shall run to you, because of Yahweh your God, and of the Holy One of Israel, for he has glorified you" (v. 5) (cf. also "you are my witnesses" in Is. 43:10,12).[3]

Several biblical texts describe the pilgrimage of the nations coming towards the centre, towards Israel, Zion and Jerusalem.

### THE PILGRIMAGE OF THE NATIONS TO JERUSALEM (Is. 2:2-4)

This is one of the most beautiful texts describing this event. But it also poses many critical problems. This same text appears in Mic. 4:1-3.[4] The conclusion of the two texts is different (compare Is. 2:5 with Mic. 4:4-5) and a few minor differences exist in the texts themselves, but despite this the two may be said to be identical. A question now arises about the origin of the texts: did Isaiah depend on Micah, did Micah depend on Isaiah, did they both borrow the text from a common source, or was the text added to these two prophets at a later date?

Some exegetes believe that the text expresses ideas which are post-exilic. Others are probably right in accepting the possibility that it comes from the time of Isaiah. Whatever the answer to this discussion happens to be, for us the present text keeps its interest because our study, as we said

---

2. O. EISSFELDT, "The Promises of Grace to David in Isaiah 55:1-5", in *Israel's Prophetic Heritage. Festschrift J. Muilenburg*, ed. B. W. Anderson and W. Harrelson, New York, 1962, pp. 196-207, or in *Kleine Schriften 4*, Tübingen, 1968, pp. 44-52; W. BRUEGGEMANN, "Is. 55 and Deuteronomic Theology", in *Z.A.W.*, 80 (1968), pp. 191-203; W.A.M. BEUKEN, "Is. 55:3-5: The Reinterpretation of David", in *Bijdr.*, 35 (1974), pp. 49-64.
3. E. SIMON, "The Jews as God's Witnesses to the World (Is. 43:10)", in *Judaism*, 15 (1966), pp. 306-318.
4. G. VON RAD, "Die Stadt auf dem Berge", in *Ev.Th.*, 8 (1948/49), pp. 439-447, or in *Gesammelte Studien*, München, 1961, pp. 214-224; H. WILDBERGER, "Die Völkerwallfahrt zum Zion, Es. 2:1-5" in *V.T.*, 7 (1957), pp. 62-81; A. FEUILLET, "La conversion et le salut des nations chez le prophète Isaïe", in *B.V.C.*, n. 22 (1958), pp. 3-22; E. CANNAWURF, "The Authenticity of Micah 4:1-4", in *V.T.*, 13 (1963), pp. 26-33; J. H. HAYES, "The Tradition of Zion's Inviolability", in *J.B.L.*, 82 (1963), pp. 419-426; J. SCHREINER, *Sion-Jerusalem Jahwes Königssitz. Theologie der Heiligen Stadt im A.T.*, S.A.N.T. 7, München, 1963; R. DE VAUX, "Jérusalem et les prophètes", in *R.B.*, 73 (1966), pp. 481-509; H. JUNKER, "Sancta Civitas, Jerusalem Nova. Eine formkritische und überlieferungsgeschichtliche Studie zu Is. 2", in *T.T.St.*, 15 (1967), pp. 17-33; M. DELCOR, "Sion, centre universel, Is. 2:1-5", in *Assemblées du Seigneur* 2, 5, Paris, 1969, pp. 6-11; A. DEISSLER, "Die Völkerwallfahrt zum Zion. Meditation über Jes. 2:2-4", in *Bi.Leb.*, 11 (1970), pp. 295-299; O. H. STECK, "Jerusalemer Vorstellungen vom Frieden und ihre Abwandlungen in der Prophetie des Alten Israel", in *Frieden–Bibel–Kirche*, ed. G. Liedke, Stuttgart, 1972, pp. 75-95; A. S. VAN DER WOUDE, "Micah 4:1-5: An Instance of the Pseudo-Prophets quoting Isaiah", in *Symbolae Biblicae et Mesopotamicae F.M.Th. de Liagre Böhl dedicatae*, ed. M. A. BEEK et al., Leiden, 1973, pp. 396-402; K. SEYBOLD, "Die anthropologischen Beiträge aus Jesaja 2", in *Z.T.K.*, 74 (1977), pp. 401-415; L. BRODIE, "Creative Writing: Missing Link in Biblical Research", in *B.T.B.*, 8 (1978), pp. 34-39.

earlier, is not diachronic but rather synchronic. Since we have the text twice in biblical tradition its importance becomes even greater for us. Many consider it as a liturgical text. All this suggests that the text expresses a more general belief and does not simply reflect the insight of just one person. There must have been a strong universal tradition behind it, even if the conclusions in Isaiah and in Micah have narrowed down its broad perspective.

> It shall come to pass in days to come (v. 2).

The pilgrimage of the nations to Jerusalem is predicted for the future. But there is speculation as to the moment when it will happen.[5] Some exegetes have translated the Hebrew expression by "in the last days". They claim that the expression appears only after the exile and that it designates the end-time. This is especially so in apocalyptic literature. But there are at least a few pre-exilic texts where the formula is used as well (Gen. 49:1; Num. 24:14; Jer. 23:20). There is also a very similar expression in Akkadian, which simply means: the future, in days to come. We therefore do not have to translate the formula here as speaking about the end of time, but as referring to the future. Even if Isaiah does not use the formula elsewhere in his book, we find a similar expression in 1:26 where "afterwards" is in opposition to "at the first", "at the beginning". These formulas mean simply "earlier" and "later" (cf. 8:23; 30:8).

The arrival of the nations in the future is foreseen. It does not mean that we must wait until the end of time to see this happen. Further, it would be incorrect to see this arrival simply as occurring in an undetermined future. It rather refers to a moment in the future when an important event will happen and a great change in salvation history will result. It will be one of those "days of Yahweh".

> That the mountain of the house of Yahweh
> shall be established as the highest of the mountains,
> and shall be raised above the hills (v. 2).

"The mountain of the house of Yahweh", which is Zion, shall be firmly "established". The verb implies the idea of duration, and of permanency, like the throne of David (2 Sam. 7:16; 1 Chr. 17:14), David's house or dynasty (2 Sam. 7:26; 1 Chr. 17:24), or the throne of Yahweh King (Ps. 93:2). The same concept is expressed in the songs of Zion. Yahweh has built his city on the rock and therefore it will not be moved, but will last (Ps. 46:6; 48:9; 87).

---

5. W. STAERK, "Das Gebrauch der Wendung *be'aḥarit hayyāmîm* im at.-Kanon", in *Z.A.W.*, 11 (1891), pp. 247-253; F. W. BUCHANAN, "Eschatology and the 'End of Days'", in *J.N.E.S.*, 20 (1961), pp. 188-193; H. KOSMALA, "At the End of the Days", in *Annual of the Swedish Theological Institute*, II (1963), pp. 27-37; E. LIPINSKI, "*Be'aḥarit hayyāmîm* dans les textes pré-exiliques", in *V.T.* 20 (1970), pp. 445-450.

That Zion will be the summit of the mountains[6] is an idea which is very rare (cf. Ps. 48:3; 78:69; Ezek. 20:40; 40:2) and rightly so, since it is not the highest mountain, geographically speaking, in the area. It is therefore a mythical theme. Man meets God on the top of a mountain, as Israel met God on Mount Sinai. One has to climb to meet God. This is the idea behind the building of the ziggurats, the tower of Babel (Gen. 11), the ladder of Jacob (Gen. 28:10 ff.). Now the mountain of the house of Yahweh will be higher than all other mountains or hills, since it is here that the meeting of God and the whole of mankind will take place. It will be seen from afar and all nations will be attracted to it.

This seems to suggest a comparison with the story of Babel (Gen. 11). There, man took the initiative: "Come, let us build... a tower with its top in the heavens" (v. 4) in order not to be scattered. The disastrous result was that mankind was dispersed over the face of the earth. Our present text is exactly the opposite. Apparently God himself raised Zion higher than all the rest and dispersed mankind will gather there to recover its unity.

> All the nations shall flow to it,
> and many peoples shall come.

Even if in Micah the word "all" is missing, it still seems to be kept in this text because of the parallel between "all nations" and "many peoples". Also, the word "many" in our languages does not necessarily mean everybody, but in the Bible it may have this meaning of totality. It is, then, in this context that we can come to a decision (cf. Is. 53:11-12; also Mk. 10:45; 14:24; Rom. 5:19). Not only a few people but all mankind is attracted by the house of Yahweh.

Further, the theme of the river is often linked with the theme of Zion, the mountain or the throne of God (Ps. 46:5; Is. 33:21; Ezek. 47; Joel 4:18; Zech. 14:8). Living waters shall flow into Jerusalem. Water gives life, refreshes, quenches thirst. Here it is a river of people streaming to Jerusalem to find real life.

> And they shall say:
> Come, let us go up to the mountain of Yahweh,
> to the house of the God of Jacob (v. 3).

We do have a technical verb for the ascent and pilgrimage to the temple. The Songs of Ascent describe the Israelites going to the sanctuary: "Jerusalem, built as a city... to which the tribes go up" (Ps. 122:3-4). The Israelites were invited in very similar terms: "Let us go to the house of Yahweh" (Ps. 122:1; cf. Jer. 31:6). The faithful went to the temple especially at the great feasts not simply to praise Yahweh (Ps. 122:4) but also to offer their gifts (Ps. 96:8), and to fulfill their promises (Ps. 76:12). Not only did they give but they also received. They came to find God's answer to their questions, to receive instruction and to be justified. This is clearly expressed in the prayers of the accused (Dt. 17:8 ff.).

---

6. J. S. KSELMAN, "A Note on Isaiah 2:2", in *V.T.*, 25 (1975), pp. 225-227.

The nations in this text come to Jerusalem with empty hands; they bring no riches and no sacrifices, but they ascend in order to receive something from God.

> That he may teach us his ways,
> and that we may walk in his paths.
> For out of Zion shall go forth the law,
> and the word of Yahweh from Jerusalem (v. 3).

What they will receive, then, is instruction. "He", namely Yahweh, will "teach" them his "ways". In several texts it is said that Yahweh teaches his way. This means he teaches a life attitude and the behaviour which he expects from men: "Teach me thy way, Yahweh" (Ps. 27:11; cf. Ps. 25:8,12; 32:8; 86:11). His "way" is also used in the plural and then it indicates the commandments, the great moral principles (Dt. 8:6; 10:12; 11:22). The nations come not only to listen to Yahweh's instruction but to be prepared to change their lives and their behaviour according to these new principles: "that we may walk in his paths". And they are willing to submit: "So you shall keep the commandments of Yahweh your God, by walking in his ways and by fearing him" (Dt. 8:6).

How Yahweh will teach the nations is perhaps explained in the rest of the text: "out of Zion", "from Jerusalem", which seems to suggest that Yahweh will work with Israel as his instrument. Israel will give them the "torah". This term was originally used for the answer given by the priest to a special "case" submitted to him, but gradually it came to mean the teaching of the priests, the instruction, the law, and finally, a whole section of the Bible. The nations too will receive "the word of Yahweh", the "dabar Yahweh" which is the oracle delivered by the prophets. The priests and the prophets were the two main teachers of Israel and, therefore, the channels of revelation: "as it is written in the law and the prophets" (Mt. 7:12). So likewise, Israel has to share the revelation with the nations. The elected people now have a priestly and prophetic function towards the nations. This is its special mission as a "priestly kingdom". At Sinai, Yahweh has given his law to Israel. Zion now becomes like a new Sinai because it is here that the nations will receive Yahweh's law.

> He shall judge between the nations,
> and shall decide for many peoples (v. 4a).

Just as the Israelites went to the temple to be justified, so, similarly, the nations will receive this privilege. Yahweh shall judge "between the nations", referring to the old practice of arbitration in the juridical procedures (cf. 1 Kgs. 3:16-28; Job 9:33). Yahweh will be such a referee between the nations who come to him with their disputes. Yahweh is not presented here as a judge punishing their unfaithfulness, as he has been seen before in some texts, but rather as one to whom the nations come freely to ask him to decide on their quarrels. By this means real justice will finally reign among all the peoples.

> and they shall beat their swords into ploughshares,
> and their spears into pruning hooks;
> nation shall not lift up sword against nation,
> neither shall they learn war any more (v. 4b).

Such justice also means the end of all wars. Men no longer have to resort to their own means to defend their rights by power and arms. These have now become useless. Instead, there will be a lasting peace: "And the effect of righteousness will be peace, and the result of righteousness, quietness and trust for ever" (Is. 32:17). The destruction of all arms[7] is sometimes attributed to God (Ps. 46:10), but this text shows that it is the nations themselves who decide to convert them into agricultural tools. Henceforth, their energies will be devoted to development rather than to destruction.

We see, then, that all the nations are coming to Jerusalem, not as to a political centre but to its temple. It is for them the place where Yahweh's throne is. In other words they are searching for Yahweh. They do not come to enrich Jerusalem. They will receive Yahweh's law and word and they will accept it. In submitting to Yahweh's justice a universal peace will reign among all the peoples of the earth.

At Mount Sinai, Yahweh revealed his law to the gathered people of Israel through his mediator Moses. If Israel accepts, she can rely on Yahweh for protection and life. This is what the covenant at Sinai conveys (Ex. 19). The text of Is. 2 can also easily be compared with this event. But now all the nations will gather at Mount Zion. They will accept Yahweh's revelation through Israel as mediator. This will bring about a universal peace. We can really consider this text as a promise of the new universal covenant which is to come.

This prophetic oracle, in which we have noticed certain liturgical overtones, expresses a very pure universalism which is centripetal. We now can briefly see how similar ideas are present in the liturgical tradition and also in the prophetic tradition, the two traditions to which this text of Isaiah belongs.

## The Liturgical Tradition

The future gathering of all the nations in Jerusalem was, of course, inspired by the regular pilgrimages of Israel to Zion. The nations come to the centre. A very special group of Psalms called "the Songs of Zion" proclaims the importance of this centre.[8]

---

7. R. Bach, "'..., Der Bogen zerbricht, Spiesse zerschlägt und Wagen mit Feuer verbrennt'", in *Probleme biblischer Theologie, Festschrift G. Von Rad*, ed. H. W. Wolff, München, 1971, pp. 13-26.
8. G. Wanke, *Die Zionstheologie der Korachiten*, B.Z.A.W. 97, Berlin, 1966; J. Jeremias, "Lade und Zion. Zur Entstehung der Ziontradition", in *Probleme biblischer Theologie*, pp. 183-198.

- *Jerusalem, mother of all nations* (Ps. 87)[9]

   2a  Yahweh loves his city
   1      founded on the holy mountain;
   2b  he prefers the gates of Zion
   2c      to any town in Jacob.
   3   He has glorious predictions to make of you
            city of God!
   4   'I will add Egypt and Babylon
            to the nations that acknowledge me.
        Of Philistia, Tyre, Ethiopia,
            "Here so and so was born" men say.
   5   But all call Zion "Mother",
            since all were born in her'.
   6   It is he who makes her what she is,
            he, the Most High, Yahweh;
        and as he registers the peoples,
            'It was here' he writes 'that so and so was born',
   7   And all shall sing, in their festive dance:
            'My home is within you'.

This text contains many problems and, because of this, several reconstructions have been proposed. The Psalm may be divided more or less into two main sections. The first part (v. 1-3) affirms that Jerusalem is not just like any other city; it is the city founded by God. He prefers her above all other places and she is destined for glorious things. Jerusalem, therefore, is not great merely for political reasons but because she is the city of God.

The second part (v. 4-7) describes Jerusalem as the mother of all nations. They are all spiritual citizens of Zion without any difference; they might be enemies of Israel like Rahab (perhaps Egypt), Babylon, or Philistia, or they may be friends as Tyre has often been. It does not matter what their colour is, as in the case of the black people of Cush (Ethiopia). All of this is of no importance, since they all now "know" Yahweh. Even if a person is born in one place and is of a particular "nationality", he may at the same time say that he is born in Jerusalem, since all nations have the same "spiritual nationality" (Gal. 4:26). So it is that all the "families of the earth" are members of the same "family".

THE PROPHETIC TRADITION

In several prophetic oracles the same theme reappears: one day the nations will come to Jerusalem. Each text has, unavoidably, its own characteristics. We will just refer briefly to some of the most important of them without entering into any discussion or going into details, since these are the texts most often commented on in the many works on universalism.

---

9. R. SORG, *Ecumenic Psalm 87: Original Form and two Rereadings with an Appendix on Psalm 110, 3*, Fifield, 1969.

- *The feast at Zion* (Is. 25:6-8)[10]

The nations are again gathered in Zion, this time for a feast. They are not coming with offerings but rather to receive something: "On this mountain Yahweh Sabaot will make for all peoples a feast..." (v. 6). It looks like a liturgical celebration. To eat together symbolizes communicating with each other; the nations are in this way in communion with Yahweh. Many covenants or treaties were performed with a communal meal, and the Sinai covenant is no exception (Ex. 24:9-11).

This oracle, Is. 25:6-8, must be compared to Is. 24:21-23, since we are at the same mountain, Zion. So, once more we have a promise of salvation following a punishment caused by "the everlasting covenant" being broken (Is. 24:5). The presence of the "elders" (24:23) confirms the reference to the banquet at Sinai in which the "elders", too, were participating (Ex. 24:9). In the analysis of Is. 2:2-4 we suggested the parallel with the Sinai covenant. This appears here once more. The covenant meal is not limited to Israel in this instance but is for all the nations.

What Yahweh did at Sinai he now does at Zion. Yahweh will reveal himself to all these peoples gathered in Jerusalem: "He will destroy on this mountain the covering that is cast over all peoples, the veil that is spread over all nations" (v. 7).

This, then, will bring about peace, life: "He will swallow up death for ever, and the Lord Yahweh will wipe away tears from all faces" (v. 8).

- *Jerusalem, city of light* (Is. 60)[11]

This text on the new Jerusalem describes the restoration of the city, thanks to the glory of Yahweh. Its light is in strong contrast with the darkness of the world. The nations are coming to this light.

> Arise, shine; for your light has come,
> and the glory of Yahweh has risen upon you.
> For behold, darkness shall cover the earth,
> and thick darkness the peoples;
> but Yahweh will arise upon you,
> and his glory will be seen upon you.
> And nations shall come to your light,
> and kings to the brightness of your rising (v. 1-3).

---

10. S. VIRGULIN, "Il lauto convito sul Sion (Is. 25:6-8)", in *Bib.Or.*, 11 (1969), pp. 57-64; J. VERMEYLEN, "La composition littéraire de l'"Apocalypse d'Isaïe (Is. 24-27)", in *E.T.L.*, 50 (1974), pp. 5-38; M. DELCOR, "Le festin d'immortalité sur la montagne de Sion à l'ère eschatologique en Is. 25:6-9 à la lumière de la littérature ugaritique", in *Salmanticensis*, 23 (1976), pp. 89-98; H. WILDBERGER, "Das Freudenmahl auf dem Zion. Erwägungen zu Jes. 25: 6-8", in *Th.Z.*, 33 (1977), pp. 373-383.

11. P. GRELOT, "Un parallèle babylonien d'Isaïe 60 et du Psaume 72", in *V.T.*, 7 (1957), pp. 319-321; ID., "La Procession des peuples vers la nouvelle Jérusalem. Is. 60:1-6", in *Assemblées du Seigneur* 2, 12, Paris, 1969, pp. 6-10.

They are all coming, this time not to receive but to bring their riches and to recognize what Yahweh has done.

> They shall bring gold and frankincense,
> and shall proclaim the praise of Yahweh (v. 6).

Their gifts will be offered on Yahweh's altar.

> ...they shall come up with acceptance on my altar (v. 7).

The general tendency of the text is that the nations have to prostrate themselves before Jerusalem rather than before Yahweh. Their riches are to enrich Jerusalem.

> Foreigners shall build up your walls,
> and their kings shall minister to you...
> ...men may bring to you the wealth of the nations
> with their kings led in procession.
> For the nation and kingdom
> that will not serve you shall perish... (v. 10-12).

Such a text is certainly very different from Is. 2:2-4, in which it is indicated that the nations came for more spiritual reasons. Here we feel some political overtones. Israel was often oppressed by others; they now come bending low before Jerusalem. It sounds, therefore, more nationalistic, more centred upon Jerusalem than upon Yahweh.

On the other hand, the nations are also coming to that light which will remove their darkness, just as the glory of Yahweh which settled on Mount Sinai at the celebration of the covenant covered it first with a cloud and then changed into light: "The glory of Yahweh settled on Mount Sinai, and the cloud covered it six days; and on the seventh day he called to Moses out of the midst of the cloud. Now the appearance of the glory of Yahweh was like a devouring fire on the top of the mountain in the sight of the people of Israel" (Ex. 24:16-17). Yahweh's glory is now upon Zion, its light is in the sight of all the nations. The nations also contribute by their gifts to the glory of Yahweh and his cult: "for my house shall be called a house of prayer for all peoples" (Is. 56:7) and "all flesh shall come to worship before me" (Is. 66:23).

- *Jerusalem, the throne of Yahweh* (Jer. 3:17)

One verse in Jeremiah expresses the same concept of centripetal universalism: "At that time Jerusalem shall be called the throne of Yahweh, and all nations shall gather to it, to the presence of Yahweh in Jerusalem, and they shall no more stubbornly follow their own evil heart".

This text is more in accordance with the teaching of Is. 2:2-4. The nations come first of all to Yahweh who resides in Jerusalem. They are willing to change their life style. Instead of following their own evil ways, they will walk in the paths of Yahweh.

- *Jerusalem, place of peace* (Hag. 2:6-9)[12]

This oracle is in the line of Is. 60. The nations come to the centre with their riches and more precisely to the temple, so that the second temple shall be more beautiful than the first. But hopefully, perhaps they will share in the peace that God promises: "and in this place I will give peace" (v. 9).

- *The favour of Yahweh in Jerusalem* (Zech. 8:20-23)

In the book of Zechariah it is said that many nations will join themselves to Yahweh who will then call them "my people" (Zech. 2:15).

Another text describes again a beautiful pilgrimage to Zion. "Peoples shall yet come, even the inhabitants of many cities; the inhabitants of one city shall go to another, saying, 'Let us go at once to entreat the favour of Yahweh, and to seek Yahweh Sabaot; I am going'. Many peoples and strong nations shall come to seek Yahweh Sabaot in Jerusalem, and to entreat the favour of Yahweh" (v. 20-22). One nation invites another and together they come to Jerusalem to find Yahweh and to receive his grace.

The following verse adds an interesting element: "In those days ten men from the nations of every tongue shall take hold of the robe of a Jew, saying, 'Let us go with you, for we have heard that God is with you'" (v. 23). A biblical tradition has linked the confusion of the languages with the building of the tower of Babel, which constituted the end of the primitive universal covenant and the exile of mankind (Gen. 11). Now people speaking different languages will again find their unity in Jerusalem. They are gathered from their exile. In an oracle which we studied earlier we spoke about "five" cities in Egypt which will speak the "language" of Canaan (Is. 19:18). We have shown its meaning. With five, one is capable of accomplishing great things, even the beginning of something more complete. The text of Zechariah speaks about "ten" men.

It is also interesting to note why and how the nations come. They are impressed by what has happened to Israel and are seemingly convinced. They, therefore, use Israel as mediator to go to Yahweh: "Let us go *with you*, for we have heard that God is *with you*". This expresses, in a very interesting way, the special position of Israel.

- *The eschatological battle, the splendour of Jerusalem* (Zech. 14)[13]

In the same book we find another text speaking about the nations coming to Jerusalem (Zech. 14). Those who have attacked Jerusalem will all be punished (v. 12) and the riches of the nations will be collected (v. 14). These nations will also be obliged to come to Jerusalem yearly: "Then

---

12. H. G. MAY, "'This People' and 'This Nation' in Haggai", in *V.T.*, 18 (1968), pp. 190-197.
13. H. M. LUTZ, *Jahwe, Jerusalem und die Völker. Zur Vorgeschichte Sach. 12, 1-8 und 14, 1-5*, W.M.A.N.T. 27, Neukirchen, 1968.

every one that survives of all the nations that have come against Jerusalem shall go up year after year to worship the King, Yahweh Sabaot, and to keep the feast of booths" (v. 16). If they refuse to do so, there will be no prosperity for them (v. 17).

- *The King of heaven in Jerusalem* (Tob. 13:11; 14:6-7)

In the book of Tobit we have two texts very similar to what we have already seen, which give a description of the new Jerusalem and show the nations coming to her:

> Many nations will come from afar to the name of the Lord God,
> bearing gifts in their hands, gifts for the King of heaven" (13:11).[14]

As mentioned in earlier texts they come to adore Yahweh and to bring him their gifts, but it is not humiliating for them.

Another text also describes the restoration of the temple of Jerusalem by the people, who have returned from exile and who have been joined by the nations.

> Then all the Gentiles will convert to fear the Lord God in truth,
> and will bury their idols.
> All the Gentiles will praise the Lord... (14:6-7).[15]

In this last text the conversion of the nations to the true God is more clearly stated.

\* \* \*

These are some of the most important texts describing the coming of the nations to Jerusalem (cf. Ps. 86:9; 102:16-17,22-23). But we would also like to refer to the beautiful prayer of Solomon at the dedication of the temple:

> Likewise when a foreigner, who is not of thy people Israel, comes from a far country for thy name's sake, for they shall hear of thy great name, and thy mighty hand, and of thy outstretched arm, when he comes and prays toward this house, hear thou in heaven thy dwelling place, and do according to all for which the foreigner calls to thee; in order that all the peoples of the earth may know thy name and fear thee, as do thy people Israel, and that they may know that this house which I have built is called by thy name (1 Kgs. 8:41-43).

All these texts have their own peculiarities; some emphasize one aspect, whereas others emphasize another. We can now try to summarize all these texts.

The description of the gathering of the nations in Jerusalem is inspired by the pilgrimage of the Israelites themselves. Like the faithful who went to the temple in Jerusalem, so also the nations will go "in days to come".

---

14. J. Goettmann, "Le chant de joie du prophète Tobie", in *B.V.C.*, n. 78 (1967), pp. 19-27.
15. J. Lebram, "Die Weltreiche in der Jüdischen Apokalyptik. Bemerkungen zu Tobit 14:4-7", in *Z.A.W.*, 76 (1964), pp. 328-331.

We have seen why the Israelites came to the temple. All this is now applied to the nations. They go simply to praise Yahweh, to adore him. They also come to make offering, and bring with them their riches. But they will also be recipients. They will receive instruction, revelation and justification. These they will accept willingly and as a result, they will be converted. So the nations give and receive.

In Jerusalem the faithful are welcomed by the priests who offer sacrifice in the name of the people and who instruct the people. In other words, the priests serve as the mediators between Yahweh and his people. Israel, chosen as the "priestly kingdom", also has this function between Yahweh and the nations coming to Zion. Several texts show clearly this role of Israel towards the peoples. But some danger is entailed in this. The priests are still human and therefore can abuse their positions. We see this well illustrated in the interesting story of the two sons of the priest Eli who profited from the offerings of the people (1 Sam. 2:11-26). In several texts we can also feel an expression of pride. When the nations, who have often humiliated Israel, come to prostrate themselves before Yahweh in Jerusalem, they must also prostrate themselves before the mediator. The gold and riches brought to Jerusalem, to Yahweh, are also brought to Israel. Several of the texts, especially those where the nations come with their offerings, are less pure than those where the nations receive the revelation.

A second theme which seems to have inspired the composition of many of these texts is the covenant of Sinai. What Israel celebrated at Sinai is celebrated by the nations in Zion. At Sinai, Yahweh gave his law to Israel through Moses. He now gives his revelation to the nations through Israel. At that time Israel was designated as Yahweh's people, but now all the nations are Yahweh's people.

The dispersion of the nations after the failure of the primitive universal covenant will thus come to an end. The nations come from everywhere. Differences of language do not matter any more. There will again be mutual understanding among all the peoples. It will be the end of war and a lasting peace will be established.

We, therefore, may conclude that a new universal covenant will exist between God and mankind through Israel's mediation.

## II. CENTRIFUGAL UNIVERSALISM

All the preceding texts predict the coming of the nations towards the centre. They come because they are impressed by what Yahweh has accomplished in favour of Israel. Israel is a living witness, able to attract them. But one may wonder if Israel was obliged to wait for this to happen "in days to come" or whether she might have taken some initiative to invite the nations, and thereby bring about or even hasten this day? In other words did Israel feel the need to go out to the nations instead of waiting until they would come to her?

Several biblical texts speak about some nations offering sacrifices to Yahweh in their own lands. These nations do not come to Jerusalem to perform these sacrifices, but rather remain in their home countries (cf. Is. 19:19; Zeph. 2:11; Mal. 1:11).[16] How then did these nations come to know Yahweh?

All this raises the following questions: Do we have any texts where the centre is going out to the nations? Does Israel go out to preach to the nations in order to share with them her revelation? Do we have texts containing what is called centrifugal universalism, or "missionary" texts in the strict sense of the word?

THE MISSION OF THE SUFFERING SERVANT

Such an idea is perhaps expressed in a few verses of the Songs of the Suffering Servant (Is. 42:1-9; 49:1-6; 50:4-9 (10-11); 52:13-53:12). These Songs certainly belong to the most problematic biblical texts. They are found in the book of Deutero-Isaiah (Is. 40-55) which is generally considered as one of the most important writings in favour of universalism[17] (despite a few exegetes who consider Deutero-Isaiah to be a nationalistic writer).[18]

All this material has been the object of several studies. The whole discussion is very understandable. There are some beautiful texts about the nations:

> for a law will go forth from me,
> and my justice for a light to the peoples.
> My deliverance draws near speedily,
> my salvation has gone forth,
> and my arms will rule the peoples;
> the coastlands wait for me,
> and for my arm they hope (Is. 51:4-5).

---

16. M. REHM, "Das Opfer der Völker nach Malachias 1:11", in *Lex tua Veritas, Festschrift H. Junker*, Trier, 1961, pp. 193-208; J. SWETNAM, "Malachi 1:11: An Interpretation", in *C.B.Q.*, 31 (1969), pp. 200-209; K. S. FRANK, "Maleachi 1:10 ff. in der frühen Väterdeutung", in *Th.Phil.*, 53 (1978), pp. 70-78.

17. H. HALAS, "The Universalism of Isaiah", in *C.B.Q.*, 12 (1950), pp. 162-170; R. DAVIDSON, "Universalism in Second Isaiah", in *Scot.J.T.*, 16 (1963), pp. 166-185; A. GELSTON, "The Missionary Message of Second Isaiah", in *Scot.J.T.*, 18 (1965), pp. 308-318; D. E. HOLLENBERG, "Nationalism and 'the Nations' in Is. 40-55", in *V.T.*, 19 (1969), pp. 23-36; A. GAMPER, "Der Verkündigungsauftrag Israels nach Deutero-Jesaja", in *Z.K.T.*, 91 (1969), pp. 411-429; P.-E. DION, "L'universalisme religieux dans les différentes couches rédactionnelles d'Is. 40-55", in *Bib.*, 51 (1970), pp. 161-182.

18. P.A.H. DE BOER, *Second-Isaiah's Message*, O.T.S. 11 (1956), especially chap. 5. The Limits of Second Isaiah's Message, pp. 80-101; H. M. ORLINSKY, "The So-called 'Servant of the Lord', and 'Suffering Servant' in Second Isaiah", in *V.T.S.*, 14 (1967), pp. 1-133; N. H. SNAITH, "Isaiah 40-66. A Study of the Teaching of the Second Isaiah and its Consequences", in *V.T.S.*, 14 (1967), pp. 135-264, especially III. The Nationalist, pp. 154-165; A. SCHOORS, *I Am God Your Saviour. A Form-critical Study of the Main Genres in Is. 40-55*, V.T.S. 24 (1973).

This is a very interesting text because in it we have a strong expression of universalism which is not centripetal. One would even be inclined to think of it as an example of centrifugal universalism: "a law will go forth...". But on the other hand there are some rather hard texts for the nations:

> Kings shall be your foster fathers,
> and their queens your nursing mothers.
> With their faces to the ground
> they shall bow down to you,
> and lick the dust of your feet.
> Then you will know that I am Yahweh;
> those who wait for me shall not be put to shame (Is. 49:23).

There is certainly no necessity to doubt that Deutero-Isaiah teaches a very strong monotheism, namely that Yahweh will be recognized by all nations, who will be saved by him (cf. Is. 45:18-25).[19]

But one may ask whether this prophet also wrote the Songs[20], or whether they were composed by somebody else? And above all, who is this Servant? Is he the same person in the Songs as in the rest of Deutero-Isaiah? Is he the same in the four Songs? In Deutero-Isaiah Israel is often called "my servant" or "his servant Jacob" (Is. 41:8; 42:19; 43:10; 44:1; 45:4; 48:20). This could be the same meaning in the Songs (cf. 49:3).[21] But on the other hand, the Suffering Servant also has a mission towards Israel (49:5), where he is represented rather as an individual. From here the discussion continues: Who is this individual? Is he the messiah? But since the Servant is sometimes spoken of as a collectivity, while at other times as an individual person, some have gone so far as to speak of him as a "corporate personality".

Whatever the answer is to all of these problems, we have Israel, or an individual representing Israel, who receives a special mission from Yahweh for the nations.[22] We will now examine those verses only where a possible "mission *ad extra*" is entrusted to Israel. These verses are to be found in the first two Songs.

---

19. W.A.M. BEUKEN, "The Confession of God's Exclusivity by all Mankind. A Reappraisal of Is. 45:18-25", in *Bijdr.*, 35 (1974), pp. 335-356.
20. Much has been written on the numerous problems related to the Songs of the Suffering Servant. One of the most recent studies where references to preceding research can be found is by J. COPPENS, "Le Messianisme Israélite. La relève prophétique", in *E.T.L.*, 47 (1971), pp. 321-339; 48 (1972), pp. 5-36.
21. N. LOHFINK, "'Israel' in Jes. 49:3", in *Wort, Lied und Gottesspruch, Festschrift J. Ziegler*, II, ed. J. Schreiner, Würzburg, 1972, pp. 217-229.
22. E. DUSSEL, "Universalismo y misión en los poemas del Siervo de Jahvéh", in *Ciencia y Fe*, 20 (1964), pp. 419-464; J. COPPENS, "La Mission du Serviteur de Yahvé et son statut eschatologique", in *E.T.L.*, 48 (1972), pp. 343-358.

> Behold my servant,[23] whom I uphold,
> my chosen, in whom my soul delights;
> I have put my spirit upon him,
> he will bring forth justice to the nations (42:1).
>
> ...he will faithfully bring forth justice (v. 3).
>
> He will not fail or be discouraged
> till he has established justice in the earth;
> and the coastlands wait for his law (v. 4).

The word translated by "justice"[24] is related to the activity of a judge. His function, as we have seen before, is that of referee between two parties. He declares one guilty, the other free. Therefore, justice means deliverance for one but punishment for the other. This is why some exegetes, who consider Deutero-Isaiah nationalistic, interpret the function of the Servant as bringing about deliverance for Israel but condemnation of the nations who have oppressed the elected people.

But the function of a judge is also that of re-establishing, through his judgment, right order or "justice". This word "justice" came to mean something close to true religion, salvation, and this is confirmed by a parallel here between "justice" and "torah", law and instruction (v. 4). We have thus the same two concepts as in Is. 2:2-4.

The verb expressing the mission of the Servant is literally: "to make go out" (v. 1,3), which seems to suggest a movement from one place to another. The servant has to "bring", "make known" and "reveal" this justice while the others "wait" (v. 4) to receive it.

There is no doubt that it is destined for everybody: "nations" (v. 1), "the earth" and "the coastlands" (v. 4).

In the same Song another verse describes further this mission of the Servant:

> I am Yahweh, I have called you in righteousness,
> I have taken you by the hand and kept you;
> I have made you as a covenant of the people,
> a light to the nations (42:6),

and a similar idea is expressed as well in the second Song:

> I will make you as a light to the nations,
> that my salvation may reach to the end of the earth (49:6).

In these texts Israel is twice called "a light to the nations". Some exegetes have given a nationalistic explanation of them, namely, that

---

23. N. L. TIDWELL, "My Servant Jacob, Is. 42:1. A Suggestion", in *V.T.S.*, 26 (1974), pp. 84-91.
24. W.A.M. BEUKEN, "*Mišpāṭ*. The First Servant Song and its Context", in *V.T.*, 22 (1972), pp. 1-30; J. JEREMIAS, "*Mišpāṭ*. Im ersten Gottesknechtslied", in *V.T.*, 22 (1972), pp. 31-42.

Yahweh will restore Israel and that this fact will be seen by the nations.[25] If this be the case, the text would only mean that the nations will acknowledge Israel's marvellous deliverance, a fact which has led one exegete to translate it: "a light respected by the nations". But the text seems to have another meaning. We have a similar expression, that Yahweh is "the light of Israel" (Is. 10:17), which means that Yahweh enlightens Israel. We may, therefore, conclude that Israel, "the light of the nations", will enlighten the others, for she will be a source of enlightenment. We may confirm this by a parallelism shown in 49:6, where Israel is the "light of the nations" who will receive Yahweh's "salvation". Such an interpretation corresponds with other biblical texts: "Yahweh is my light and my salvation, whom shall I fear?" (Ps. 27:1). Here we have the same two words being used (cf. also Ps. 43:3; Is. 60:19,20). The idea that Yahweh's salvation must "reach to the end of the earth" could therefore suggest a kind of outgoing movement.

The other expression is even more difficult to understand. The Servant is appointed as "bᵉrît ᶜam".[26] This is the only text where such an expression appears and it has been interpreted in several different ways, a disparity which depends a lot on the identity of the Servant. Some of those who consider the Servant as an individual conclude that this person is destined as a "covenant of the people". Normally the "people" refers to Israel, while the covenant is a link between the two partners; the Servant will thus be a "covenant(-bond) of the people [i.e. of Israel]". He would then have a double mission. He would be a link between Yahweh and Israel, as well as a light to the nations. But if the Servant is Israel herself, then two main interpretations are possible. The first would be that Israel is called the "covenant people"; she is the elected people, the chosen one with whom Yahweh concludes a covenant and who is now destined to become a light to the nations. Another interpretation considers covenant as a link, and sees in "people" a parallel with "nations". The word "people" may have, on exceptional occasions, the meaning of "all mankind". This is the case in the preceding verse (42:5) and thus the servant Israel then becomes the link between Yahweh and mankind, the "covenant(-bond) of the people [i.e. all the nations]", and is in parallel with the expression "a light to the nations".

---

25. H. M. ORLINSKI, "The So-called 'Servant of the Lord' and 'Suffering Servant' in Second Isaiah", in *V.T.S.*, 14 (1967), pp. 1-133, Appendix: "A Light of Nations"—"A Covenant of People", pp. 97-117; or "'A Covenant (of) People, A Light of Nations'— a Problem in Biblical Theology", in *Essays in Biblical Culture and Bible Translation*, New York, 1974, pp. 166-186.
26. G. SCHWARZ, "'...zum Bund des Volkes'? Eine Emendation", in *Z.A.W.*, 82 (1970), pp. 279-281; J. J. STAMM, "*Bᵉrît 'Am* bei Deuterojesaja", in *Probleme biblischer Theologie, Festschrift G. von Rad*, ed. H. W. WOLFF, München, 1971, pp. 510-524; E. HAAG, "Bund für das Volk und Licht für die Heiden (Jes. 42:6)", in *Didaskalia*, 7 (1977), pp. 3-18; D. R. HILLERS, "Bᵉrît 'ām: 'Emancipation of the People'" in *J.B.L.*, 97 (1978), pp. 175-182.

Most of these ideas and even the terminology are found in the text quoted above (Is. 51:4-5) which says nothing of how this salvation will come about. The Songs, on the other hand, attribute this to the mission of the Servant.

This cursory investigation, then, shows us the numerous problems which we encounter when we try to understand these particular verses. Unlike a very small number of exegetes who find here nationalistic feelings, we are inclined to affirm that a teaching of universalism is present. Yahweh's salvation is destined not only for Israel, but for all nations. All nations will share in it through the mediation of the Servant who has to fulfill his mission as if he were a prophet. According to some, the text seems to suggest even a going out to the others. This must be considered as a possibility only because of the numerous unsolved problems which these texts raise.

Some exegetes are inclined to see a confirmation of this in a few other texts in Deutero-Isaiah, such as "listen to me in silence, o coastlands" (41:1). The nations are not asked to come to Jerusalem but to receive the revelation in their own land. It is equally true that all these verses might simply signify that restored Israel, while living faithfully, is a light attracting the others.

The Mission of Jonah

Another example often invoked as a true "missionary" text is the story of the prophet Jonah.[27] Technically, this is not considered a prophetic book, since it does not contain oracles of the prophet as do all other prophetical books; rather, it tells the story of a prophet. It is often considered a fine polemical writing against some narrow-minded tendencies in Israel. Some believe that Jonah symbolizes Israel. But again, whatever the answer is to all these critical problems, we have here the story of a prophet (whether he represents the mission of a prophet or merely represents Israel) who goes to preach in Nineveh.

But the prophet refuses his divine call and flees to Tarshish, where he experiences the well-known adventures on the sea. One interesting event for us is that the pagan sailors pray to Yahweh and "then the men feared Yahweh exceedingly, and they offered a sacrifice to Yahweh and made vows" (1:16). Yahweh is, as we see here, adored by foreigners who do

---

27. A. Feuillet, "Les sources du livre de Jonas", in *R.B.*, 54 (1947), pp. 161-186; Id., "Le sens du livre de Jonas", in *R.B.*, 54 (1947), pp. 341-346; Id., "Le livre de Jonas", in *R.Cl.Afr.*, 18 (1963), pp. 509-521; C. A. Keller, "Jonas, le portrait d'un prophète", in *Th.Z.*, 21 (1965), pp. 329-340; R.B.Y. Scott, "The Sign of Jonah. An Interpretation", in *Interpr.*, 19 (1965), pp. 16-25; J. E. Wrigley, "An Old Testament Ecumenical Message", in *The Bible Today*, 25 (1966), pp. 1763-1769; G. M. Landes, "The Kerygma of the Book of Jonah. The Contextual Interpretation of the Jonah Psalm", in *Interpr.*, 21 (1967), pp. 3-31; R. E. Clements, "The Purpose of the Book of Jonah", in *V.T.S.*, 28 (1975), pp. 16-28.

not have to go to Jerusalem to offer sacrifices.

Finally, Jonah decides to accomplish his mission and then goes to Nineveh to proclaim his message: "Yet forty days, and Nineveh shall be overthrown" (3:4). The people accept this message and fast, and "when God saw what they did, how they turned from their evil way, God repented of the evil which he had said he would do to them; and he did not do it" (3:10).

This displeases Jonah (4:1 ff.), who gets angry, and after another story, Yahweh explains to his prophet: "and should not I pity Nineveh, that great city...?" (4:11).

We evidently have a "mission *ad extra*". Jonah is sent to a far region, Nineveh. He has to leave his own country to preach there. But as a first observation we note that he does not go willingly. He first refuses, and when his mission succeeds, he gets angry. We certainly do not find a great desire on his part to share anything with others but rather the contrary. A second point which is even more important is that Jonah preaches the future punishment of Nineveh. In a certain sense this has to be compared with the "oracles against the nations" which we have studied before (cf. Am. 1-2; Ezek. 29:1-12). It is the same severe punishment of a sinful nation. The only difference is that Jonah goes to tell them in their own country. If Yahweh can punish them, he is their master and they are responsible before him (1:2). We have thus the same kind of universalism as contained in the "oracles against the nations". Jonah is certainly not preaching the good news; he is not sharing the revelation with the nations. Nineveh still lacks Yahweh's revelation. They pray to God and fast in the hope that God may repent. It is interesting that there is never any reference to "Yahweh" but always to "God" in relation to the inhabitants of Nineveh. It is not even Jonah who invites them to conversion; he just preaches the impending punishment. It is rather the king of Nineveh who invites his people to conversion: "Let every one turn from his evil way and from the violence which is in his hands" (3:8). The people are asked to live an honest life, through a moral conversion, following what we have earlier referred to as the "natural law" (cf. also 3:10), but they have no knowledge of Yahweh and his "revealed law".

In other words this book teaches, as so many other texts do, that the nations too are responsible before God, who will punish the unfaithful but will save the one who converts. It would be difficult to call this a real "missionary" text, though it seems to invite Israel to open up to the world, if only as a reaction against the bad interpretation of her election. Yahweh's pity is really universal.

## "Tell among the peoples his deeds" (Psalms)

The Psalms very often refer to the nations. Since these prayers reflect the different religious beliefs and tendencies of Israel, we find in them all the different aspects of universalism which we have studied. Several essays have been written on this topic.[28] Let us now examine a few texts that may contain a possible expression of centrifugal universalism.

In many Psalms we find an *invitation, addressed to the nations to praise Yahweh*. A typical example is Ps. 117.[29]

> Praise Yahweh, all nations!
> Extol him, all peoples!
> For great is his steadfast love towards us,
> and the faithfulness of Yahweh endures for ever.
> Praise Yahweh!

This invitation is frequently repeated in the Psalms (33:8; 47:2; 66:1, 4,8; 67; 68:32-33; 86:9; 96:1,7-9; 98:4,7; 99:3; 100:1-3; 113:3; 148:11; 150:6). It is instructive to see the context of these verses. The nations are invited to praise Yahweh, but often with them nature is invited to do the same: heavens, sea, rivers, fields, trees, hills, animals, etc. (cf. 96:7 ff.; 98:4 ff.; 148). It is, therefore, difficult to consider this as a preaching to the nations, thereby giving them the revelation. These texts rather express the hope that the whole world may adore Yahweh and grow in faith in Yahweh's universal power over the whole world.

Even more interesting are a few texts in which we find an *invitation to proclaim Yahweh's deeds among the nations*:

> Declare his glory among the nations,
> his marvellous works among all the peoples
> (Ps. 96:3; cf. also Ps. 9:12; 96:10; 105:1).

This can be compared with similar expressions in the book of Tobit: "Acknowledge him before the nations, O sons of Israel; for he has scattered us among them" (Tob. 13:3; cf. also 13:8). This text of Tobit clearly says that the people are in exile, since they are far from the promised land, and, therefore, under the circumstances they may still continue to praise Yahweh.

And finally in a few texts *the psalmist promises that he will sing the praises of Yahweh among the nations*:

> I will give thanks to thee, o Lord, among the peoples;
> I will sing praise to thee among the nations (Ps. 57:10; cf. also Ps. 18:50; 108:4).

Wherever he is, he will sing the praises of God.

These texts certainly express a dynamic desire to tell others about Yahweh and his marvellous deeds. The Israelites certainly must have spoken about all of this to the foreigners who came to Jerusalem or those whom they met when they were themselves in foreign lands. But the prime motive seems to have been gratitude to Yahweh for what he had done for Israel rather than a desire to share the revelation with other nations.

---

28. A. STROBEL, *La Conversion des gentils dans les Psaumes*, Paris, 1950; J. DE FRAINE, "Les nations païennes dans les Psaumes", in *Studi sull' Oriente e la Bibbia, Festschrift G. Rinaldi*, Genova, 1967, pp. 285-292.
29. H. DUESBERG, "Le Psaume d'invite aux nations", in *B.V.C.*, n. 14 (1956), pp. 91-97.

The results of our investigation on centrifugal universalism are rather meagre. A few more texts are sometimes quoted as "mission" texts (e.g. Is. 48:20; 66:19; Jer. 31:10 ff.). From the preceding discussion we may conclude that we have a number of texts which clearly express centripetal universalism; namely, that the nations will receive Yahweh's revelation in Jerusalem. There are several other texts which suggest what could be called a decentralized universalism; namely, that the nations can offer and adore Yahweh in their own lands and do not have to come to the centre. There are only a few texts where the beginning of what could be called centrifugal universalism, the desire to go out to others, is perhaps expressed. However, these latter texts are still far from clear and it would be an exaggeration to suggest that they speak of a real mission movement at this point in biblical tradition.

THE MISSION OF THE DISCIPLES (Mt. 28:18-20)

Since the missionary character of the Old Testament texts has remained hypothetical, and because Jesus himself during his life showed great reservations towards the "nations", we have to wait until the end of the second period of salvation history, which concludes with Jesus' resurrection, before we find what is often considered to be Jesus' command to go out to the nations (Mt. 28:18-20). Now finally we may have a very clear text which constitutes the summit of the biblical tradition on universalism.

This text is probably most quoted in studies on the biblical foundation of mission and has inspired many in their missionary zeal. But if one tries to determine its precise meaning, one is immediately confronted with several problems, as is evident from the great number of studies that have been made of this particular text.[30] Because of the important value

---

30. W. VOGELS, "La proclamation de l'alliance universelle en Mt. 28:18-20", in *Z.M.R.*, 58 (1974), pp. 258-272, where an extensive bibliography on this particular text can be found, pp. 271-272, or the same study in *Kerygma*, 8 (1974), n. 22, pp. 1-20, bibliography pp. 18-20. Several studies have appeared since then: J. LANGE, *Das Erscheinen des Auferstandenen im Evangelium nach Mattäus: Eine traditions- und redaktions-geschichtliche Untersuchung zu Mt. 28:16-20*, Würzburg, 1973; H. FRANKEMÖLLE, *Jahwebund und Kirche Christi: Studien zur Form- und Traditions-geschichte des "Evangeliums" nach Matthäus*, Münster, 1974; B. J. HUBBARD, *The Matthean Redaction of a Primitive Apostolic Commissioning: An Exegesis of Matthew 28:16-20*, Missoula, 1974; J. D. KINGSBURY, "The Composition and Christology of Matt. 28:16-20", in *J.B.L.*, 93 (1974), pp. 573-584; J. J. MCGOVERN, "Mission Commands. Programs for Humanity", in *The Bible Today*, n. 73 (1974), pp. 36-46; K. ROMANIUK, "'Gehet hin in alle Welt!'. Biblische Hinweise für eine Meditation über den Missionsbefehl Jesu", in *Z.M.R.*, 58 (1974), pp. 1-7; C. H. GIBLIN, "A Note on Doubt and Reassurance in Mt. 28:16-20", in *C.B.Q.*, 37 (1975), pp. 68-75; D.R.A. HARE and D. J. HARRINGTON, "Make disciples of all the Gentiles (Mt. 28:19)", in *C.B.Q.*, 37 (1975), pp. 359-369; J. P. MEIER, "Salvation-History in Matthew: In Search of a Starting Point", in *C.B.Q.*, 37 (1975), pp. 203-215; S. BROWN, "The Two-fold Representation of the Mission in Matthew's Gospel", in *S.T.*, 31 (1977), pp. 21-32; J. P. MEIER, "Nations or Gentiles in Matthew 28:19?", in *C.B.Q.*, 39 (1977), pp. 94-102; ID., "Two Disputed Questions in Matt. 28:16-20", in *J.B.L.*, 96 (1977), pp. 407-424; H. SCHIEBER, "Konzentrik im Matthäusschluss. Ein form und gattungskritischer Versuch zu Mt. 28:16-20", in *Kairos*, 19 (1977), pp. 286-307.

attributed to this passage, we propose now to analyse it in more detail and to discuss some of the more technical problems which it presents.

The *historicity*[31] of Mt. 28:18-20 is rejected by a number of writers for several reasons. This text should not be attributed to Jesus but to the primitive church. It does not express Jesus' command on missionary activity but rather it is a formulation of the primitive church to justify its own expansion politics. These objections would seem to arise from different levels. Some are based on literary criticism: the formulation of these words cannot be attributed to Jesus but have the characteristics of a later liturgical tradition. This kind of discussion on the *ipsissima verba Jesu* is of less importance for us since it does not change the profound reality which interests us here. The text of Matthew is not an isolated case; we have several parallel texts (Mk. 16:15; Lk. 24:47 ff.; Jn. 20:21; Acts. 1:8). They all seem to refer to the same basic desire of Jesus. Though the precise wording of texts may have changed, we may still ask the question: Did Jesus really intend that type of mission? Thus we come to the problem of historical criticism which we must now examine.

First of all, according to some exegetes, this text seems to be in direct contradiction to *the attitude adopted by Jesus himself during his life*. Indeed the intention of Jesus would seem to have been to limit himself to Israel, not only in his preaching but also in his activity. In this respect a few examples also taken from the gospel of Matthew will throw even more light on this paradox. To the request of the Canaanite woman Jesus' answer is surprising: "I was sent only to the lost sheep of the house of Israel" (Mt. 15:24).[32] Jesus is one of the many prophets of Israel, and like them, his mission is towards the chosen people. When he sends his disciples on a mission, he gives them some recommendations, one of which is completely contrary to our so-called missionary text: "These twelve Jesus sent out, charging them, 'Go nowhere among the Gentiles, and enter no town of the Samaritans, but go rather to the lost sheep of the house of Israel'" (Mt. 10:5-6).[33]

This apparent contradiction between the way in which Jesus limited himself to Israel and his last words has often been studied.[34] We have to distinguish clearly here two periods in the life of Jesus of which he him-

---

31. On this question: E. L. COPELAND, "The Great Commission and Missions (Mt. 28: 19 ff.), in *Sw.J.T.*, 9 (1967), n. 2, pp. 79-89; W. TRILLING, "De toutes les nations, faites des disciples Mt. 28:16-20", in *Assemblées du Seigneur*, 2, 28, Paris, 1969, pp. 24-37.
32. T. LOVISON, "La pericopa della Cananea Mt. 15:21-28", in *Riv.Bib.It.*, 19 (1971), pp. 273-305; A. DERMIENCE, "Tradition et rédaction dans la péricope de la Syrophénicienne, Marc 7:24-30", in *R.T.L.*, 8, (1977), pp. 15-29.
33. F. W. BEARE, "The Mission of the Disciples and the Mission Charge: Matthew 10 and Parallels", in *J.B.L.*, 89 (1970), pp. 1-13; J. RADERMAKERS, "La Mission, engagement radical. Une lecture de Mt. 10", in *N.R.T.*, 93 (1971), pp. 1072-1085; J. WILKINSON, "The Mission Charge to the Twelve and Modern Medical Mission", in *Scot.J.T.*, 27 (1974), pp. 313-328.
34. Cf. J. JEREMIAS, *Jesus' Promise to the Nations*, S.B.T. 24, London, 1956; J. P. MEIER, "Salvation-History in Matthew", pp. 203-215; S. BROWN, "The Two-fold Representation", pp. 21-32.

self is conscious. Jesus was sent by his Father with a mission in the line of the other prophets and in this respect he continues the revelation which began with Abraham. In his salvation plan, Yahweh chose Israel, but with a view to service towards the nations. Israel is called to communicate to them the revelation which she has received first. It is through the elected people that the others will find salvation. But nobody can give what he has not himself received. Israel must first receive the fullness of revelation before she can share it with others. Jesus limited his action to Israel during his earthly life in order to bring to fulfilment the revelation to the elected people. But already during this period of Jesus' life we find some indications, some anticipations, of universal salvation (Mt. 22:1-14; 24:14). Even if Jesus expresses some reservations to the Canaanite woman, he finally grants her what she asks for (Mt. 15:28). With the death and resurrection of Jesus, God's revelation has come to its completion and Jesus may then invite his disciples to let the nations share in it.

The attitude of Jesus does not constitute a valid objection to the historicity of our text. Jesus has played his role as part of the history of salvation as we have seen it up until now. In this perspective the universal mission had to start after the complete revelation had been given to Israel. The command to start this mission is, therefore, very appropriately expressed verbally by the risen Jesus.

A second objection against the historicity of the text seems to originate from *the attitude of the primitive Church*. If Jesus really had given such an order to his disciples, why was the Church so slow to embrace the uncircumcised (Gal. 2:7) and, likewise, what necessitated all the discussions which pertained to the acceptance of the Gentiles into the community? Further, why was this command never used to solve the problem and to stop the discussion? Why did Peter need a special vision before he could accept the fact that the Roman centurion Cornelius could be baptized, and what are we to think about the whole discussion which this baptism caused (Acts. 10:1-11:18; 15:7-11)?[35]

Surely the delay of the primitive Church is not any different from that which is common to all men, especially when adjustments to new situations have to be made. Nothing seems to suggest any real rejection of the universal mission. There is no reason to doubt the *theoretical* consciousness of this universal mission in the primitive Church; the difficulties are more at the level of the *practical* implications. Was it necessary for Gentiles who were baptized to undergo circumcision and, likewise, was it necessary for the law of purity and all the prescriptions of the Jewish cult to be followed? There really, then, seems to be no reason

---

35. P. CATRICE, "Réflexions missionnaires sur la vision de St. Pierre à Joppé. Du Judéo-christianisme à l'Église de tous les peuples", in *B.V.C.*, n. 79 (1968), pp. 20-39; K. STENDAHL, "It took a Miracle to launch the Mission to the Gentiles. (The Cornelius Story—Act. 10-11:18)", in *Risk*, 13 (1977), pp. 56-57.

to refer to the command of Jesus since everybody had agreed to it in principle; but the "how" did raise problems.

The attitude of the primitive Church, therefore, does not seem to be a real objection to the historicity of our text. On the contrary, the primitive Church, which had inherited the reserved attitude of the Old Testament and also that of Jesus himself towards the Gentiles, would most probably not have opened up so actively to the pagan world had it not been forced to do so by direct command from the Lord.

This mission to the nations was, indeed, the desire of Jesus but was executed by the Church only after certain hesitations and opposition common to all men when confronted with change.

18. And Jesus came and said to them:
    —'All authority in heaven and on earth has been given to me,
19. —Therefore, while going, make disciples all nations,
    baptizing them in the name of the Father and of the Son and of the Holy Spirit,
20. teaching them to observe all that I have commanded you;
    —And lo, I am with you always, until the end of the world'.

The structure of this text is very simple. Three parts appear very clearly: a *presentation* (v. 18b), a *command* (v. 19-20a) and a *promise* (v. 20b). The link between the three sections is very strongly marked: the command is introduced by "therefore" and the promise by "and lo". The connection between the three parts is thus very logical and the unity of the text evident.

This very unified structure gives a kind of solemnity to the text, which is reinforced by the repetition four times of the word "all". The general and universal dimension of the text is thus very strongly underlined.

The interior composition of the second part, the command, is rather complex. Four verbs describe the activity of the disciples. Only one of these verbs is in the imperative: "make disciples". The three others, "go", "baptize" and "teach", are participles. So the most important element of this command is certainly "make disciples". This is introduced by one participle ("while going") and is followed by two participles which explain how to make disciples: "baptizing them" and "teaching them".

There is no agreement about the *literary genre* of the text and several opinions have been proposed.[36]

One group of authors classifies the text as belonging to the *genre of enthronement* or coronation[37] by comparing it with Dan. 7:13-14. "All authority has been given to me" (v. 18) recalls "to him was given authority" (Dan. 7:14), with the same verb "give" and the same noun

---

36. B. J. MALINA, "The Literary Structure and Form of Mt. 28:16-20", in *N.T.S.*, 17 (1970), pp. 87-103; J. P. MEIER, "Two Disputed Questions in Matt. 28:16-20", pp. 416-424.
37. E.g. J. J. JEREMIAS, *Jesus' Promise*, pp. 38-39.

"authority" being present. Yet still another similarity can be noted, namely, "all nations" (v. 19) and "all peoples, nations" (Dan. 7:14). The text of Daniel is considered to be the enthronement of the Son of Man. It would therefore seem that we have the same literary genre in the text of Matthew, but in this case it is the enthronement of Jesus himself which he had foretold (Mt. 26:64).

The elements of this genre are: elevation, presentation or proclamation and enthronement of the new king. This genre is used in the Egyptian texts and possibly in certain texts of the New Testament, where Christ is enthroned (1 Tim. 3:16; Phil. 2:9-11; Heb. 1:5-14); some have also identified these three elements in our text: v. 18, v. 19-20a, v. 20b.

But if one were to examine the texts more closely, one would find important differences. Our text does not speak about the enthronement of Jesus. In the text of Daniel, God enthrones the Son of Man: "to *him* was given"; in Matthew, Jesus is conscious of his authority: "all authority has been given to *me*". He has already been enthroned; he already has the authority. Jesus is not presented; rather he presents himself and gives the orders. If one judges from the "therefore" which links v. 19 to v. 18b, it appears that the elevation of Jesus does not constitute the main object of this passage but is only the basis for the order which he gives.

Other authors, therefore, classify this text as belonging to the literary *genre of commission* or order of mission.[38] This classification is based upon the importance of the command given by Jesus.

But to determine the literary genre of a text, one has to take into account all the elements of its structure and the links between them. The first interpretation is based especially on the first element of the structure, the second interpretation on the second element. The genre which best respects each of the elements and their interior links is the *genre of the proclamation of the covenant*.[39] Recent research on the covenant is the guideline through this book and illustrates how the whole theology of the covenant is built around certain characteristic elements: (I) the *historical prologue*; the suzerain presents himself to his new vassal and recalls everything he has done for him in the past, in order to inspire him with confidence and gratitude; (II) consequently, the suzerain expects an answer and thereby expresses his *stipulations*, commandments and orders to his vassal. It entails above all a total and faithful submission of the vassal towards his suzerain; (III) in return, the suzerain *promises protection* to his vassal by granting him his blessings. These are the three main elements of the genre. They correspond well with the three elements of the structure of our text as described earlier.

---

38. E.g. B. J. HUBBARD, *The Matthean Redaction*.
39. R. R. DE RIDDER, *The Dispersion of the People of God. The Covenant Basis of Matthew 28:18-20 against the background of Jewish, pre-christian proselyting and diaspora, and the apostleship of Jesus Christ*, Kampen, 1971. In this line also, H. FRANKEMÖLLE, *Jahwebund und Kirche Christi*.

(I) The *historical prologue* or the narration of a past historical event: Jesus presents himself, proclaiming that he has just received a universal power (v. 18b).

(II) This event constitutes the basis of the *order* which he gives; this is what the "therefore" indicates, which introduces this command (v. 19-20a).

(III) This order is linked with a *promise* by "and lo" (v. 20b).

To understand more fully the real purpose of the text of Matthew, we can compare it with the text of the conclusion of the Sinai covenant (Ex. 19:3-6) which we have already studied. There we discovered the same structure: (I) the historical prologue (v. 4); (II) what constitutes the basis for a request for submission (v. 5a); and (III) finally, the text finishes with a guarantee of protection (v. 5b-6). The event takes place at "the mountain" (Ex. 19:3) as in Matthew: "the mountain to which Jesus had directed them" (Mt. 28:16) and the mountain is the place of the revelation (Mt. 5:1; 15:29; 17:1; 24:3). We also have a covenant sign, which is baptism.[40]

At Sinai, Yahweh the suzerain concludes a covenant with Israel, the newly formed people, as his vassal. We now assist at the conclusion of another covenant, this time between the risen Jesus, enthroned as suzerain, and the people called to include all nations. Mankind now is the new vassal. We have here the proclamation of the new universal covenant.

(I) *Historical prologue:*

All authority in heaven and on earth has been given to me (v. 18b).

Several exegetes have compared this verse with Dan. 7:14, since both verses contain the same verb "give" and the same noun "authority", and have concluded that the text belongs to the genre of enthronement. Since the text of Daniel speaks about a judgment (7:10), they also suggest that the Lord in Matthew received the power to judge.

We have already noticed the considerable differences between the text of Daniel and the text of Matthew. We, therefore, have to determine with more precision the meaning of the term "authority" in our text. Matthew says already of Jesus during his earthly life that he has "authority": an authority to teach (7:29), to perform miracles (8:9; Jesus gives this same authority to his disciples 10:1) and to forgive sins (9:6 and especially 9:8, where it is said that God has "given" him this authority). His authority comes from the Father: "All things have been delivered to me by my Father" (11:27), and therefore he invites people to become his disciples (11:29). This last passage suggests an interesting comparison with the text in which the risen Jesus declares that he has received all power and therefore asks to make disciples. Having received the authority of

---

40. M. G. KLINE, *By Oath Consigned. A Reinterpretation of the Covenant Signs of Circumcision and Baptism*, Grand Rapids, 1968.

his Father, Jesus exercises the authority of God himself, which in the biblical tradition indicates the divine power over the created world and over the history of mankind.

The difference between the authority of Jesus during his earthly life and the authority of the risen Jesus is that the authority he received is now extended "in heaven and on earth". This biblical expression refers to the totality of creation: "In the beginning God created the heavens and the earth" (Gen. 1:1); the same expression is used elsewhere in Matthew (5:18; 24:35). The Father, who is creator, is Lord of heaven and earth (Mt. 11:25). During his life, Jesus limited his action to Israel; by his death for the salvation of mankind (Mt. 26:28), his salvific power is now extended over the whole universe. The Father, creator of everything which exists, gives Jesus this universal salvific power. It is not so much a power to judge, as was the case in the text from Daniel, as a power to save.

The historical prologue of the Sinai covenant contains this refrain: "I am Yahweh, your God, who brought you out of the land of Egypt, out of the house of bondage" (Ex. 20:2). Yahweh has offered salvation to his people by freeing them from the slavery of Egypt and by revealing himself to them. Jesus, who through his death became the universal saviour of mankind, has the power to free men from the slavery of the death of sin and to give knowledge to mankind (this is the meaning of "power", to perform miracles, to forgive and to teach). Like Yahweh, who as saviour of his people requested an answer from them, so also does Jesus address a demand to his disciples.

(II) *The request*: (v. 19-20a)

In texts which are composed using the covenant formulary, the request or stipulations are always closely linked with the historical prologue which constitutes the basis of the request itself. This link is often expressed by "now therefore" (Ex. 19:5; Jos. 24:14). Here we have "therefore". By his death, Jesus became the universal saviour and for that reason he now wants this salvation, of which he is the source, to be communicated to all mankind.

The essence of the request is expressed by the verb "make disciples". The gospel of Matthew is the only one of the synoptic gospels to use this term (13:52; 27:57; 28:19). To be a "disciple" of Jesus is not the privilege only of those who have lived with the Jesus of history. Rather, all are invited to be disciples and indeed, everyone can become his disciple if only they will listen to him and follow him. But one does not become a disciple on one's own initiative; one has to be called. Jesus has called some individuals to become his disciples. These in turn will then invite others. This call is addressed to "all nations".[41] The biblical tradition often

---

41. Cf. D.R.A. HARE and D. J. HARRINGTON, "Make Disciples", pp. 359-369; J. P. MEIER, "Nations or Gentiles in Matthew 28:19?", pp. 94-102.

opposes "the nations" to "my people" Israel. Therefore, some exegetes conclude that, since the "nations" are now called, Israel is indirectly rejected. But other texts, where Matthew uses the expression "all nations", clearly indicate that he speaks of all mankind (this is certainly the meaning of 24:9, of 25:32 and probably also of 24:14). "The nations" and "Israel" are called without any restriction. The call is not addressed to the nations as collectivities but to the individuals who compose these nations. This fact can be concluded from the participles that follow: "baptizing them" and "teaching them", which are in the masculine plural. They would have been expressed in the neuter gender if they referred to the nations as collectivities. Dan. 7:14b mentions also "all nations", but only to show that they are all under the authority of the Son of Man. Here they are invited to share in the salvation.

A special difficulty of the text lies in the form of the verb "to go". In Mt. 10:5-7 this verb expresses clearly the idea of a missionary sending of the disciples, but here the verb is in a participle form: "while going".

Several authors consider that this participle, because of its association with the main verb which is an imperative, also has the value of an imperative and consequently they translate: "Go, make disciples", a translation which underlines the aspect of "mission". The eleven are sent to the nations; they have to leave, to go out. Some authors also go as far as to put the emphasis on going, on travelling, since the participle precedes the verb "make disciples".

On the other hand, certain authors consider this participle as a kind of auxiliary without any particular meaning. Its purpose is only to stress the importance of the main verb which follows: "while going, make...". And some even say that we have here a grammatical form which need not even be translated. According to these interpretations, it would then be wrong to put much stress on the aspect of going out. As examples of such a pleonastic use of a participle there is the text of Matthew: "While going, learn what this means, 'I desire mercy, and not sacrifice'" (Mt. 9:13; it is clearly not necessary to "leave" to learn), and the text of Luke: "When you are invited, while going, take the lowest place" (Lk. 14:10; to take the lowest place does not imply that one has to "leave"). But we have to note that in other texts such a participle of the verb "to go" implies clearly an idea that one has to go, to leave. This is the case in: "Go and tell John" (Mt. 11:4; they have to return to John to give him the answer); also in "Go and tell that fox" (Lk. 13:32; they have to leave to go and tell him). The most significant example is the parallel text of Mark: "While going into all the world, preach the gospel to the whole creation" (Mk. 16:15 which has the same construction as in Matthew, but a "going to" or a "leaving" seems clearly to be implied by "into all the world").[42]

---

42. P. TERNANT, "La prédication universelle de l'Évangile du Seigneur. Mc. 16:15-20", in *Assemblées du Seigneur*, 2, 28, Paris, 1969, pp. 38-48, especially p. 43.

We could perhaps suggest that whenever we have the formulation "while going, proclaim, tell etc...", it implies at the same time a "going out" and a "proclaiming".

But even if one adopts the option to translate this text using the words "while going", it becomes apparent that the text refers, at least implicitly, to a going of the eleven to the nations; but this is not what is essential in the request of Jesus. The disciples in fact have gone to the nations. But whatever hypothesis one adopts, the main element of the request is to make disciples. If this is what is essential, one has then to conclude that each one has to make disciples wherever he is: while going... wherever you go, wherever you are. According to Matthew, the most important point, then, is to make disciples so that men come into a personal relationship with Jesus. According to Mark (16:15) and Luke (24:47) the missionary activity consists first of all in proclaiming the good news. It seems, therefore, in view of these facts, that the request as formulated in Matthew is more demanding.

How to "make disciples" is specified by the two participles that follow: "baptizing them" and "teaching them". Even if baptism is quoted before the teaching, this does not reflect on the practice of the primitive Church, for a certain degree of teaching must have preceded baptism. But what Matthew shows is that one becomes a real disciple of Jesus by baptism and by the observance of his commandments. Through baptism the disciple enters into a relationship of belonging to the Lord and a very close link is created between them: "in the name of...". And like any other covenant, the new universal covenant has its own sign, which is baptism.

We are also told that the disciple must "observe". This term in Matthew refers to an obedience to the divine commandments to which his fidelity must be expressed in deeds and not merely in words (19:17; 23:3).

The disciple has to observe "all that I have commanded you", an expression which would appear to have its origin in the Old Testament (Ex. 7:2; 29:35; Dt. 1:41; 4:2). The verbs "observe" and "command" are often used in the Old Testament, and especially in the Book of Deuteronomy, for the requests of God towards his people of the covenant. Here it refers to the totality of Jesus' preaching which is presented here as a "commandment", like the torah or the doctrine of life in the biblical tradition. He came indeed to accomplish the law and to bring it to perfection. Jesus, following his predecessors, the prophets, has completed their preaching. It is all this that has to be communicated to the nations so that they may be able to observe it. The expression "all that *I* have commanded you" does not mean an abstract theory, but rather a personal relationship. One has to submit to a person, to Jesus himself. Just as in all other covenants, this submission consists of a global and total acceptance of the will of the Lord. This acceptance is symbolized in the rite of baptism but has to be lived concretely in obedience to specific stipulations.

The essential point of the request of the Lord, then, is to "make disciples". The real disciple of Jesus is therefore he who makes other disciples.

(III) *The promise of protection*:

And lo, I am with you always, until the end of the world (v. 20b).

The last part of the structure is closely linked with what precedes it and expresses a guarantee of protection for those who fulfill what is commanded.

The expression "I am with you" has its origin in the Old Testament.[43] It recalls the name of Yahweh himself. Yahweh became the God of the covenant by offering Israel freedom. He revealed himself as "I am who I am" (Ex. 3:14), an expression which is to be understood in the sense of "I am with you" (Ex. 3:12). It is often said that Yahweh "is with...". He may be with individuals or with the people Israel, to accomplish a mission or to inspire confidence in a difficult situation (Gen. 26:24; 28:15; Dt. 20:1,4; Jos. 1:5,9; Jgs. 6:12; Is. 41:10; 43:2,5; Hag. 1:13).

This protection offered by Yahweh to his people or to his messengers in the past is now promised by Jesus, the universal saviour, to the new people of this universal covenant. It is interesting to note how Matthew starts his gospel with this idea when he tells the story of the annunciation: "Behold, a virgin shall conceive, and bear a son, and his name shall be called Emmanuel, which means, God with us" (Mt. 1:23), and he also closes his gospel with the same promise of protection.

This promise concerns not only the eleven but all those who will become disciples, in other words, the whole people of God. The protection which he promises will be effective "always", thus constantly, and will last until "the end of the world".

The solemnity of this text and its position at the end of the gospel clearly show the very special importance which Matthew has given to it. It is evident that the end of a book is always very precious, as is the beginning. But the text becomes even more important and meaningful if we consider its function in the whole of biblical tradition.

The prehistory describes the first period of the history of mankind (Gen. 1-11): "In the beginning God created the heavens and the earth" (Gen. 1:1). We have called this the primitive universal covenant which through the failure of men ended with the exile of mankind.

God wanted to restore this universal covenant. He chose Abraham to make a people, and in "him" (Abraham-people) all the others would receive blessings (Gen. 12:1-3). With this people God concludes his historical covenant. But Israel's election is to share her revelation with others. Jesus, as the last of the prophets and the very Word of God himself

---

43. H. D. PREUSS, "...ich will mit dir sein", in *Z.A.W.*, 80 (1968), pp. 139-173.

(Heb. 1:1-2), has continued this divine plan and limited his teaching mainly to Israel (Mt. 15:24; 10:5 ff.).

This second period came to an end with the death and resurrection of Jesus. The time has now come for that Israel which had accepted the whole revelation to communicate the richness of this revelation to the nations. We have now reached the new universal covenant which will be the complete restoration of the first one. Indeed Jesus even predicted and celebrated this new covenant on the eve of his death: "And he took a cup, and when he had given thanks he gave it to them, saying, 'Drink of it, all of you; for this is my blood of the covenant, which is poured out for many for the forgiveness of sins'" (Mt. 26:27-28).[44]

Here Jesus clearly uses a formula borrowed from the covenant with Israel (Ex. 24:8) which he now extends to include the whole world. The last words of Jesus in the gospel of Matthew appear, therefore, as the promulgation of this new covenant. The text refers partly to the first verse of the Bible (Gen. 1:1), where we find the same expression "heaven and earth" (Mt. 28:18) and, as in Genesis, an element of time is also mentioned, but instead of "in the beginning" it becomes "until the end of the world" (v. 20). Matthew likes to refer in his gospel to Abraham, to whom the promise of a people was made and through whom all the nations will receive a blessing. He starts his gospel by connecting Jesus to Abraham: "son of Abraham" (Mt. 1:1). He also speaks about Abraham when he predicts the time of the nations: "I tell you, many will come from east and west and sit at table with Abraham, Isaac, and Jacob in the kingdom of heaven" (Mt. 8:11).[45] But now the moment to invite "all nations" (Mt. 28:19) has arrived; the promises given to Abraham and the prophecies of the Old Testament are fulfilled.

We certainly have here, in the conclusion of the gospel of Matthew, one of the great "mission" texts of the biblical tradition. The confirmation of this text by its parallel texts no longer leaves any doubt as to the centrifugal movement of the revelation.

We find many details in the New Testament about the "how" of sharing with others. But this is outside the scope of this study. We just want to quote the mission concept of John, which might be very appealing to our times.[46]

---

44. V. WAGNER, "Der Bedeutungswandel von $b^e rît\ h\breve{a}d\bar{a}\check{s}\bar{a}h$ bei der Ausgestaltung des Abendmahlsworte", in *Ev.Th.*, 35 (1975), pp. 538-544.
45. J. DUPONT, "'Beaucoup viendront du levant et du couchant...' (Mt. 8:11-12; Luc. 13:28-29)", in *Sc.Eccl.*, 19 (1967), pp. 153-167; D. ZELLER, "Das Logion Mt. 8:11 f./ Lk. 13:28 f. und das Motiv der 'Völkerwallfahrt'", in *B.Z.*, 15 (1971), pp. 222-237; 16 (1972), pp. 84-93.
46. W. VOGELS, "Mission–Communion en Jean 17:18,21-23", in *Kerygma*, 5 (1971), n. 3-4, pp. 149-160; E. MALATESTA, "Consecration and Mission", in *The Way Supplement*, 13 (1971), pp. 3-13; J. P. MIRANDA, *Der Vater, der mich gesandt hat. Religionsgeschichtliche Untersuchungen zu den johanneischen Sendungsformeln*, Bern, 1972; P. S. MINEAR, "Evangelism, Ecumenism, and John 17", in *Th.Tod.*, 35 (1978), pp. 5-13.

Mission has a *vertical* dimension:

> As thou didst send me into the world,
> so I have sent them into the world (Jn. 17:18).

The Father has sent the son, who sends others. This centrifugal movement is initiated by God. One is sent by someone to someone.
But it also has a *horizontal* dimension:

> That they may all be one;
>     even as thou, Father, art in me,
>     and I in thee,
> That they also may be in us,
>     so that the world may believe
>         that thou hast sent me...
> That they may be one,
>     even as we are one,
>         I in them
>     and thou in me,
> that they may become perfectly one,
>     so that the world may know
>         that thou hast sent me (Jn. 17:21-23).

What, then, is essential is to bring about the unity between all men and between mankind and God, a unity which was destroyed and ended when the primitive universal covenant was broken.

We then see the people of God starting to bring about this work of universal salvation: "You shall be my witnesses in Jerusalem, and in all Judea and Samaria and to the end of the earth" (Act. 1:8) and moving further and further from the centre to reach all nations.[47]

We recall that in chapter three we saw how the nations were lacking one thing to live in a real covenant relationship with Yahweh. This was, in their case, the revelation which only Israel had received.

In this last chapter we have studied how the nations will one day be called to enter into this one and only covenant by sharing in the divine revelation. In view of this fact, God has used as his instrument the people he has chosen for this special function, but only once they have received the fullness of the revelation through Jesus.

Many biblical texts have predicted this great event by describing the coming of the nations towards the centre to receive there the divine teaching. On the other hand only a few texts even vaguely suggest a centrifugal movement of the centre towards the nations. But all of these texts remain only predictions. However, at the moment of the death of Jesus, an era was concluded, as is expressed for us by the words: "And behold the cur-

---

47. W. VOGELS, "La prédication de l'Évangile selon le livre des Actes", in *Kerygma*, 4 (1970), n. 2, pp. 14-30; A. B. RUTLEDGE, "Evangelistic Methods in Acts", in *Sw.J.T.*, 17 (1974), n. 1, pp. 35-47; R. C. GUY, "The Missionary Message of Acts", in *Sw.J.T.*, 17 (1974), n. 1, pp. 49-64.

tain of the temple was torn in two, from the top to the bottom" (Mt. 27:51). The era of the nations could begin. After his death and resurrection Jesus declared that that moment had arrived. Until then, we had only promises of a new universal covenant to come; this third period of the salvation history has now started, the work has begun, and it will continue until the end of time.

# Conclusion

It is only at the end of a book that the introduction can be clearly understood. We indicated there the purpose of our study. It might be well to state once more the scope of our investigation, in order to avoid all misunderstanding.

This work is a study on one particular theme of the biblical tradition and this can easily be misleading. It gives only one aspect of the total richness and, even though the theme of universalism is of utmost importance, the election of Israel appears much more frequently and is more central, as we have already said.

But what our intention here has been, and hopefully what we have been able to convey, is a new approach to universalism and its intimate relationship to covenant. Election has no meaning without universalism. The two are very closely related to each other.

Consequently, our study has developed some texts and omitted the use of others. We admit that many texts other than those we quoted express a negative attitude towards the nations. Some texts even express hatred, but this current has not prevailed. Also, in addition to the very positive texts which we have used regarding the nations, many more could have been cited. These other texts have been frequently studied in books on universalism and, therefore, we saw no necessity to include them in our study.

Very often we have simply quoted the better-known texts, without analysing them in detail. What we have developed instead are those texts where covenant vocabulary, structures and theology are applied to texts not speaking of Israel but rather of the nations. It is this fact which we hope expresses the originality of this work. We have analysed these texts as precisely as possible, but we have tried at the same time to avoid the use of technical language. This explains why there is a certain disproportion in the attention which some texts receive in comparison to others.

Our purpose has not been to write the history of universalism and to explain when and how Israel became conscious of her call of service to the nations. Many different tendencies existed in Israel. Sometimes there were interior conflicts and opposed positions. Other books have tried such a diachronic study of universalism, with more or less success since it is not very easy to date all biblical texts. Further, we did not develop "how" the elected people had to share, how they had to approach the nations, or what they themselves would receive from them. It is self-evident that nobody gives without receiving.

Our approach has been synchronic. We have taken God's plan of salvation as presented in the biblical tradition in its totality, which includes the commonly accepted division of the Old and New Testaments. These two sections constitute the whole history of salvation. The Israel called to share the revelation with the nations is that Israel which accepted the totality of revelation including the one of the last prophet, Jesus.

This history of universal salvation seen as covenant theology is divided into three periods.

The first was God's primitive universal covenant with mankind. There was no question of an elected people and other nations. Mankind was in direct relation with God, but this ended through sin in disaster and was followed by the dispersion or exile of mankind (*Chapter One*).

God wanted to restore this covenant and to come to the rescue of mankind. Then the second period started and the distinction between the elected people and the nations appeared. God chose one nation as his instrument. He concluded a covenant with Israel and started revealing himself to her. During many centuries he formed that people to prepare them to accomplish their service to the nations. But this does not mean that God totally neglected the others. This covenant was made with those other nations in mind. They had already had something to do with it in several ways (*Chapter Two*) and what was even better, during this period God cared for the nations directly and ordained their history. They, however, lacked the revelation and, therefore, were not living a covenant relationship which indeed presupposes a mutual knowledge (*Chapter Three*).

When Israel herself finally received the fullness of revelation the third period began. Israel was now capable of sharing her privilege with the others. And so, finally, the distinction between the elected people and the nations disappeared in order to make room once more for a direct mutual relationship between mankind and God, namely, that of a new universal covenant. Universalism, therefore, in the biblical tradition is unitarian (*Chapter Four*).

The future is described as being as beautiful as the first beginning. Will it remain a dream, or will it become reality?